The Literary
Haunted House

The Literary Haunted House

Lovecraft, Matheson, King and the Horror in Between

Rebecca Janicker

McFarland & Company, Inc., Publishers

Jefferson, North Carolina

Library of Congress Cataloguing-in-Publication Data

Janicker, Rebecca, 1978– author.
   The literary haunted house : Lovecraft, Matheson, King
and the horror in between / Rebecca Janicker.
     p.   cm.
   Includes bibliographical references and index.

   ISBN 978-0-7864-6573-6 (softcover : acid free paper) ∞
   ISBN 978-1-4766-1928-6 (ebook)

   1. Horror tales, American—History and criticism.
   2. Gothic revival (Literature)—Influence. I. Title.

PS374.H67J38 2015
813'.0873809—dc23   2014046217

British Library cataloguing data are available

Front cover image © 2015 Antonis Liokouras/iStock/Thinkstock

Printed in the United States of America

*McFarland & Company, Inc., Publishers
  Box 611, Jefferson, North Carolina 28640
   www.mcfarlandpub.com*

This book is dedicated to Lincoln

Table of Contents

Acknowledgments

This book began as a Ph.D. project at the University of Nottingham and there are several members of the academic staff there whom I must thank for their guidance and support. My original supervisor, Peter Messent, deserves acknowledgment and gratitude for all his work towards shaping and guiding the project early on. Special thanks go to Nick Heffernan, who later took over that role and whose constructive feedback and encouragement helped steer the project to completion. I also offer thanks to my Ph.D. examiners, Matthew Pethers and Lorna Jowett, as well as to all those staff members and Ph.D. students who participated in the Work in Progress seminars that I undertook as part of my studies.

Beyond the University of Nottingham, there are several other academics for whose expertise and support I wish to express my gratitude. Having been a regular presenter at the annual National Popular Culture/American Culture Conference since undertaking the Ph.D., I would like to thank the area chairs, co-presenters and panel-attendees for the Gothic, Horror and Stephen King Areas at these events. This opportunity to share my research, receive constructive criticism and simply to discuss my scholarly interests with like-minded researchers over the years has been invaluable. For their support in providing funding for my participation in these conferences, I would like to thank the Centre for Cultural and Creative Research at the University of Portsmouth. Having been a part-time lecturer at that university since 2005, and a permanent lecturer since 2009, I have many supportive colleagues there to thank—especially in the School of Creative Arts, Film and Media—and have also made some good friends. In particular, for their various contributions, I wish to thank Emma Austin, John Caro, Imogen Jeffrey, Van Norris, Deborah Shaw, Esther Sonnet, Graham Spencer and Jackie Walker.

Acknowledgments

Heartfelt thanks go to my family, whose practical and emotional support helped me to continue with what has been, at times, a very challenging endeavor. Many, many, many thanks go to my parents, Laurie and Kathy Janicker, as well as to Diane and to Malcolm Geraghty. Far and away the deepest thanks go to my husband Lincoln Geraghty, whose editorial skills, general ability to lead by scholarly example and, above all, love and encouragement, have helped to make this book possible.

Preface

As a fervent reader of the horror and Gothic genres for most of my life, I am wholly aware of the unsettling power of such fiction to linger with the reader long after a book has been closed and replaced upon the shelf. Vampires titillate and monsters horrify, and these unnatural creatures and the supernatural unrest they incite have ever enjoyed the capacity to thrill, to alarm and to disturb in equal measure. Yet it is the ghost story, with its eerie atmosphere and nerve-shredding intimation that something, somewhere, is not right, and that that something will ultimately demand recognition, that strikes us closest to home. For ghosts are—or were—people, all-too recognizable figures that embody the past and act as striking reminders that what has gone before may yet come back to worry the living.

It was precisely this sense of the potency of ghosts that led me to my doctoral research into fiction about haunting. There are numerous books on the Gothic, as well as on ghosts in American literature and culture, yet there is a dearth of work dedicated to the power of haunting and of haunted space in popular American fiction, and my research addresses this critical lack. Specifically, this book examines popular American Gothic fiction through a critical focus on what I call the *haunted house motif*. I argue that this motif creates a singular type of narrative space characterized by liminality—the state of being in between normally-distinct states, such as life and death—in which past events can literally impact upon the present. Haunted house stories provide imaginative opportunities to keep the past alive while highlighting the complexities of the culture from which they emerged. My chosen authors, H. P. Lovecraft, Richard Matheson and Stephen King, use the haunted house motif to engage with political and ideological perspectives important to an understanding of American history and culture.

In the Introduction, I consider important aspects of the Gothic as a genre, explaining how the haunted castle of European Gothic transmuted into the haunted house associated with American Gothic. Here, discussions of space and liminality are drawn together with discussions of genre to establish the critical concept at the heart of my study: the haunted house motif. The chapters provide a largely chronological reflection on ways in which this motif, when applied to the work of my chosen authors, offers insights into American society throughout the sweep of the twentieth century. In Chapter One, I argue that H. P. Lovecraft uses haunting in "The Dreams in the Witch House" (1933) to address concerns about industrialization, urbanization and modernization in the early part of the twentieth century, endorsing both progressive and conservative ideologies. In Chapters Two and Three, I show that Richard Matheson's use of haunting highlights issues of 1950s suburbanization in *A Stir of Echoes* (1958) and changing social mores about the American family during the 1970s and 1980s in *Earthbound* (1982; 1989), critiquing conformist culture while stopping short of overturning it.

Chapters Four, Five and Six are devoted to that most prolific and high-profile author of horror and Gothic, Stephen King. As a product of the counterculture, King explores new kinds of haunted spaces relevant to the American experience from the 1970s onwards. In *The Shining* (1977) he draws on haunting to problematize inequalities of masculinity, class and capitalism, and in *Christine* (1983), at a time of re-emerging conservative politics, he critiques Reaganite nostalgia for the supposed "golden age" of the 1950s. At the close of the twentieth century, haunting in *Bag of Bones* (1998) reappraises American guilt about race and the legacy of slavery. Overall, this book works to show that the haunted house motif adapts to the ever-changing conditions of American modernity, and that the liminal power of haunting offers a way of processing the challenges that such changes bring.

Introduction

The Haunted House Motif
in Popular American Fiction

The evocation of the haunted house initially takes a visual form. To speak of such a place is to conjure up an image of an archaic building, dark, decrepit and cavernous. Typically shunned by all but the most tenacious of characters, latent with memory and pregnant with menace, this kind of place is a byword for the dark side of domesticity and the underbelly of normal society. So iconic is it that the label *haunted house* has become synonymous with the potent supernatural energies that its appearance suggests it inevitably harbors.

The union of setting and theme has become sufficiently entrenched, in both publishing and cinematic terms, to warrant designation as a sub-genre in its own right. This consists of a clearly-defined body of fiction that takes haunted houses as its primary focus. This book focuses on works by three authors—H. P. Lovecraft, Richard Matheson and Stephen King—that deal with such places. From fairgrounds to campfire gatherings, haunted houses are an enduring presence in popular culture.[1] Jan Harold Brunvand stresses that narrative folklore has persisted in America in the form of urban legends, many of which fixate on horror and haunting, not least because of the messages or morals contained therein.[2] In *Danse Macabre*, his overview of the horror genre, Stephen King describes tales like these as archetypes and emphasizes the unsettling power they exert.[3] As will be argued in this study, fictive treatments of the haunted house represent imaginative opportunities to keep the past alive and vie with the complexities of culture.

However, written fictions belonging to this sub-genre do have a clear literary heritage. In order to trace this lineage, the first part of this

3

introductory chapter will briefly address the nature and origins of British Gothic, while American Gothic will be examined in greater detail in the next section. Such works have their roots in English romantic literature and the Gothic tradition. As Eino Railo has observed, the trope of the "haunted castle"—perhaps the first form of haunted building and the prototype for what would follow—originated in both literal and literary form with the eighteenth-century English writer Horace Walpole.[4] In *The Castle of Otranto*, published in 1764 and generally held to be the first Gothic novel, the eponymous building has an eerie and imposing atmosphere crucial to the book's success. Walpole's novel recounts a brutal series of incidents, finally shown to be the product of the castle's past usurpation, and exploits the supernatural throughout to suggest its grim heritage. This link between a place and its history, forged time and again in Gothic fictions, is integral to my argument.

Otranto marks the origin of such literary "hauntings," yet the events it describes are so fleeting and fragmentary as to be crude symbols of menace rather than the meaningful encounters with complex supernatural entities that appear in later haunted house fiction.[5] Railo argues that a further important element of such fiction emerged with Clara Reeve's *The Old English Baron* (1778).[6] Reeve's apparitions appear where the body of Lovel Castle's murdered rightful owner lies concealed. More sophisticated than those of Walpole, these ghosts exhibit motivations and memories and thus function in narrative terms as characters with agency and not as mere echoes of the past.[7] Building on Walpole's basic idea of a troubled space, Reeve links the supernatural events to a meaningful physical place and adds an element of psychological depth to create a more coherent type of haunting. These issues are at the heart of the present study, and subsequent chapters will explore how haunting works through precisely such means. In essence, this book foregrounds the physical spaces in which fictional hauntings occur, emphasizing that these spaces are bound up with the events played out within them. As such, it maintains that haunting gives its protagonists and, by implication, its readers, special access to the histories and ideologies contained within these supernatural locales.

These early Gothic texts were written towards the end of the eighteenth century, at a time when rationalism was beginning to replace religion as the basis for knowledge. The darker side of human existence, embodied in notions of sin and the Manichean conflict between good and evil, was pushed aside in favor of the new emphasis on reason and understanding, on ordering the world through human, rather than divine, agency.[8] Such Enlightenment thinking cast the Middle Ages as a barbaric and superstitious past derisively known as "Gothic."[9] Yet these beliefs were unable to supplant entirely the older worldview, with its emphasis on human fallibility and the inevitability of evil and darkness. The need for such ideas did not recede and Gothic fiction, in its "attempts to explain what the Enlightenment left unexplained,"[10] provided a forum for exploring them. With its medieval trappings of castles, aristocrats and knights rescuing damsels in distress, Gothic fiction represented a prose extension of Romanticism,[11] while its distinctive tropes of occult phenomena and hauntings worked to engage with the baser human impulses and the wider themes of spiritual darkness that they represented. Maggie Kilgour notes that its rise has been interpreted as a "need for the sacred and transcendent in a modern enlightened secular world which denies the existence of supernatural forces."[12] So it was in such eighteenth-century European literature that ghosts and atmospheric places started to take hold of the imagination of the reading public, as Gothic met the need to address what the new worldview, with its emphasis on rationality and logic, attempted to smooth over.

Early British Gothic was thus characterized by an atmosphere of mystery and antiquity. For Eve Kosofsky Sedgwick, key Gothic conventions comprise "sleep-like and deathlike states; subterranean spaces and live burial; the discovery of obscured family ties … the poisonous effects of guilt and shame; nocturnal landscapes and dreams [and] apparitions from the past."[13] To these features can be added heroes and villains, physically repugnant and psychologically unsettling locations and situations of domestic and social unrest.[14] Following in the footsteps of Walpole and Reeve, other classic Gothic works such as Ann Radcliffe's *The Mysteries of Udolpho* (1794) and Matthew Lewis's *The Monk* (1796) establish supernatural disturbances, evocative settings and troubled pasts as Gothic staples—all qualities still readily discernible in contemporary exemplars of the genre. Closer scrutiny reveals, however, that these tales are essentially infused by a sense of engagement with history—both personal and social—and this study claims that it is precisely this concern that lies at the heart of the Gothic.

Both Walpole and Reeve use their Gothic novels as a fictional means of rectifying bygone wrongs such as murder and treachery. Later novelists follow suit in having their tales level criticisms at targets which, in earlier eras, would have seemed beyond reproach. Acknowledging the political faculties of the genre, with its emergence in the context of the Enlightenment, Mark Edmundson remarks that "Gothic thrives in a world where those in authority—the supposed exemplars of the good—are under suspicion."[15] With their dissolute holy men and villainous aristocrats, the works of Lewis and Radcliffe are bound up with critiques of institutionalized power.[16] In a changing world, Gothic fiction was a vehicle for challenging social establishments and the ideologies wielded by them, and I argue that this facility for political interrogation remains integral to the genre.

Building on this idea of the fundamental significance of history to the Gothic, it must further be noted that the genre has an emphasis on what many critics describe as the *return of the repressed*.[17] Such repression might result from what Anne Williams calls "the frustrations of too much emphasis on Reason"[18] in the eighteenth century. For Noël Carroll, at least broadly speaking, the horror genre addresses uncomfortable, and therefore repressed, issues by portraying them as "horrific creatures."[19] Indeed, Gothic and horror fictions have ever been associated with monsters seen as symbolic of the unpalatable. In his essay "The 'Uncanny'" (1919), Sigmund Freud argues that that which is called "uncanny" (in German this is *unheimlich*, literally "unhomely" in English) can also mean the exact opposite: it can mean "homely" and therefore "familiar."[20] Yet that which is familiar to the mind can be rendered unfamiliar "through the process of repression."[21] The resurgence of something repressed, which may well produce fear, will therefore be something known rather than something unknown. Because of this, Freud states that we can understand "the uncanny as something which ought to have remained hidden but has come to light."[22] In the context of Gothic fiction, this view of repression translates into a thematic preoccupation with the past encroaching on the present: often in a violent fashion beyond the bounds of accepted reality. This may occur in a quite literal manner, as when those believed dead somehow resurface to disturb the living, perhaps in the form of ghosts, vampires, zombies or other unnatural beings.

Many of the generic conventions described above—death, decay, unsavory locales, shameful secrets and the eruption of the past into the present—converge in haunting, which is the primary focus of the current study. For Edmundson, the idea that "to be human is to be haunted"[23] is central to Gothic, and Valdine Clemens points to the genre's focus on keeping the living linked to the dead through "forging an imaginative connection with the archaic past."[24] She also notes the Gothic imperative to lay bare secrets.[25] As discussed above, early Gothic tales recount ghostly activities that work to uncover the past and especially to reveal hidden wrongs. "If a ghost walks," avers Julia Briggs in her study of the English ghost story, "there must be a reason."[26] Such actions clearly signify ineffective attempts to keep the past buried. These may include individual transgressions or instances of wider social injustice that inevitably come to light.[27] So the act of repressing the past, as well as what is actually repressed, may be individual or social in nature—concerned with the subject and his or her family history, or with the larger social history of which he or she is a part. Similarly, when the past returns to the present, it may be the contents of the individual or the social subconscious forcing their way back towards recognition.[28]

So Gothic texts in general, and tales of haunting in particular, depict physical and metaphorical representations of history brought into the present. Although, unlike many critics of the Gothic, I do not provide psychoanalytical readings of my chosen texts, I find the idea of repression to be a valuable one because of its historical dimensions. The obsession haunted fiction has with the power of the past is central to my argument, as the Gothic fictions taken as the critical focus of my study are fundamentally concerned with the interrogation of history. The earliest Gothic novels—with their relatively clear-cut portrayals of wrongdoing—tend to employ haunting as a device for uncovering and redressing unlawful past deeds and thus render it an instrument of justice. However, the twentieth-century haunted fictions I analyze throughout my later chapters do more to engage with the complexities of ideology inevitably wrought by social change. While they still serve to expose secrets, in contrast with earlier forms of the Gothic they are often unable to provide easy resolutions to the issues they raise. Catherine Belsey contends that "the work of criticism is to release possible meanings,"[29] and my study works to interrogate what these texts reveal about the socio-historical context from which they emerge. As my chosen authors, Lovecraft, Matheson and King, are generally regarded as popular authors, it will be necessary to discuss the nature of popular—as opposed to literary—fiction, and the implications of this will be addressed later.

Having outlined key conventions of the Gothic, I will now turn attention to the pivotal concept with which I opened this introduction: the haunted house. David A. Oakes goes so far as to argue that "the most prominent and common element of Gothic literature is the haunted castle and its later derivations."[30] This suggests that the medieval setting of eighteenth-century literature, over the decades leading into the twentieth century and beyond, has transmuted into a rather more domestic one— a house rather than a castle. A lack of medieval architecture led to American Gothic's focus on more commonplace dwelling spaces.[31] Stemming from the original castle, the later term of "haunted house" begins to symbolize more than that suggested by a merely literal interpretation. For Stephen King, haunted house tales are just one variety of the hauntings so prevalent in Gothic fiction, including his own: "The archetype of the Ghost is, after all, the Mississippi of supernatural fiction."[32] As both consumer and creator of fictional works of horror, King suggests that such places invoke deeply-held superstitions, aptly reducing them to their simplest state with his observation that "we might call this particular archetype the Bad Place."[33] This study follows King's idea of "bad places" in allowing a discussion of fiction about haunted houses to include fiction about haunted space more generally. It will thus extend the original term by incorporating such fiction and designating it, along with the more rigidly-defined "haunted house" texts, under the broader term of "haunted fiction."

Contemporary fiction about haunting clearly exhibits themes and functions that are not tied to the historically-prescribed set of circumstances represented by the original Gothic castle insofar as it typically no longer harks back to an archaic setting or to an imagined past. Yet there is still a literary impetus to turn to the Gothic as a means of contending with history. In recognition of how this key Gothic trope has evolved, my discussion of tales that deal with haunting and haunted spaces throughout this study will employ the term *haunted house motif*.[34] There are three main ideas embedded in this concept: that haunted fiction draws upon various types of space, that such space has special properties, and that it therefore performs certain functions. The haunted house in this sense—as a *motif* rather than merely a *building*—refers to a set of literary themes and conventions that appears throughout the sub-genre of haunted fiction. These features of the sub-genre, embedded within the Gothic, can be detected in my chosen texts. It is my contention that this motif, which combines a diversity of physical settings with the Gothic trope of haunting, creates a special kind of narrative space in which fictional characters and those who read about them can engage with the histories these narratives portray.

While the decrepit and timeworn literary castle may appear vastly more conducive to fear and horror than its humble modern equivalents, both have found frequent expression in haunted fiction. Clean, contemporary spaces that are without centuries of history, yet still haunted by supernatural entities, can indicate problems, memories and dark forces of various types that can cause just as much distress as those embodied in the ancient, moldering buildings of traditional Gothic literature. A look at the development of haunted fiction shows that, although the places and the nature of the troubles may change, the idea of a troubled space with the power to harm remains.[35] After the rise of Gothic in the late eighteenth century, early nineteenth-century Romantic poetry and historical romance novels, including those of Sir Walter Scott, continued to utilize gloomy castles as settings, drawing upon their concomitant Gothic themes of tragedy, secrecy and supernatural horror in so doing.[36]

With the passage of time, other types of setting began to appear in Gothic tales. Towards the middle of the nineteenth century, American author Edgar Allan Poe, in addition to using dungeons and castles and their attendant subject matter, began to feature domestic settings in his fiction, as well as shifting the focus to *internal*—rather than purely *external*—depictions of horror.[37] Such developments—the use of familiar and everyday spaces and the emphasis on psychological sources and experiences of fear—helped pave the way for the ghost story: an identifiable trend in Gothic fiction in the nineteenth century and a new direction for the sub-genre.[38] Moving into the twentieth century, Julia Briggs argues that M. R. James's practice of placing ghost stories within a banal rather than an overtly antiquated setting set the ghost story apart from its more purely Gothic literary predecessors.[39] This study maintains, however, that those key Gothic conventions identified above still endure in contemporary fictional hauntings, even when transplanted into identifiably modern-day settings.

In the twentieth century, then, Gothic fiction has retained many of its traditional tropes and themes, adapting earlier features of the genre to more modern and even quite contemporary concerns and situations.[40] Such flexibility is clearly in evidence in the haunted fictions with which the present study is concerned. Yet, as though reflective of the convoluted sweep of history which they show, these recent narratives seem unable to supply the resolutions found in the earliest Gothic tales of haunting. In moving with the times, these fictions reflect the kind of problems alluded to above, which may stem from highly individualized circumstances like personal trauma, or take on a more social dimension in engaging the cultural and historical past. One example of late twentieth-century Gothic which concerns both is Toni Morrison's *Beloved* (1987), which addresses the legacy of slavery and racism by reconstructing in literary form "the story of Margaret Garner, a recaptured fugitive slave who killed her child rather than see her returned to slavery."[41] Sethe, the fictionalized version of Garner, is troubled by the memory of the child who died at her hands. Space plays a part in this tale, as the modest home Sethe continues to occupy, "the gray and white house on Bluestone Road [which] didn't have a number then, because Cincinnati didn't stretch that far,"[42] is also haunted by the ghostly child. Despite its status as a literary novel, *Beloved* not only shares the Gothic preoccupation with the legacy of the past, but also acts out that preoccupation through the device of haunting so characteristic of that genre.

Once again, the above example demonstrates that fictional haunting is a way of accessing history, with all the troubles and complexities it may contain, in order to engage with ideological struggles which linger into the present. Further, haunted fiction is sufficiently versatile, thematically and stylistically, for the motif to which it gives rise to be employed in less traditional settings while still retaining core aspects of its original meaning. As this study will show, modern haunted spaces like the suburban homes of Richard Matheson's *A Stir of Echoes* (1958) and even the eponymous car of Stephen King's *Christine* (1983) can—and do—work to engage with history in the same way that a more traditional setting, such as the fictionalized version of Salem's Witch House in H. P. Lovecraft's "The Dreams in the Witch House" (1933) does.

Much scope for writers and readers has certainly been found within the sub-genre. Steven J. Mariconda has observed that, even within the relatively-constricting parameters of that fiction which concerns a home disturbed by supernatural events, "the haunted house story has proved amazingly flexible in accommodating a wide variety of themes: good versus evil, science versus the supernatural, economic conflict, class, gender, and so on."[43] This list can be augmented with examples from my own chosen authors, whose works about haunting also encompass such subject matter as capitalism, consumerism, domestic turmoil and race. In short, I argue that such fictions deal with ideology and that they work especially to highlight the contradictions and complexities contained therein. My contribution to this field of criticism is to posit the haunted house motif as a way of understanding the ideologies contained within these fictions. The motif to which, I argue, this sub-genre gives rise affords a distinctive type of literary encounter with ideological forces, one tied to specific socio-historical contexts through the physical spaces in which the hauntings occur. A crucial component of this motif is its liminal properties. Somewhat akin to Michel Foucault's notion of heterotopias, those places in which culture may be "represented, contested, and inverted,"[44] liminal spaces are arenas in which social values and norms may be confronted. The nature and application of this motif will be discussed later in this introduction and argued by means of textual analysis throughout the remainder of this work.

The topic of the haunted house is addressed via three key terms to be used in the book as a whole: genre, space and liminality. It is necessary to commence the remaining sections by making further observations about genre, particularly in terms of how Gothic plays out in America, a society unencumbered by the weight of European tradition and preoccupied instead with carving out a new society away from such precedents. Furthermore, with its turn to more domestic settings, it is there that the type of haunted house fiction I will be analyzing can be said to find its clearest expression. Then a consideration of critical work on space will reveal how various uses of this term have been bound up with history and ideology. Throughout this study, the term "space" will be used primarily to denote physical places, though sometimes it may also be extended to include mental states and processes, e.g. "getting some space" in the sense of removing oneself from a situation. In the fiction I explore, haunted spaces inevitably impact upon the emotions and psychology of those subjected to them. This second section on space will, however, focus primarily on the former, more concrete usage.

The third section, on liminality, will outline the important theoretical ideas and terminology on which my later analyses will draw. Liminality refers to those spaces that exist on the margins of society. Haunted places are one such example. With its roots in social anthropology, the term *liminality* derives from work on the temporarily "in between" positioning of those undergoing changes in status within social groups. Such experiences typically involve immersion in temporal and spatial zones that are separate from everyday life. They are thus readily applicable to the Gothic as a genre which routinely transgresses accepted boundaries such as those between fundamentally distinct states like past and present and life and death. This section will also discuss the impact of these spaces on those who encounter them. The concept of liminality epitomizes the kind of borderland territory so crucial to the present study. As such, liminality is intrinsic to the haunted house motif and a vital attribute of the haunted fictions analyzed in this study. For example, haunting sets Tom Wallace of Matheson's *A Stir of Echoes* apart from his daily life, enabling him to gain a perspective on his community which was unavailable to him so long as he remained within it.

Finally, these three strands will be brought together in a discussion of haunted fiction to show that the haunted house motif provides the kind of literary spaces that allow access to, and interrogation of, the particular times and places it evokes in each tale. I maintain here that haunted space is liminal space, allowing characters access to, and a perspective on, histories and ideologies that they would otherwise not experience. While there may be distinctions drawn between different types of haunted space, according to the texts under discussion, overall my contention is that all such spaces have similarly revelatory functions. This argument will inform later chapters, where a close analysis of haunted texts will reveal the diverse circumstances in which this function may operate.

American Gothic

American Gothic and the larger family of which it is a part (the Gothic) are complex and multi-dimensional generic areas. From its inception the Gothic came to be associated with antiquated settings and supernatural events. Yet, despite this seeming disregard for contemporary reality, the genre has ever been used to engage with immediate issues of injustice and oppression. It works variously to expose social ills, critique the structures that have given rise to and sustained them, and question previously-unchallenged norms and values. Critics have traced the differences between American Gothic and the eighteenth-century European works from which it derives, noting how this specific American variant, as with its European counterpart, continues to develop into the twenty-first century. For the purposes of the current study, I identify a number of areas for relatively brief discussion in this section: the adaptation of British Gothic to an American literary and social context and the defining features and purposes of the latter.

Some overtly European features, such as issues of aristocracy and hereditary rights, as well as the places to which they pertain, appear rather less pressing in the case of the United States, given its status—at the very time that the European Gothic was popular—as a still-new and relatively unformed nation, lacking precisely those ancient buildings and long-established social institutions on which the first instances of the genre depended. Yet, even with these differences, David Punter affirms the European influence on early American literature with the observation that "where English Gothic has a direct past to deal with, American has a level interposed between present and past ... an often already mythologised 'Old World.'"[45] Indeed, Poe's Gothic is notable for its deployment of a "quasi-European setting"[46] rather than for an identifiably American one.

This peculiarity has given rise to the view that American Gothic is intrinsically paradoxical—whereas America connotes newness, the term *Gothic* invokes the past.[47] Teresa Goddu contrasts it with the more established European Gothic in noting, "Unlike the British gothic, which developed during a definable time period ... and has a recognized coterie of authors ... the American gothic, one of several forms that played a role in the development of the early American novel, is less easily specified in terms of a particular time period or group of authors. There was no founding period of gothic literature in America."[48] Removed as they were from the European context and based in a nation "born of Enlightenment ideals,"[49] the earliest American authors in the Gothic tradition, like Charles Brockden Brown, were not described as such at the time.

Yet despite America's drive towards futurity the genre was clearly found to be of continuing relevance to this young nation whose fears were different from, yet no less grave than, those of Europe, encompassing both anxiety about the past it had fled and concern for the future it was trying to build. As Mark Jancovich argues, "It was horror fiction's concern with the relationship between the past and the present which made it so appealing to American writers."[50] With its desire to avoid past mistakes in forging a better society in the New World, America was concerned with history from the outset, and this was reflected in its literary output.

Indeed, America brought its own special anxieties to the Gothic. In addition to those concerns which it shared with its British forebear—horror, madness, death, the supernatural—distinctively American concerns included the untamed wilderness and those "profane presences [it] might harbour."[51] Regarded as fundamentally uncivilized and peopled by dangerous savages, the land itself was a natural source of fear for an early American audience concerned with creating a new nation in the face of a hostile frontier experience and in isolation from the Old World. This issue can be detected in such early works of American Gothic as Charles Brockden Brown's *Edgar Huntly* (1799), in which Brown's own preface designates "the incidents of Indian hostility, and the perils of the western wilderness"[52] as vital components of the American experience.[53] Allan Lloyd-Smith indicates the "compulsion of the settler to kill and to signal his triumph over the barbaric."[54] For Jared Gardner, *Edgar Huntly* portrays a late eighteenth-century America which saw its very identity as contingent upon Indian removal,[55] and Renée L. Bergland echoes this in noting that Huntly's personal struggle to develop a civilized self mirrors the struggle taking place at a national level.[56]

As with the trauma of prolonged conflict with and wrongful treatment of indigenous peoples, the horror of institutionalized slavery has had far-reaching effects on American culture and literature. Herman Melville's "Benito Cereno" (1856), the tale of the eponymous captain of a Spanish slave ship ousted by his slave Babo, addresses this concern. It illustrates the anxieties attendant upon such a tenuous state of authority and, in having a Northern American captain assist with bringing Babo to justice, insinuates "a hypocritical collusion of the North with the Peculiar Institution of the South [slavery] at the time of impending pre–

Civil War tension."[57] Though this is not a supernatural story, the ship—haunted by the brutality of the recent revolt—functions as a version of the Gothic castle, and a sense of dark secrecy pervades the entire narrative, structured as it is by a convoluted quest for the truth.[58] In the same way that the religious imperatives of Puritanism to establish a model society left their mark,[59] an early history marred by violence and racism left America to contend with what Lloyd-Smith terms "the political horror of a failed utopianism."[60]

Thematically, it can be seen that the above conventions point once again to the Gothic emphasis on the return of the repressed—this time in terms of American history and experience. Despite its relative youth then, America seems no less bound up with history than its European ancestor. Its brief history has provided ample scope for a uniquely Gothic literature to emerge, one shaped by its own nascent political concerns such as land ownership and the control of resources. To take one canonical example, in discussing *Edgar Huntly*, Leslie Fiedler delineates how the adaptation of European genre conventions for an American milieu also means a crucial shift in the ideological meaning of the Gothic: "The heathen, unredeemed wilderness and not the decaying monuments of a dying class, nature and not society becomes the symbol of evil. Similarly not the aristocrat but the Indian, not the dandified courtier but the savage colored man is postulated as the embodiment of villainy. Our novel of terror … is well on the way to becoming a Calvinist exposé of natural human corruption rather than an enlightened attack on a debased ruling class or entrenched superstition."[61]

In contrast with the examples of British Gothic considered above—tales that often challenge the existing social order and can thus be construed as radical—Fiedler argues that the political thrust of American Gothic is essentially conformist and reactionary. Whereas, he contends, "the European gothic identified blackness with the super-ego and was therefore revolutionary in its implications; the American gothic … identified evil with the id and was therefore conservative at its deepest level of implication, whatever the intent of its authors."[62] Fiedler's claim that American Gothic developed as an inherently conservative literary form is valuable in both acknowledging the genre's historical roots and drawing attention to its capacity for political engagement. Yet this unequivocal position needs to be tempered in light of how the genre has evolved. In adapting to various cultural milieus over time, the haunted house motif lays bare the complexity of twentieth-century American history and culture. This results in the depiction of diverse—often incompatible—beliefs and ideologies and thus, over the course of the present study, my own examples of haunted fiction exhibit a blend of conservative and radical impulses.

It is important to consider why such an identifiably antiquated genre has been repeatedly employed by authors up to, and into, the twenty-first century.[63] American Gothic's engagement with its national past has been—and continues to be—a tentative means of addressing fears, crystallizing anxieties and exploring how tension might be channeled (and perhaps controlled) through a text. Lloyd-Smith suggests that Gothic may be better suited than realist fiction for probing unresolved conflicts and concealed impulses "because it is in some ways freed by its status as absurd fantasy."[64] The efficacy of these works in situations characterized by some kind of stress could account for their continued popularity, and the status of Gothic as a *popular* fictional form will be examined in greater detail below.

With its competing drives towards the present and the past, the Gothic has ever sought to linger simultaneously on the impact of history while looking ahead to the future,[65] and this tension seems especially pertinent to an American audience. When such fiction first emerged, it served as a means through which its writers and readers could reflect on an era of change. The horror in European Gothic centered on oppressive social structures, while horror in American Gothic stemmed from the lack of—and need to develop—such civilizing frameworks. Gothic has thus dealt with the extent to which people continue to feel tied to a troubled past, even in the context of a new, more future-oriented, world. A desire for this endures in the present day, as the genre clearly meets a need for those millions who continue to consume it. Authors like Stephen King, tied to their literary ancestors through the conventions and tropes outlined above, have periodically dominated the bestseller lists for decades,[66] engaging the fears and anxieties of a national (even international) audience. However, as later chapters will show—and bearing in mind what Fiedler contends is the conservative bent of American Gothic—the popular fictions about haunting analyzed in the present study typically explore issues so intractable as to elude any possibility of a definitive resolution.

American Gothic fiction's thematic concern with the lingering impact of the past has clearly tied it to distinct kinds of physical places, both wild and civilized. Stylistically, because it seeks to exploit uncertainty and generate suspense in its readers, it is a genre ultimately reliant on the development of atmosphere insofar as descriptions of physical space are used to create mood. These depictions may then be used to connote themes. American Gothic is concerned both with setting and with the significance of that setting, just as is European Gothic. For example, Bergland notes that Gothic tropes have been adapted to address American fears about the hostility of the wilderness they occupy: "When cliffs are substituted for castle towers, and caves for dungeons, the threats and dangers of the natural world replace the threats and dangers of ancient aristocratic power structures."[67] Such tales are typically placed in a certain type of physical environment or structure which is used to produce tension. This may then create a sense of "atmosphere" in the mind of the reader. To put this in another way, Gothic spaces work to convey the historical, cultural and, therefore, ideological, anxieties which underpin Gothic fictions. The following section seeks to address this feature of the genre.

Space

It has often been noted that setting is a central motif of Gothic fiction,[68] and it has certainly continued to play a vital role in American Gothic. Indeed, Dale Bailey argues that "in few other genres does setting play such a significant and defining role."[69] Locations have included man-made spaces, such as the traditional castle, and the wild, sublime landscapes in which they are situated. Such early settings have altered to suit changing times; gloomy castles were historically more intimidating, but contemporary authors have utilized a wide range of settings to update the field. And the Gothic trope of haunting uses space to perform particular functions. This section will therefore explore notions of space in relation to genre. In particular, it will consider how this relationship finds special expression in Gothic through the haunted house motif.

Of crucial importance to this study is space in the physical sense and, for my purposes, the term is used to encompass a rather more diverse range of physical locations than is found in early Gothic fictions.

I will show that Anne Williams's observation about early Gothic—that the "imposing house with a terrible secret"[70] is central—expands, in modern Gothic fictions, to include all manner of troubled spaces. From Lovecraft's fictionalized versions of genuine New England historical dwellings to Matheson's post–Second World War mass-produced tract houses, my chosen American Gothic texts demonstrate how the haunted house motif works to transplant Gothic conventions into a variety of domestic spaces, even those seemingly least conducive to traditional manifestations of haunting. And, as will be shown with King's fiction, the motif also extends to include other locations—from an unremarkable family car to a whole luxury hotel.

Space may also suggest freedom from oppression or routine and the concomitant chance to benefit from such release. Space in this sense suggests an emotional and psychological distancing, as from a traumatizing event or from stultifying circumstances. Obtaining this kind of space implies obtaining a valuable opportunity: perhaps to achieve some measure of renewal, or at least to find a fresh perspective on a challenging situation through stepping beyond its immediate confines. As my case studies will show, it is not uncommon for protagonists of contemporary Gothic fictions to be in need of such an experience as their stories commence. To take some examples, David Cooper of Matheson's *Earthbound* (1982; 1989) takes his wife back to where they spent their honeymoon after they begin to experience marriage difficulties, while Mike Noonan from King's *Bag of Bones* (1998) retreats to his vacation home to get his life back on track after the untimely death of his wife. As the tales advance, and the protagonists encounter supernatural events, the properties of the haunted house motif subject them to a distinctive version of this emotional and psychological space, one bound up with the physical spaces they occupy.

Having considered the nature and function of space in relation to this study, there is a need to consider how it relates to memory and identity. In her work on prosthetic memory and its relation to identity politics in American culture, Alison Landsberg makes the observation that "memories are central to a person's identity—to one's sense of who one is and who one might become ... they become the building blocks from which to construct narratives of the present and visions for the future."[71] In other words, memory makes people and communities, even entire nations, who they are—or who they think they are. And memory is often tied directly to, perhaps even contingent upon, a physical space.[72]

In Gothic fiction, it is the trope of haunting that links memory to space. Haunting is thus a special kind of memory. In her study of haunting in the Hudson Valley, Judith Richardson observes that ghosts are the outcome of the communal lives that report them and are thus tied to physical space. Designating them as a "kind of social memory, an alternate form of history-making in which things usually forgotten, discarded, or repressed become foregrounded,"[73] she acknowledges ways in which tales of supernatural entities from ages past can reveal as much about the present as about the history they represent. Her work, more on history and folklore rather than on literature, nevertheless highlights the importance of both writer and reader in such Gothic fiction. The comment that "the main work of haunting is done by the living"[74] shows that fictional ghosts and haunting are not just about the dead, but rather about those who remember them, whether writing about them, reading about them or experiencing them through fiction. Jancovich observes that Gothic and horror often feature physical spaces like houses which act as "a manifestation of the past which comes to threaten or dominate the present."[75] Such spaces thus give material form to the genre's recurring theme of bringing the past into the present.

In talking of architectural and physical space, the house is naturally of peculiar interest. Gaston Bachelard's study of "eulogized space"[76]—that which is seen and loved on the basis of its special status—provides a philosophical reflection on the emotions attached to human experience of space. He observes, "The house, quite obviously, is a privileged entity for a phenomenological study of the intimate values of inside space."[77] As revered locales, houses may seem obvious places for us to go to escape from any dangers that may assail us. Yet, in acknowledging that houses are exceptional kinds of space, we also acknowledge that they can be a prime site for provoking fear.[78] Anthony Vidler avers that the uncanny finds architectural expression in the form of the house that "pretends to afford the utmost security while opening itself to the secret intrusion of terror."[79] Because of this close association with family and stability, houses, when used as settings of fear, are especially good at provoking tension and anxiety in most people—both about the relationship of individual to family and of family to larger social and historical whole—a fact continually borne out by horror fiction.[80] This shows the genre's drive towards isolating and exploiting key areas of sensitivity in its readers and, perhaps, in its writers too. It is doubtless for this reason, chiefly if not exclusively, that the haunted house has been an important locale for inspiring anxiety and conflict in so many works of horror fiction in America and elsewhere.

However, it can be argued that there is no need to restrict the kind of fears associated with the violation of personal space (in American Gothic, this personal space has traditionally taken the form of the house, as the domestic version of the Gothic castle) merely to residences. Bachelard continues his reflections to observe that "all really inhabited space bears the essence of the notion of home."[81] The definition of personal, or intimate, space could then very well be extended to incorporate what might be described as extensions of the home, like the haunted vehicle of King's *Christine*, or to public versions of the home, such as King's Overlook Hotel in *The Shining*. Indeed, any space which is regularly used by, and thus bears the mark of, human occupants can fundamentally be seen as a kind of "home away from home."

This book will show how my chosen authors use haunting to engage with history and ideology. Richardson's study shows that ghosts have much to reveal about how people relate to the spaces they occupy. The sense that these spaces have been shaped by the past—and sometimes conceal unpleasant, frequently ignored, histories—is crucial to this. With reference to the examples mentioned above, a space like a vintage 1950s automobile can act as Gothic territory ripe for exploring the contradictory impulses induced by nostalgia. And a prestigious hotel, with its roots in the Gilded Age, can provide a fictional arena for interrogating the inequalities entrenched within corporate capitalism. It can thus be seen that space has a special part to play in American Gothic, particularly with regard to haunted fictions. With this in mind, attention will now be turned to how this relates to the other key component of the haunted house motif: liminality.

Liminality

Liminality is a term that has come to epitomize boundaries, as well as transition and progress.[82] Arnold van Gennep's work on initiation practices led to his identification of so-called *"rites de passage"* (original emphasis),[83] which he describes as a "series of rites of separation, transition, and incorporation,"[84] common to many societies, in which those about to undergo a change in status—such as those participating in tribal initiations or training for the priesthood—temporarily separate from society in order to return to a higher state within it. This transitional or liminal phase is characterized as a sacred time, apart from the normal experience of society, in which the novitiate or liminar has the time and opportunity to absorb the kind of knowledge so vital to their anticipated progress.[85]

Borrowing from Van Gennep's work, Victor Turner explains that such knowledge might take the form of tribal lore, myths and access to sacred objects.[86] For Turner the liminar, as a passenger travelling from a state of separation from society through to a state of re-aggregation, can be described as "ambiguous, neither here nor there, betwixt and between all fixed points of classification; he passes through a symbolic domain that has few or none of the attributes of his past or coming state."[87] So a liminal period, in terms of space and time, is characterized by its relative isolation. It is a time apart from normal everyday experience, a place for confrontation, trial and theoretically for progress. Being defined as a transitional place between two positions in a status sequence,[88] liminality is an ideal, even necessary, arena for individual development and growth. The liminar holds a precarious position in terms of structural invisibility, being outside of society's normal boundaries and confined to a space shrouded in mystery for those who do not share it.[89] Essentially, liminars are temporarily freed from mundane concerns in order that they may contemplate the wider mysteries of life,[90] then learn to become more rounded and mature members of their society.

Critics have taken this concept of liminality from its anthropological roots and extended its use to the study of literature. Arguing that "literary texts are in themselves liminal spaces," Hein Viljoen and Chris N. van der Merwe see fiction as a potential vehicle through which readers may see the world anew.[91] I argue here that the trope of haunting performs such a function in Gothic literature. Manuel Aguirre, Roberta Quance and Philip Sutton stress that those texts and genres which are designated as liminal take as their focus "a crossover, a transgression or an entry into the Other."[92] Such properties can certainly be attributed to fictions about haunting. From Matheson's tainted suburban spaces to King's bleak depictions of the underbelly of rural communities, the current study examines encounters with ghostly presences that work to estrange protagonists from their daily lives, forcing them to see previously-accepted versions of their "reality" in a very different light.

However, whereas the anthropological account of the nature and outcome of liminality emphasizes the individual's reintegration into society, the same may not be true of liminality in literature. This is especially discernible in the case of Gothic fiction. Having undergone a challenging time of separation from society, the liminar discussed by Van Gennep and Turner is ultimately permitted to achieve re-integration. Yet, although the liminal Gothic protagonist will become separated from the mainstream of society and gain knowledge as a result, such re-integration—or even a real resolution of any kind—is typically denied them. Because the literary usage of liminality is frequently so different from that of anthropology, it has been observed that "the liminal can be a place of threat as well as of promise."[93] As such, it may be "progressive or conservative, productive or destructive."[94] The narrative treatment of the hauntings discussed here thus has ideological implications. When these hauntings (characterized as they are by revelatory insights) fail to effect change, when there is a failure to progress "to a postliminal state,"[95] then this fiction fails to realize its radical potential and falls back instead into conservatism.

To return to the anthropological origins of liminality, although the term refers to a period of time, it may also denote a physical space apart; possibly a purpose-built space such as a "seclusion lodge or camp."[96] This physical space provides the necessary conditions, solitude and access to vital knowledge, for the liminar to develop. For my purpose then, liminal space may take the form of a haunted building or other edifice: a space that functions as a space apart from the ordinary, one in which to explore the boundaries and interactions between life and death, past and present, unearthly and earthly, self and society.[97] With regard to the former concept of margins and thresholds, liminality may denote a phase between more discrete stages such as childhood and adulthood, innocence and enlightenment, life and death. The term *liminal* may then be used to refer to that which occupies the borderland between such states. Building on this is the latter notion of change and development: if liminality is a borderland, then it is arguably a place, in the more abstract sense of the word, which permits reflection and, perhaps, growth.

Linking this back to genre, it has been observed that Gothic fiction is fundamentally liminal.[98] Indeed it has ever pushed at the boundaries of what is considered socially acceptable in both its subject matter and style. As Botting observes, the genre was heavily criticized on the basis that it "produced emotional effects on its readers rather than developing a rational or properly cultivated response."[99] And, as noted earlier, the genre originated in a historical era characterized by tensions between Enlightenment rationalism and the older belief that religion was the means of explanation and salvation in a world where evil and darkness threatened to overwhelm humanity. Further to this, Gothic habitually deals with boundaries and boundary-crossing in taking murder, incest, kidnapping and so forth as its subject matter. The early Gothic supernatural tropes combine with later features such as vampires, werewolves and zombies (blending with the horror genre in doing so) to provide an excess of violence, embodied by these liminal creatures that cross natural boundaries between normally-distinct states. As well as crossing boundaries of taste and decency, such fiction is renowned for exploring the line between life and death, natural and supernatural, fantasy and reality, childhood and maturity, ignorance and awareness. Of chief interest here is Gothic's provision of liminal spaces and experiences through the trope of haunting.

In terms of space, liminality deals with both the physical and the psychological applications of the term. In allowing its protagonists (and, vicariously, its readers) to have bodily and emotional distance from the day-to-day, the Gothic genre engages with space in its tangible and less-tangible forms. Evocative locations, such as places of confinement or sites of traumatic past events, may serve as places where characters encounter horrors which readers are asked to interrogate; perhaps in the form of oppression from the ruling classes in early Gothic, or the legacy of slavery in later American Gothic. Beyond this, however, if a physical setting, aberrant in some way, is facilitative of some kind of change, in the form of personal development or the acquisition of knowledge, it can be described as liminal. Such spaces will typically be isolated, enjoying a special status because only certain people will be privy to their powers, a factor which ties in with Turner's designation of liminal space as that which is apart from daily life. These locations therefore perform special functions in allowing those who enter the spaces to undergo a kind of rite of passage, akin to those described in Van Gennep's work and developed by Turner with reference to liminality, yet complicated by the awareness that liminality in literature often permits no move to the post-liminal state that these critics describe.

In combining considerations of Gothic space with those of liminality and the potential it entails, the above analysis leads on to the final section of this introduction which deals specifically with that key Gothic theme, the return of the repressed, epitomized by the haunted house motif itself.

The Haunted House Motif

Bringing the three strands of genre, space and liminality together, this final section will demonstrate that Gothic space is intrinsically liminal in both nature and function. Given that haunted fiction is necessarily concerned with ghosts and with the past, it is my contention that the liminal nature of haunting is particularly relevant and helpful because the liminality of such fiction affords an engagement with the histories it evokes—one that demands a confrontation with the competing ideological forces found therein. Crucially, it is the haunted house motif that unites these areas, and this concept is at the very heart of my argument. In order to clarify this fundamental notion, this part of the chapter will situate the current study alongside existing criticism on fictional haunting and elucidate how, in fusing the three components discussed throughout the Introduction, the idea of the haunted house motif offers a distinctive and original means of understanding haunted fiction. It will also provide a brief introduction to the authors from among whose works my case studies have been selected. As they are deemed to be popular, this will be done in conjunction with an appraisal of the nature and uses of popular fiction, maintaining that popular haunted fiction has the capacity to interrogate the socio-historical contexts from which it emerges.

A survey of previous criticism reveals some common ground with the current study regarding the qualities and purposes of haunted fiction. In *The Contested Castle: Gothic Novels and the Subversion of Domestic Ideology* (1989) Kate Ferguson Ellis stresses that, despite its supernatural tropes and lurid themes, early Gothic literature is most emphatically not escapist and specifically works to expose the underbelly of everyday life of the time.[100] Similarly, in *The Closed Space: Horror Literature and Western Symbolism* (1990), Manuel Aguirre sums up the key criteria of the literary haunted castle as "the confining building, the atmosphere of dread, the crime committed *in illo tempore* (original emphasis), the secrecy, the ghost demanding reparation."[101] With the genre's migration to the New World came the shift from castle to house, as described above, and Eric Savoy notes that "the house is the most persistent site, object, structural analogue, and trope of American gothic's allegorical turn."[102] This alignment of horror with the ordinary home—rather than the bastions of Old World aristocracy—calls to mind once again the uncanny, as that which is "strange within the familiar,"[103] as a central concern of American Gothic. Haunted houses, with their connotations of identity and security, harbor secrets and thus address fears about the individual and their place within society: fears that adapt over time as the nation changes. I join with these critics in seeing Gothic as a means of probing—even challenging—unpalatable aspects of American history and culture that might otherwise be overlooked, though the twentieth-century tales on which I focus typically lack the kind of closure discernible in the first examples of the genre. Further, through the idea of the motif, I extend the properties attributed to fictional haunted houses to other types of space.

These critics, along with those discussed earlier in this chapter, tender insights expressly on the subject of haunted space. There are works devoted to haunting and ghosts in American history and culture, like Richardson's study of the Hudson Valley and Bergland's analysis of the figure of the Indian, as well as works on ghosts in English stories and in literary American fiction. While Railo's book is on the haunted castle, Bailey's *American Nightmares: The Haunted House Formula in American Popular Fiction* (1999) examines haunted houses in American Gothic. In seeking to separate fiction that takes haunted houses as its exclusive focus from the broader category of haunted fiction, Bailey's work is confined to an analysis of troubled domestic space. His haunted house formula incorporates variations on four areas—setting, characters, plot and themes—that he identifies across numerous instances of this fiction.[104] Themes encompass class and gender conflict, fiscal hardship and the "consequences of the past,"[105] which latter subject I would cast as that perennial obsession of the Gothic genre, the return of the repressed. For Bailey, these themes "present deeply subversive critiques of all that [Americans] hold to be true," and he avers that the "formulaic construction" of these tales is a key component of their critical success.[106] His analysis undoubtedly isolates key areas of interest for those wishing to examine the place of this type of fiction in American culture.

Illuminating as Bailey's case studies are, the stress he places on singling out such a blueprint renders his account of haunted fiction an excessively reductive one. In this rigid formula, the more divergent aspects of this most ingrained and adaptable of story-types go unobserved. Therefore, I argue that he places too great an emphasis on establishing the repetitive formal elements within the genre and not enough on its inherent thematic flexibility. I do concur with his claim that these tales yield apt observations about problematic aspects of American culture. Partly—and in opposition to Bailey's views—it can be seen that the formulaic nature of such fiction may actually disallow the implementation of solutions to the problems it depicts, e.g., when haunted dwellings like *The Shining*'s Overlook Hotel are destroyed while no firm resolution is provided to the competing ideologies they work to represent. Yet, as discussed previously, I argue that it is the thematic density of these tales—in terms of the complexity of the ideas they raise—and not merely their status as genre fiction, which sees many of them conclude with scenarios that fail to impart the kind of resolutions which were possible in early Gothic. So, although these conventions might very well recur, there is significantly more to haunted fiction than a simple focus on its formulaic nature would suggest. My conception of the haunted house motif not only encompasses fiction that incorporates more wide-ranging hauntings than Bailey's haunted house tales, but also draws on liminality in order to complicate the role of genre fiction.

In tandem with critical work on Gothic and on haunting, then, the main theoretical framework that underpins the present study is liminality—a model drawn originally from the work of Van Gennep and

Turner in anthropology and then adapted for the study of literature. This is the key concept that informs the case studies, selected from among the publications of three American authors, which make up the chapters of this book. The methodology employed to analyze their fiction is textual analysis. Close and detailed textual readings of these haunted fictions reveal that, time and again, the haunted house motif works as a critical device through which to interrogate important facets of American culture.

The authors have been isolated for analysis on the basis of their distinctive and innovative contributions to American Gothic in general and to depictions of haunting in particular. The first author, H. P. Lovecraft (1890–1937), was a native of Rhode Island renowned for the New England regionalism which permeated his work and whose supernatural stories appeared principally in pulp magazines. The second, Richard Matheson (1926–2013), was active as a screenwriter and producer of horror and science fiction from the early 1950s. Finally Stephen King (1947–), whose career began in the 1960s and 1970s, remains a phenomenally prolific writer of novels, short stories, comic books, Internet publications, and film and television screenplays, which often take horror as their chief focus.

As they run the gamut of the twentieth century, from the inter-war years to the close of the 1990s (and beyond), and have consequently been able to inspire, react against and respond to each other's oeuvres, these writers represent significant trends in American Gothic over the previous century. The work of all three authors resonates with the time in which they write—from Lovecraft's modernist take on Gothic, to Matheson's emphasis on the daily lives of ordinary citizens, to King's endeavors to explore new kinds of space relevant to the American experience. Cementing their status as key figures in the evolution of the genre, their fictions—with the various kinds of haunted spaces they describe—demonstrate how the haunted house motif adapts to the ever-changing conditions of American modernity and how the liminality of haunting addresses the concomitant social unease that such changes bring.

My chosen focus on haunting—an aspect of their fiction largely unexplored by critics—means that this book provides an examination of texts that have received little or no previous scholarly attention.

Throughout the remaining chapters, examples of their fiction will be studied chronologically in order to show how the Gothic provides a literary space for reflection upon the diverse phases through which American culture has passed during the twentieth century. Liminality, with its faculty for boundary crossing, is an integral feature of these fictional hauntings, which confound accepted notions of time and space in order to call the socio-historical contexts which they depict into question.

Although the case has been made for placing their work within a more broadly literary tradition, this book focuses on writers of popular fiction. It is therefore necessary to consider the implications of this categorization. Ken Gelder commences his study of popular fiction by defining it in opposition to literature. Whereas the latter is held in high esteem on the basis that it is fundamentally meaningful, intellectual and creative, popular fiction is seen instead as inconsequential, sensuous and formulaic.[107] As a corollary to this, readers of literature are purportedly more contemplative than those who read popular fiction.[108] A crucial distinction between literary and popular authors is the latter's intention to produce novels with a mass, rather than a critical, appeal.[109] Indeed, Clive Bloom's work on popular fiction is concerned with what he terms "the history of bestsellers."[110] So, while literature is "enmeshed with the art world,"[111] popular fiction is derided as mere mass-produced entertainment, inherently lowbrow because of its blatant commercialism. As mere consumers, rather than active participants in the society to which they belong, those who "consume" such "products" are necessarily rendered passive. So the prevalence of these mass products is seen to lead to a standardized and unmotivated populace.

Yet critics are not united in dismissing mass culture and its manifestations as intrinsically worthless. In the 1980s, the rise of cultural studies saw some academics embrace the study of popular culture, turning critical attention towards areas such as audience studies.[112] While my work is not concerned with the audience per se, it is certainly concerned with those texts which, in line with the definitions of popular fiction supplied above, might be construed as of interest to a general audience. For Scott McCracken such fiction is a worthwhile object of academic study because, in order to achieve broad appeal, it has to anticipate the needs of its audiences.[113] On this basis, he argues, "narratives read by large numbers of people are indicative of widespread hopes and fears."[114] Such fiction is arguably as capable as literature of upholding and contesting ideologies.[115] This means that, for McCracken, popular fiction can only properly be understood within its socio-historic context.[116] As explained above, I will analyze my chosen texts as products of the particular moments at which they appear in twentieth-century America.

Specifically, the general audience evoked in the preceding paragraph can be defined as one with a taste for *genre*. Both Gelder and McCracken align popular fiction with genre fiction, concurring that— among others—romance, crime, science fiction and horror are all major genres in the popular domain. It is, to a large extent, this alliance with genre that has led to popular fiction being denigrated as formulaic, conservative and therefore lowbrow.[117] For this study, it is important to note Bloom's avowal that "gothic is *the* genre against which critics attempted to separate serious fiction from … popular entertainment and escapism."[118] He casts Poe as a kind of bridge between literary and popular fiction, as his fiction draws on artistic and philosophical preoccupations while simultaneously achieving a broad appeal for its obvious entertainment value.[119] Gothic is a genre which has continued to attract both literary and overtly populist authors, and sometimes the boundaries become extremely blurred between the two. To take one highly pertinent example, Stephen King—whose "popularity" in the simplest sense of sales volume can hardly be denied—has also been celebrated as a literary author. In 2003, he was awarded the Medal for Distinguished Contribution to American Letters from America's National Book Foundation. Observing that the majority of those previously honored thus were authors of literature, Gelder acknowledges that "King was a different kind of recipient."[120] Not only is it debatable that literary fiction is suitable for academic critique in a way that popular fiction is not, but also that the distinction between the two fields is clearly demarcated.

With these observations in mind, my study provides a new way of looking at popular fiction by means of the haunted house motif. Haunting is arguably the clearest manifestation of Gothic's deep-seated fixation with the return of the repressed—its drive to expose forgotten, ostensibly vanquished, past events that cannot lie forever dormant. The time-honored means of conveying this impulse—the haunted castle of Old World Gothic—is transformed into the haunted house in the New World, yet the haunted house motif extends this generic fascination with place and setting to spaces beyond mere dwellings and thus encompasses still more facets of the human experience. Liminality is the key notion that informs this concept. Haunting and haunted space are liminal in nature, as they are borderlands straddling life and death, past and present, and they function as spaces, and times, apart from everyday life which afford the opportunity for these things to be examined. The haunted house motif shows that, in fictional treatments of haunting, notions of "time apart" and "space apart"—both central to Turner's account of the liminal experience—start to merge, to powerful critical effect. My argument is that haunting and haunted spaces are intrinsically liminal. As textual examples will show, in being set apart from daily society, liminars gain the chance to see it anew. From Lovecraft's regional space to Matheson's quotidian settings and King's revisioning of haunting, this study shows that popular haunted fictions can, and do, provide narrative spaces in which authors interrogate history and through which readers engage with the complex ideologies to which they give rise.

CHAPTER ONE

"The changeless, legend-haunted city of Arkham"

Cosmicism, Regionalism and Liminality in "The Dreams in the Witch House"

In demarcating the nature and function of the haunted house motif, the Introduction has established that the physical settings in which Gothic fictions play out are fundamentally liminal. As a result, haunted fictions enable authors and readers to engage with a range of often clashing histories set in motion by liminal spaces and sites. Such engagements with the past might be driven by a desire to reconcile history with the present, but this proves to be no easy task. Indeed, the depictions and evocations of American history and culture examined here foreground intractable forces and generate testing encounters which brook no easy resolution. The liminality of haunting conjures up a narrative arena, set apart from the everyday, in which the complex and frequently contradictory nature of American society is revealed.

This book commences with a chapter examining the haunted fiction of H. P. Lovecraft, a figure central to the development of twentieth-century American Gothic. Born in 1890 in Providence, Rhode Island,[1] Lovecraft's close involvement with amateur publishing from his early twenties stoked a lifelong enthusiasm for writing.[2] Several of his tales appeared in amateur publications, though most were published in genre-based pulp magazines like *Weird Tales* and *Amazing Stories*.[3] Though writing within a recognizably Gothic tradition, whereby physical space occupies a central role and the threat of the return of the repressed seems ever present, Lovecraft nonetheless offered a peculiarly modern twist to the genre and is therefore crucial to this study. Besides his horror fiction, his worldviews have been well documented in the extensive correspondences he undertook regularly with family members and the wide array of friends and acquaintances made through his writing. These letters help inform a reading of his tales—fabricated from the turn of the century until his death in the late 1930s—which he used as a response to the turbulent decades of early twentieth-century America, particularly with regard to industrialization, urbanization and modernization.

Distinguishing the first two decades of the 1900s as an age that saw "backward-looking images and ideas contesting with the voices of prophecy, the reactionary coexisting with the subversive,"[4] Peter Conn thus delineates the "divided mind" of America at the start of the twentieth century from which his study derives its title. Yet cultural historian Lawrence W. Levine perceives that such a tension is by no means unique to this era. Rather, he identifies an enduring "belief in progress coupled with a dread of change; an urge towards the inevitable future combined with a longing for the irretrievable past" which constitutes the "central paradox of American history."[5] Avowing that it is the 1920s—the decade following Conn's chosen timeframe—that best exemplifies this conflict, Levine points to anxieties about national purity, immigration and modernity which provoked in many Americans a desire "to return, at least symbolically, to a golden past."[6]

Making the shift into modernity at this time, America was thus a nation poised on a threshold: as anxious about what lay before it as about what lay behind. Bound up as it is with the tension between clinging to the past and yielding to complex and powerful processes of modernization, Lovecraft's fiction reflects this ambivalence. One of his later tales, "The Dreams in the Witch House" (1933) tells of a gifted young student living in the house—named after a former occupant incarcerated for witchcraft—to study the implications of so-called "magic" for contemporary science. The backdrop of Salem, Massachusetts, grounds this fictional treatment of social change in the real world. As befits its late 1920s setting, the story addresses the impact of science on culture and explores the changing modes of explanation that were in evidence at that time. Further, with an overtly New England location—as well as a deliberate reworking of known regional history—its portrayal of evolving demographic patterns and shifts in living arrangements indexes the rapid changes wrought by modernity.

Broadly speaking, then, Lovecraft's fiction is marked out by an air of conflict. As will be explored throughout this study, usages of liminality differ between my chosen authors, reflecting the various eras and themes with which they contend. Recalling Leslie A. Fiedler's claim about the conformist nature of American Gothic, it can be seen that liminality in Lovecraft's work unleashes progressive notions while endorsing conservative ideologies. Forward-thinking in its depiction of knowledge and yet highly reactionary in its handling of social matters, "The Dreams in the Witch House" is a contradictory maelstrom of radical and conservative impulses. With no resolution to the dilemmas created by these competing pressures, and thus reflective of Lovecraft's unease with modernity, the tale rejects any possibility that the liminar might learn from his experience and concludes with his destruction. It is through the liminality of haunting that these historical and ideological clashes—which the author never moves to fully reconcile—are activated.

Some brief biographical facts will help frame an understanding of Lovecraft's distinctive contribution to horror. Despite prolonged hiatuses in his formal education,[7] he eagerly devoured the likes of Grimms' *Fairy Tales*, the *Arabian Nights* and the works of Edgar Allan Poe from a young age.[8] His youthful "predilection for natural science"[9] drove him to study disciplines like chemistry and astronomy even while at home.[10] These influences shaped his worldview and laid the foundations for his own brand of Gothic, and it is of note that "The Dreams in the Witch House" draws on such seemingly-disparate spheres of interest as "quantum physics [and] folklore."[11] Astronomy was to exert an especially profound effect on Lovecraft's understanding of the universe and the place of the human race within it. In a letter from 1924, he recollected his brush at first-hand—via his astronomy studies—with "the myriad suns and worlds of infinite space" as one of the "most poignant sensations of my existence."[12] This personal encounter with a wider universe caused him to regard human life from a markedly detached perspective. Struck by the smallness of Earth in relation to the vastness of space in which it sat, he reminisced that "by my thirteenth birthday I was thoroughly impressed with man's impermanence and insignificance, and by my seventeenth ... I had formed in all essential particulars my present pessimistic cosmic views."[13] These reflections reveal the roots of the "cosmism"—the belief of the insignificance of humanity in the context of a vast, inevitably indifferent cosmos—for which his writing is renowned.

Lovecraft's absorption with science and discovery, along with his aforementioned literary taste for the fantastic and macabre, gave rise to a highly idiosyncratic generic blend of Gothic and science fiction.[14] Accustomed to reading and critiquing horror fiction—his celebrated essay *Supernatural Horror in Literature* (1927) ranges from early British Gothic through Poe and Nathaniel Hawthorne to Arthur Machen, Algernon Blackwood and M. R. James—he was certainly familiar with the literature which preceded his own efforts. Although favorably impressed by many of these authors, Lovecraft was scornful of hackneyed attempts to frighten. In a 1924 letter to Edwin Baird, the first editor of *Weird Tales*, he bemoaned the cautious tendencies of many of his contemporaries: "Good and evil, teleological illusion, sugary sentiment, anthropocentric psychology—the usual superficial stock in trade, and all shot through with the eternal and inescapable commonplace... One can't write a weird story of real power without perfect psychological detachment from the human scene."[15] As this passage conveys, his cosmicism led him to reject the kind of horror fiction that still adhered slavishly to conventional notions of a human-centered universe. Indeed, though ostensibly treading familiar territory, "The Dreams in the Witch House" ultimately forges its own path.

This break with the past led to a distinctively contemporary type of Gothic that, as will be discussed throughout this chapter, reflects the turmoil of life in the early decades of twentieth-century America. Lovecraft imparts his view of what he came to term "weird fiction" in the introduction to *Supernatural Horror in Literature*, arguing that the "true weird tale has something more than secret murder, bloody bones, or a sheeted form clanking chains according to rule."[16] Thus jettisoning horror conventions, he moves on to outline those elements which he deems essential to such fiction and which have since been seen as precisely the hallmarks of his own writing: "A certain atmosphere of breathless and unexplainable dread of outer, unknown forces must be present; and there must be a hint, expressed with a seriousness and portentousness becoming its subject, of that most terrible conception of the human brain—a malign and particular suspension or defeat of those fixed laws of Nature which are our only safeguard against the assaults of chaos and the daemons of unplumbed space."[17] Picking up on these ideas, S. T. Joshi also favors the label "weird tale" for horror of this type.[18] However, given

Lovecraft's continual emphasis on the impact of the past on the present—and my own focus on depictions of haunting—I choose rather to place him in the American Gothic tradition.

As evidenced by his desire to return to Providence after two years in New York,[19] Lovecraft always held a great affection for New England in general and his native Rhode Island in particular.[20] In an epistle recounting his homecoming train journey some weeks after his return, he famously wrote: "I am Providence, and Providence is myself."[21] Charles L. Crow, in his recent history of American Gothic, casts Lovecraft as "a writer of New England Gothic"[22] and in so doing highlights the centrality of regional space to his fiction. Many of his best-known tales—including "The Colour Out of Space" (1927), "The Dunwich Horror" (1929) and "The Shadow Over Innsmouth" (1936–) take real, or thinly-fictionalized versions of recognizably real, New England locales for their settings. Although this affinity for native space seems to stand in opposition to the "perfect psychological detachment from the human scene" that Lovecraft sought in his horror fiction, both his regionalism and his cosmicism can be understood as reactions to the challenges posed by an era when the "scale and scope and speed of change were unprecedented"[23] and will be explored as such in the remainder of this chapter.

Living through these tumultuous decades, Lovecraft saw his world change around him in ways he found both exhilarating and perturbing. Many of the subjects by which he found himself gripped, and which he wove into his fiction, can be seen as being of broader significance to American culture at this time. As examined above, he strove to expand the horizons of American Gothic even as he upheld the regionalist tradition established by authors like Hawthorne. Consciously distancing himself from traditional notions of supernatural horror, he laced his fictions with a trademark sense of disquieting "contact with unknown spheres and powers"[24] which, in the words of Stephen King, "make[s] us feel the size of the universe we hang suspended in."[25] Set in a fictionalized version of Salem—and thus in a "haunted" site replete with regional and national meaning—"The Dreams in the Witch House" represents a fresh take on haunted fiction while still responding explicitly to Gothic conventions. The liminality of the haunted house motif affords a narrative space apart from the everyday in which the protagonist—

and the reader—encounters a taxing onslaught of irreconcilable social and historical forces representative of the conflict at the heart of early twentieth-century American culture.

Symbolic Salem: Modern Living, Regionalism and Knowledge

Written in the early 1930s and first published in *Weird Tales* in 1933,[26] "The Dreams in the Witch House" exemplifies both the tensions engendered by the upheavals of modernity and the ways in which Lovecraft responded to these through his haunted fiction. Though his work has drawn considerable critical attention, consideration of how Lovecraft's fiction employs the Gothic trope of haunting is lacking.[27] While offering the time-honored Gothic trappings of a sinister old house— here purportedly haunted by the specter of an evil witch—Lovecraft's cosmicism makes this an updated version of this type of horror tale. Further, the New England locale positions the story as one reflective of his regionalist proclivities. As noted above, Lovecraft lived through a time when America was desirous of moving forward, yet uneasy about tackling change. Equally, his work displays a profound ambivalence about both the future and the past. Haunting provides a narrative arena in which the protagonist is compelled to contend with these competing ideologies. Liminality in this bleak tale permits no final escape for its protagonist, as no resolution seems possible to the challenges posed by such incompatible forces.

From an opening paragraph that states, "Behind everything crouched the brooding, festering horror of the ancient town" (*TDWH*: 300), Lovecraft loses no time in establishing how vital the setting is to the horror which is to follow. This ominous contextualizing remark is reinforced by a more specific description of the town in question as "the changeless, legend-haunted city of Arkham, with its clustering gambrel roofs that sway and sag over attics where witches hid from the King's men in the dark, olden days of the Province" (300). Lovecraft's Arkham—featured in several of his tales and described in "The Thing on the Doorstep" (1937) as "witch-cursed, legend-haunted Arkham,"[28] and a town tainted by "horror, madness, and witchcraft" in "The Shadow Out of Time"

(1936)[29]—serves as a fabricated version of Salem, a real place that has attained mythic proportions in the American imaginary. Taking the Salem Witch Trials as its guiding impetus, this tale incorporates themes concerning regional identity, as well as modern shifts in living arrangements and in prevailing attitudes towards science and religion, invoking the inherent anxiety of modernity in doing so.

In their introduction to *Salem: Place, Myth, and Memory* (2004), Dane Anthony Morrison and Nancy Lusignan Schultz remark upon "the sea of myths and memories" that renders Salem a deeply symbolic site.[30] With its origins as an outpost in the wilderness, it is a place with a long history—harking back to the formative days of the nation—and one which "embodies the Puritan vision and religious foundations of America."[31] Yet this is a vision of freedom tarnished by the tragic events of 1692—described by historian Carol F. Karlsen as a "paroxysm of accusation and counter-accusation, confession, denial, and death"[32]—in which almost two hundred people were accused of witchcraft, twenty were executed and several others fated to perish in jail.[33] The historical events pertaining to witches and witchcraft there during the 1600s have "seized the American imagination … consecrating Salem as a civic shrine."[34]

Transcending history, Salem has a literary tradition—dependent in no small part upon the legacy of Nathaniel Hawthorne—running down to Arthur Miller and beyond, establishing it as "a place that looms large in American cultural memory."[35] Scholars have noted Hawthorne's preoccupation with history and his insistence that past events—particularly instances of wrongdoing—have the power to resurge into the present.[36] Via his Gothic fiction, in which he "enacts the presence of the past,"[37] he sought to explore, confront and somehow redeem troubled—and perpetually troubling—aspects of private and communal history. Because of its fall from grace, Hawthorne saw Salem as emblematic of "the battle between good and evil in American culture,"[38] and its power to convey the sinister underbelly of life in the Edenic New World endures. American Gothic has been partly shaped by anxious imperatives to forge a better life in the New World. Whereas the ominous castles of British Gothic denote horrors pertinent to a European context, the literary evocation of Salem—the site of a uniquely American experience of darkness—performs a similar function within American Gothic. Donald R. Burleson notes that "Lovecraft found endless fascination with

Hawthorne's shadowy interest in and ancestral connection with New England Puritanism and witchcraft persecution."[39]

So, as a historical site and a metaphor for darkness, Salem constitutes a liminal place—one encompassing past and present, fact and fiction—fashioned to a considerable degree by Hawthorne and later developed by Lovecraft's distinctive brand of Gothic. The physical description of the old town, the dark heart of which is the Witch House, provides a setting that is regionalized by way of an overt entrenchment in New England's historic past. Yet this use of local color is not confined to history, as the tale also acknowledges the kind of changes apparent in that area with the advent of the twentieth century. In the same way that Salem is a liminal place where aspects of history may be encountered, it also a site—here re-imagined as Arkham—where the intrusion of modernity can be explored. To establish this, the tale's handling of two notable features of modern living—science and shifts in living practices—will be explored in turn.

"Strange and significant information"— Science in modern society

Integrating some of the newest features of science and mathematics into "The Dreams in the Witch House," Lovecraft ensures that this horror tale is contemporaneous with its setting in the inter-war years. Miskatonic University student Walter Gilman elects to lodge in the attic quarters of an infamous witch, Keziah Mason, whose vanishing from jail in 1692—seemingly as a result of "the curves and angles smeared on the grey stone walls" (*TDWH*: 300) of her cell—hints at an unparalleled grasp of advanced science. Drawn to the Witch House because of the "hushed Arkham whispers about Keziah's persistent presence in the old house and the narrow streets" (301) and rumors of a "small, furry, sharp-toothed thing which haunted the mouldering structure and the town" (301–302), Gilman looks to ensconce himself in an overtly haunted house. The claim that no spot in the city was "more steeped in macabre memory than the gable room which harboured him" (300) designates this as the most troubled place in a troubled town, yet also as the site most likely to yield an understanding of the witch's power.

Consistent with the mood of the era, Lovecraft's tale demonstrates a marked ambivalence about science. Although it is still feared by many Arkham residents, Gilman occupies the Witch House in the hope that studying the "magic" for which Mason achieved her notoriety will enhance his own cutting-edge research. Via a radical fusion of contemporary physics, mathematics and folklore, he desires to "trace a strange background of multi-dimensional reality behind the ghoulish hints of the Gothic tales" and thus fathom "the properties of space and the linkage of dimensions known and unknown" (301). Taking into account the "explosion of medical and scientific interpretations"[40] of Salem at the turn of the century, whereby witchcraft came to be explained in medical and psychological terms by the late 1920s,[41] this tale in which "alleged supernatural phenomena are instead accounted for in scientific terms"[42] is at one with the leanings of the time.

Certainly, science in its various forms had begun to permeate American culture by the onset of the twentieth century. High-profile visits by Sigmund Freud in 1909 and Albert Einstein in 1921 appealed initially to intellectuals, then—following the publication of their works for a mass audience—their ideas caught the popular imagination.[43] Susan Currell sees these developments as part of "a new dissemination of science in popular culture" at that time, as the Science Service news syndicate was formed in 1921 for the purpose of conveying scientific theories and findings to the American public.[44] Yet the public appetite for science was not confined to the realms of scientific fact. Detailing the genesis of pulp magazines in America, Mike Ashley points to the existence of a "growing generation of writers fascinated with the possibilities of science" whose work infused popular magazines from the early 1900s.[45] Hugo Gernsback, who coined the term "science fiction" in the 1920s, aimed to educate ordinary Americans about science and technology with publications like *Modern Electrics* and *Science and Invention*.[46] His *Amazing Stories*, which appeared in 1926, was intended as a palatable forum for achieving a similar goal.[47] This didactic ethos sits readily with Lovecraft's own method of informing fiction with fact, albeit with a measure of extrapolation, and his science fiction tale "The Colour Out of Space" was featured in *Amazing Stories* in 1927.[48]

Lovecraft retained an interest in science and scientific discovery throughout his life. For instance, he was fascinated as a child by polar expeditions, asserting well into adulthood that "the *Antarctic Continent* is really paramount in my geographico-fantastic imagination" [original emphasis].[49] The 1930 discovery of Pluto—"a thing which excites me more than any other happening of recent times"—was a source of wonder to him because of its scientific significance and the imaginative possibilities it represented: "I have always wished I could live to see such a thing come to light—& here it is! The first real planet to be discovered since 1846.... One wonders what it is like."[50] David A. Oakes remarks that Lovecraft "responded to some of the most prominent debates and controversies of his time," such as Einstein's theory of relativity and the mechanization of American society, often including examples of "contemporary discoveries" in his fiction.[51] Physicist Paul Halpern and his co-author, philosopher Michael C. LaBossiere, comment upon "how he remarkably weaves the scientific and philosophical discourse of the age" into his writing.[52]

Though they appear in a context of horror, Lovecraft's depictions of science are by no means purely negative. In his fiction, science makes extraordinary contributions to human knowledge and technological advancement. In "Beyond the Wall of Sleep" (1919), human contact with an extraterrestrial entity is enabled by the use of a "cosmic 'radio,'"[53] while "From Beyond" (written in 1920) features a machine that renders such creatures visible. "Cool Air" (1928) sees a physician prolong his own conscious existence for years after his bodily death. Lovecraft's central characters are often well-versed in disciplines such as biology, geology, engineering and physics.[54] Erudite and measured, these gentleman-scholars prove reliable witnesses to the incredible phenomena they encounter, as in *At the Mountains of Madness* (1936) where a pioneering geological expedition uncovers the ancient presence of alien life forms on Earth. With the aid of science, the protagonists of "The Shunned House" (written in 1924) are even able to defeat the monstrous creature lurking beneath that eponymous residence.

The scientific discoveries on display in "The Dreams in the Witch House" are equally ground-breaking and awe-inspiring. Excessively devoted to his studies—to the extent that his "professors at Miskatonic had urged him to slacken up" (*TDWH*: 301)—Gilman is a scholarly protagonist very much in the Lovecraftian mold. He soon gleans that, besides its connection to Mason, the actual construction of her garret room has imbued this space with some enigmatic power. For Manuel Aguirre, Gothic structures are often characterized by physical irregularity, and he suggests that "this basic distortion yields mystery, precludes human control and endows the building with a power beyond its strictly physical structure."[55] The attic seems to be one such structure, as its slanting walls render it of "queerly irregular shape" (*TDWH*: 302), distorted to the extent that two sealed apertures are clearly discernible— one between the room's inner and outer walls and one between the room and the roof above. Gilman speculates that this strangely-angled place has a "mathematical significance" of clear interest to the witch, "for was it not through certain angles that she claimed to have gone outside the boundaries of the world of space we know?" (303).

Gilman's haunted lodgings, deemed conducive to furthering his research, do not disappoint. Before long, he experiences disconcerting dreams comprising "plunges through limitless abysses of inexplicably coloured twilight and bafflingly disordered sound" (304) wherein the witch and her familiar make themselves manifest. At the same time, his capacity for mathematics develops significantly and he "astonishe[s] Professor Upham by his comprehension of fourth-dimensional and other problems which had floored all the rest of the class" (306). As the tale unfolds, Gilman comes to understand that these are not mere dreams but rather dream-like voyages to other dimensions. In one instance, he finds himself on a terrace above what appears to be an alien city and breaks off part of the metal balustrade. Discovering it in his room the next day, he realizes that this alien object can only have come to Earth because he has travelled elsewhere and brought it back with him. In line with his expectations, his time in the Witch House gradually provides him with unforeseen experiences that lead to exceptional scientific insights.

The liminality of haunting here sets Gilman apart from his everyday experience, giving him time to acquire specialist knowledge as yet denied to even the most advanced scientists of the day. His formal studies at the university, as part of the recognized system through which such knowledge is traditionally acquired, provide a framework for explaining them but furnish him with only part of the answer. Once isolated from his peers, he has a new-found state of "solitary eccentricity" (307) that helps confirm his initial conjecture that Mason is not haunting in the accepted supernatural sense. Rather, she is harnessing forces that, via science, humanity might only just be capable of grasping. As suspected, the physical environment is vital to this discovery and the liminality of the Witch House offers space, as well as time, away from daily reality. Gilman's studies in mathematics, calculus and quantum physics—at a time of "startling transition in the world of science"[56]—lead to the realization that knowledgeable people might be able to perform feats, such as travelling through space and time, once seen as the exclusive preserve of those with magical abilities. Science here thus presents "picturesque possibilities" (*TDWH*: 322) and opens up exciting new avenues for humanity.

Yet this new enthrallment with the power of science and technology brought its own set of challenges. Historian Michael E. Parrish writes that although many Progressive Era thinkers were confident that reason and efficiency could improve society, this buoyancy waned after the First World War.[57] Critics such as Henry Adams stressed that the absence of a binding force like religion that had characterized older societies meant these post-war advances "would fuel only individual greed and social disintegration."[58] For many, then, science represented a break with old ways of thinking which was as testing as it was stimulating. One thinker who was acutely influential on Lovecraft was Joseph Wood Krutch, author of *The Modern Temper* (1929).[59] Parrish remarks that Krutch, though mindful that science had improved the human condition, tempered enthusiasm about progress with the observation that "along with these benefits had come a scientific explanation of the universe and of man's place there that reduced the meaning of life to a set of mathematical equations about the behavior of atoms, molecules, neurons, and synapses."[60]

Such new modes of explanation, in accentuating the "impersonal forces governing the world"[61] and thus putting to rout myth and religion, effectively relegated humanity from its former status—presumed to be at the center of the cosmos—and undermined conventional notions of the universe operating according to an inherent moral order.[62] Given Lovecraft's youthful conviction of the transience of human life and the inadequacy of religion—which led him later to dismiss the "immortality myth [as] too childish to talk about"[63]—it is hardly surprising that the disturbing implications of Krutch's views resonated so strongly with him in his later years. In a letter of 1916, he comments that the explanatory power of science works to undermine those religions which apparently afforded humanity its position of privilege in the natural order: "What right has man arbitrarily to assume his own importance in creation? Science can trace our world to its source.... We are able to comprehend that the human race is but a thing of the moment; that its existence on this planet is extremely recent, as infinity is reckoned; and that its possible existence in all the expanse of illimitable space is but a matter of yesterday."[64] The scientific revelations of modernity affirmed for Lovecraft what he had long supposed—that all religion was illusory—and his philosophy of cosmicism can be gleaned from these reflections.[65]

This cosmic line of thought can be detected in the work of other American authors dating from the first decades of the twentieth century. Mark Twain's *Letters from the Earth* (1909) represents a satirical examination of religion—particularly Christianity—from the perspective of someone looking at humanity from the outside. Addressed to the archangels Michael and Gabriel, the letters are written by Satan after he is banished from the heavens and chooses to visit Earth. The creation of Earth, outlined at the start of the piece in keeping with the Biblical account, is attributed to the Creator's/God's desire for experimentation, and Satan is intrigued to see how this has turned out. Describing the place and its inhabitants as insane, he notes with incredulity that "Man is a marvelous curiosity.... He even believes the Creator loves him... He prays to Him, and thinks He listens ... although no prayer of his has ever been answered."[66] Turning his attention to the Christian Bible, Satan heaps scorn on the human notion therein that the vast universe in which Earth sits was engineered by the Creator solely to "furnish light for this little toy-world. That was his whole purpose; he had no other."[67] Similar ideas are expressed in "The Damned Human Race" (circa 1905–1909), where Twain ironically concludes, "If the Eiffel Tower were now representing the world's age, the skin of paint on the pinnacle-knob at its summit would represent man's share of that age; and anybody would perceive that that skin was what the tower was built for."[68]

With the onset of modernity, science had shown the old notion of a human-centered, moral universe to be obsolete and, for Lovecraft, horror fiction had to evolve in order to reflect this seismic shift. His own contribution to Gothic is most clearly exemplified by the tales known collectively as the Cthulhu Mythos and "which share as their common background a system of invented lore."[69] This lore pertains to a pantheon of "gods"—monstrous extraterrestrial entities like Cthulhu which precede, transcend and threaten to overwhelm human life—and the Mythos portrays liminal encounters with these beings in a fictional space somewhere between the old belief systems and the new scientific principles which have come to supplant them.[70] The driving force behind this fiction, Lovecraft's belief that "common human laws and interests and emotions have no validity or significance in the vast cosmos-at-large,"[71] can readily be linked to early twentieth-century preoccupations about the destabilizing power of science.

Literally a liminal place, the Witch House is a threshold between Earth and "other spaces beyond" (*TDWH*: 301). Yet liminality here is also figurative, permitting an overlap between past and present, known and unknown. Gilman's insight that Mason is not dead—she has lived on in these other dimensions—distinguishes this tale from those of conventional Gothic, where haunting is attributed to the spirits of the deceased. Rather, Mason's sporadic visits give the impression that she "haunts" Arkham. During Gilman's dreams, she urges him to sign his name in the Book of Azathoth "now that his independent delvings had gone so far" (310). Through his research into esoteric folklore, he knows of "the mindless entity Azathoth, which rules all time and space from a curiously environed black throne at the centre of Chaos" (319). As Oakes contends, such a being "redefines God from a benevolent force that protects and guides the universe to a chaotic, mindless power that has no awareness of humanity or anything else,"[72] and this tale thereby conforms to the cosmicist tenets of the Cthulhu Mythos. Halpern and LaBossiere remark that early science fiction shows science to be dangerous, as "tragedy occurs because a character tampers with an otherwise benign natural order." Here, however, science is dangerous simply because it reveals the horrifying truth about the natural order: "[Gilman] does not create a monster by tampering with nature. Rather, he discovers that reality is a monstrous horror and thus meets his doom."[73] Through liminality, in this modernist brush with science, the initial thrill of discovery is quickly surpassed by the horror it brings. This liminal encounter offers groundbreaking revelations while, in an essentially conservative fashion, insinuating that such insights are best overlooked.

Oakes concurs with Halpern and LaBossiere in stressing that what Lovecraft does here is explain what was once seen as *supernatural* as something *natural*, i.e., he makes the supernatural part of science.[74] In this regard, the tale is emblematic of an era that many saw as characterized by "the removal of magic and meaning from life"—what Max Weber famously termed "the disenchantment of the world"—as a result of scientific and technological progress.[75] As discussed above, this new level of scientific insight seems to imply a reassuring grasp of how the world works along with a concomitant denunciation of more primitive modes of explanation and of superstition, as in the case of early twentieth-century medical explanations for the events at Salem. However, Lovecraft's fiction resolutely fixates on the incongruous notion that science is inherently bound up with horror. Moreover, it is often the case that science is inextricably enmeshed with the very horrors it seeks to elucidate—as is the case here with witchcraft. Indeed, the very essence of scientific enterprise—the sheer drive towards explanation—is a cause for repulsion here.

Lovecraft's predilection for mining this new worldview for horror has been noted by previous critics. What tends to be downplayed though—and is especially intriguing—is his insistence on wedding it to the occult and thus to those modes of explanation he purports to decry. Despite her impressive achievements, Mason is invariably cast in terms of her wickedness and described as "evil" (*TDWH*: 306), "monstrous" (312), "devilish" (313) and with regard to her "hideous malevolence" (310). Thus, she is construed entirely as an evil occultist rather than as a visionary. Her stipulation that Gilman sign the Book of Azathoth, an allusion to the historical belief that witches were granted power on signing the "Devil's book,"[76] equates this cosmic entity with the Satan of Christian doctrine as much as it does with God. It transpires that she worships this being, abducting children as sacrificial victims each "Witches' Sabbath," when "hell's blackest evil roamed the earth and all the slaves of Satan gathered for nameless rites and deeds" (*TDWH*: 309).

These elements conspire to cast Mason in a rather conventional Gothic role: that of an evil worshipper of an even more evil supernatural being. Yet, in their very anthropocentrism, these notions of "good" and "bad" seem at odds with rationalism, especially in the context of a body of cosmicist fiction that aims to eschew such human values in light of a more scientific worldview. Mason's initial offense seems chiefly to have been her inclination to push at the boundaries of human knowledge, which Gilman himself does under the aegis of the university. His stance that her knowledge and experience—both of which he actively seeks—are still "forbidden" (301 and 322) is curiously antiquated in an age looking to cast off superstition in favor of science. In a similar vein, her veneration of the "mindless" Azathoth sits uneasily in a tale which ostensibly supersedes religious explanations with scientific ones. Such facets of the story thus undermine the sense that Lovecraft has rejected superstition outright. In investing his treatment of *science* with all the trappings of the superstitious *mythology* which preceded it, he clings to notions of morality and even reverts to earlier modes of explanation. The implications of cosmicism, alarming though they may be for humankind, are by their very nature incompatible with notions of good versus evil (as Lovecraft himself declared) and a tension between scientism on the one hand and mythical thinking on the other thus emerges here. While noting that modernity has been seen as the end of supernatural modes of explanation, Alex Owen argues that "significant religious beliefs and behaviors" persisted into the early decades of the twentieth century nonetheless.[77]

So it is clear that Lovecraft is torn between his enthusiasm for and his anxiety about the explanatory power of science. As argued throughout this chapter, this conflict is characteristic of the time in which he wrote. Despite his stated embrace of scientism, he also exhibits a tendency to adhere to ingrained superstitions. However, in pointing to the penchant of turn-of-the-century authors for depicting "fabulous environments that were nevertheless ... couched in the language of science,"[78] Michael Saler indicates the extent to which that era was infused with a tension between science and the supernatural. For him, Lovecraft's fiction epitomizes such trends to "re-enchant the modern world without compromising the rational and secular tenets of modernity."[79] In this tale Lovecraft does not entirely succeed in "dismiss[ing] the supernatural and fully embrac[ing] the rational."[80] Yet he certainly succeeds in conveying the impact of science on human understandings about their place in the wider universe, and Saler's comments serve to underscore the conflicted attitudes towards science at this point in American history. Seen in this light, "The Dreams in the Witch House" offers a narrative submersion in a liminal realm where science is as potentially detrimental to humanity as it is valuable and haunting here allows an engagement with such irreconcilable social forces. Further, as will be explored next, this tendency of Lovecraft to cling to the past also extends to other areas of his fiction.

"Something ... which did not belong there"

The first part of this chapter has shown that the portrayal of science in "The Dreams in the Witch House"—a tale which is both receptive to, and fearful of, the worlds of possibility which new kinds of knowledge came to represent—is in many ways expressive of the period in which it was written. In addition, Lovecraft's fiction exhibits another key discernible tension, that between his cosmicism and his aforementioned regionalism. While views like cosmicism are not hard to understand in isolation, once placed within the context of early twentieth-century thinking, which saw humanity merely as one tiny component of a vast universe, Lovecraft's prominent cosmic literary stance is very much at odds with his simultaneous investment in such flagrantly human matters as local history and identity. As will be shown, this emphasis on humanism can be seen as a contradictory and compensating response to his preoccupation with cosmicism. By the same token, his interest in the regional constituted a reaction to the shifts in living patterns brought by modernity and is as indicative of his era as the kinds of ambivalence previously highlighted. "The Dreams in the Witch House," with its symbolic placement in Salem, offers an engagement with the impact of progress on historical regional space.

Lovecraft's connection to the New England region is thus symptomatic of a generalized sense of apprehension about change. Although he always held a great affection for his hometown, his attachment increased with his return to Providence in 1926. A letter written shortly after his homecoming, in recounting his train journey from New York, extols the delights of gazing upon "stone walls, rolling pastures, and white church steeples—imagining them when none were in sight"[81] and rather suggests that, in many ways, he actually favored an imagined New England over the real one. This bucolic vision bears a remarkable similarity to one supplied in a missive three years later to the same person on the same subject, where he describes "the stone-wall'd rolling meads and white farmhouse gables of the Arcadian realm of Western Rhode-Island."[82] In building up to the sentiment, "The past is *real*—it is *all there is*" (original emphases),[83] Lovecraft reinforces this sense that he was haunted by an idealized regional past intensified by the two years he spent in a rapidly-developing metropolis.

A few years later, he was to explain his uneasy blend of cosmicism—with all its connotations of the futility of human endeavor—and partiality for regional life in the following way: "With me, the very quality of being cosmically sensitive breeds an exaggerated attachment to the familiar and the immediate—Old Providence, the woods and hills, the ancient ways and thoughts of New England."[84] Echoing the summation of those contradictory views already acknowledged by Lovecraft himself, Joshi suggests that regionalism provided him with a kind of "bulwark against cosmic meaninglessness."[85] David Simmons notes that Lovecraft began to write stories with a more regionalist bent on his return there. Whereas he attributes this to Lovecraft's desire to accept the lived reality of his own surroundings,[86] I would suggest rather that Lovecraft's idealized vision of the region was partly shaped by those nostalgic tendencies earlier identified as the counterpoint to modernity by the likes of Levine.

A striking feature of Lovecraft's perception of New England is its pastoral tranquility. In addition are its visible links—predominantly in terms of architecture—to its past, as evidenced by his enthusiastic identification of "Georgian alleys" and "ancient roofs" on his return to Providence in the mid–1920s.[87] With its "clustering gambrel roofs" (*TDWH*: 300) and "eldritch brown houses of unknown age" (302), the Arkham of "The Dreams in the Witch House" epitomizes this penchant for history, going back even further in time than the Georgian era in which Lovecraft particularly reveled. These visions of rusticity and history stand in stark contrast to the reality of life for many Americans in the 1920s. One notable early twentieth-century development identified by Conn was the swelling population of America's cities, resulting from a combination of foreign immigration and internal migration.[88] For instance, in the early 1900s large numbers of African Americans moved to northern cities, particularly in response to increased demands for labor during the war, which led to heightened tensions along race lines.[89] This influx of people into built-up areas meant a shift towards urbanization, and "by 1920, a slight majority of all Americans lived in cities."[90]

As well as symbols of modernity and sites in which culture and the arts could flourish, cities were associated with squalor, poverty and moral degradation.[91] Lovecraft displayed a pronounced distaste for the modern urban environment and his antipathy centered on the city which, in the words of Douglas Tallack, was seen as "*the* modernist city of the twentieth century"[92] New York. Though initially taken with the romantic symbolism of Manhattan—he "had been profoundly moved by the first stunning visual impression of the distant skyline at night"[93]— he soon developed a loathing for the reality of the city when experienced at close quarters, which was doubtless heightened by the burglaries, unemployment and subsequent poverty he endured there. His negative sentiments are conveyed in the stories he produced during his stay in Brooklyn. The narrators of "He" (1926) and "Cool Air" (1928) cast the city as a place "full of unsuspected horrors"[94] and as a "nest of squalor and seediness"[95] respectively, while "The Horror at Red Hook" (1927) depicts that Brooklyn neighborhood as a "maze of hybrid squalor."[96] Besides his notorious fixation on the city's immigrant populations,[97] Lovecraft was also preoccupied with ambient factors such as noise, the shabbiness of buildings and the potential for menace to thrive in the labyrinthine streets of such a populous locale, and was desperate to return to a home which he saw as a refuge from such torments.

Lovecraft's regional turn can therefore be understood as a coping mechanism for dealing with the challenges of modern living, one chiming with the wider "force of nostalgia" detected by Levine in 1920s America.[98] Joseph A. Conforti describes the state-sponsored promotion of the image of New England, especially of the more northern states, as "the unchanging, pastoral Yankee heartland" during the early part of the century.[99] A case can thus be made for regionalism as an intrinsic part of the national mindset at that time. Bodies like the Society for the Preservation of New England Antiquities (SPNEA), founded in 1910, strove to safeguard the region's past by acquiring and renovating buildings deemed worthy of such attention,[100] and by undertaking heritage work to augment "the colonial revival's reconstruction of the region's early history,"[101] while museums were established to combat the threat posed to cultural memories by the encroachment of modernity.[102] This outlook endured and, by the 1930s, regionalism was gaining currency as part of a movement to "establish American culture on native grounds."[103] An enthusiastic traveller, Lovecraft explored most extensively within his native New England and expressed his love of the region by seeking out particularly those "antiquarian oases ... where the past lingered almost unchanged to the present."[104] I join with Timothy H. Evans who discerns that, though Lovecraft's views and fictions contain tensions, they nonetheless clearly resonate with the era in which he wrote.[105]

Lovecraft's correspondences certainly provide evidence of his fascination with the regional past. He proclaims a trip to Salem in the early twenties, when he visited the Witch House and the House of the Seven Gables, to be "an aesthetick and historicall orgy of delight,"[106] commenting specifically on his tour of a Salem house which was "finely preserv'd and restor'd"[107] by the SPNEA. Later, he uses glowing adjectives— "delightful," "graceful" and "splendid"—to tell of the sights of the country around Salem and Danvers, describing the trip as one "to stimulate the antiquarian soul."[108] As this excursion—and the letter detailing it—progresses, he relates: "I now put the aera of Colonial refinement behind me, and hark'd back farther still to an age of darker and weirder appeal— the age of the dreaded witchcraft."[109] Dovetailing as they did with his worldviews, visits such as these helped inform Lovecraft's fictional engagements with the past.

There are various elements of known history woven into "The Dreams in the Witch House," as Lovecraft blurs the boundaries between reality and imagination. For instance, the details of Mason's trial have some basis in established historical events. Noting that the witch was kept under the jurisdiction of Cotton Mather, Gilman studies the records of her confession to John Hathorne at the "Court of Oyer and Terminer" (*TDWH*: 301), the actual term for the special court set up by Sir William Phips, newly-appointed governor to the Massachusetts Bay Colony in 1692, "to 'hear and determine' the enormous backlog of witchcraft cases."[110] That Judge Hathorne and Mather, minister at Boston's First Church, held some sway over the proceedings is also a matter of record.[111] Such details, in conjunction with Mason's power to "haunt" the town, ensure that Gilman and the reader are placed in a liminal encounter with history.

It is important to distinguish another kind of ambivalence here, insofar as Lovecraft appears simultaneously to relish and to revile this regional space. The fictional Arkham often serves to place its real-life counterpart in a very unflattering light, with its "shadowy tangles of unpaved musty-smelling lanes" (*TDWH*: 302) and the "rotting walls of ancient houses" (323), coupled with its history of horror and superstition. Given that he was writing Gothic horror, and with the genuine intention to disconcert, his efforts to ensconce the reader—immediately and unrelentingly—in an environment conducive to this end are to be expected. Yet there seem to be wider issues at work here which are indicative of an attraction to a past—however horrifying—perceived by many as under threat from the modern age. In saying that Salem offers access to an "age of darker and weirder appeal," Lovecraft implies that he is thrilled and repulsed, perhaps in equal measure, by the dark and disturbing elements contained within regional history and geography. So, though it is tempting to conclude that he was overwhelmingly disturbed by what he found in these regional spaces, there is also some indication that he was drawn to them for those same qualities—even when they contradicted his very modern investment in the explanatory power of science. The liminality of haunting offers a fictional encounter with the intractable forces so characteristic of this period of American history.

Aside from its dark past, however, there are other reasons why Arkham is portrayed as repellent here. Conn points to a number of factors which contributed to the "peculiar turbulence" of the early 1900s.[112] In addition to the urbanization which seemed to endanger traditional understandings of life in New England, another remarkable trend was the huge influx of immigrants which took America's population "from about 75 million in 1898 to roughly 100 million in 1917."[113] Immigrant numbers started to rise around the turn of the century, especially for those of Italian, Jewish and Polish Catholic origin, and levels climbed to unprecedented heights in the years after 1900 until, as historian Donna R. Gabaccia observes, "by 1910, almost 15 percent of the American population was of foreign birth."[114] The effects of these radical shifts in demographic patterns shored up a sense that the nation was changing beyond all recognition, as signaled by anxious ruminations on the demise of the Yankee—that long-time representative of a supposedly authentic American culture—in such publications as *Yankee* magazine.[115]

Parrish detects a certain "ambivalence of the American people on this subject" as, although the country had a history of welcoming foreigners to its shores, increased numbers in the late 1800s "provoked rising demands for restriction based on crude notions of racial inferiority and hereditary determinism."[116] The 1907 Dillingham Commission, appointed by Congress to study and help legislate on immigration, proceeded on the assumption that these new types of immigrants—who came from Eastern and Southern Europe—were inferior to their Teutonic predecessors from Britain and Northern Europe.[117] Madison Grant's best-seller *The Passing of the Great Race* (1916) drew on pseudo-scientific ideas to venerate those "blond conquerors of the North"[118]—whom he perceived to be racially superior—and to maintain that restrictions on immigration were the only way to prevent the dilution of American stock by inferior ethnic minorities.[119] Such eugenicist thought persisted into the 1920s, as many saw these trends as a threat to the comfort and livelihood of American citizens and a continued danger to the nation's racial purity.[120] There was a clear sense of mounting evidence that "Nordic America" would be swamped by this undesirable movement,[121] and this racist unease, grounded in a "new racial ideology [of] scientific racism," was to shape the Immigration Restriction Act of 1924.[122]

Lovecraft, who asserted in a letter as early as 1915 that "the one supreme race is the Teuton,"[123] often expressed his own fears that immigration was weakening America. Writing to one of his aunts from New York in 1926, he commented that "America has made a fine mess of its population."[124] Though critics and biographers have noted the moderation of Lovecraft's more extreme views with his shift from conservatism to socialism in his later years,[125] his racist attitudes—centering on a belief in racial difference and the attendant need for segregation—persisted. In a letter written in 1936, the year before he died, he declared that "the races are *equal*, but *infinitely different* [original emphasis]"[126] and looked back to the immigration legislation of 1924 as commendable in its drive to exclude "the immigration of racial elements radically alien to the original American people."[127]

Such views are expressed throughout "The Dreams in the Witch House." With the exception of his course-mate Frank Elwood, Gilman's fellow tenants in this squalid house, along with its landlord, are designated as Polish. Numerous derogatory descriptions of the "whining prayers" and "long, rambling stories" of the likes of lodger Joe Mazurewicz serve to dismiss their feelings about "the ghost of old Keziah" (*TDWH*: 308) as the products of mere weak-minded superstition, rooted in Catholicism and ultimately unable to account for the true nature of the haunting. Via its anxious abundance of foreign names—Dombrowski, Mazurewicz, Choynski, Desrochers, Iwanicki, Wolejko, Czanek, Stowacki, Malkowski—this tale is laced with reminders of what was for many an undesirable development in America's social demographics. Accounts of those areas in Arkham where immigrant populations were concentrated are especially negative. A dream prior to the witches' sabbath of Walpurgis Night sees Mason take Gilman to a "dark, muddy, unknown alley of foetid odours" (323) from whence she procures a young child for the upcoming sacrifice. The next day, he realizes that this must be the kidnapped son of "a clod-like laundry worker named Anastasia Wolejko" (325). Strikingly, his foray into this impoverished neighborhood is almost as repellent as his encounters with the witch. Gilman's liminal experiences with the ghostly Mason thus force an unpalatable confrontation with the reality of modern life in Arkham.

Positioned as superior because he is a "native" New Englander—from Haverhill, Massachusetts—rather than an immigrant, and because of his status as a student, Gilman has both privileged access—and, through the liminality of haunting, exceptional insight—to knowledge which helps explain the powers of the witch. Yet it is clear from the outset that his superstitious neighbors are fully cognizant that Mason and her familiar haunt their home and that their influence is malicious. The ethnicity and religious beliefs of these characters are targets for scorn, though this tale endorses the ostensibly primitive beliefs and rituals of these characters by showing that the "ghostly" Mason does indeed worship a higher power and, in so doing, poses a threat to Arkham. The crucifix given to Gilman by Mazurewicz and "blessed by the good Father Iwanicki" (321) actually proves efficacious in inducing sufficient "panic" (328) in the witch for Gilman to end her haunting powers by finally taking her life.

It is noteworthy that this anxiety about the effects of social change on America in general and New England in particular should be associated with Salem. Henry James, famously self-exiled from the United States on the cusp of the late nineteenth and early twentieth centuries, commented on such shifts in *The American Scene*, an account of his travels through America in 1904 and 1905. Of one eagerly-anticipated visit, "a search … for the New England homogeneous," intended to take in "Hawthorne's Salem, and the witches,"[128] he comments on the inevitability of his meeting a "flagrant foreigner" when inquiring about the way to such celebrated sites as the House of the Seven Gables. As a result of this disconcerting exchange, James experiences a sense of alienation both in terms of his own seemingly "foreign" status and in his finding such a fundamentally American place less "American" than he had anticipated. Lovecraft's tale supplies a Gothic reflection on precisely such brushes with estrangement.

Set apart from the common stream of humanity through the liminality of haunting, Walter Gilman is afforded exceptionally privileged insights at a time when science began to offer unprecedented understandings of the workings of the wider universe. Yet his death, coupled with the declaration that "Gilman's dreams and their attendant circumstances have never been explained" (*TDWH*: 332), represents a bleak indictment of such an achievement. Far from a being a conventional warning of the dangers of science, however, this is a taxing encounter with the clashing forces of history and modernity, superstition and rationality, opened up by the liminality of haunting. Lovecraft here uses his liminal spaces to let loose forces for which he can see no prospect of a resolution. Further, the Gothic device of haunting permits encounters with a broad sweep of social changes in the symbolic regional space of Salem. The culmination of this tale—in "the inevitable razing of the decrepit structure" (332–333) of the Witch House some years after Gilman's demise—underscores Lovecraft's deeper unease about the plight of regional history in the face of a changing America.

Conclusion

Drawn to the horror genre, with its long-standing power to shake complacencies and force readers to see the familiar world in a new light, yet determined to bring it in line with the demands of contemporary intellectual and social life, Lovecraft represents a figure of fundamental importance in the trajectory of twentieth-century American Gothic. Gilman's repeated dismissals of the "wild whispers" (*TDWH*: 301) of "superstitious foreigners" (321) call attention to this drive to take haunted fiction in a new direction, one befitting the experiences and revelations of modernity. In "The Dreams in the Witch House," Lovecraft thus utilizes established Gothic techniques and exploits the symbolic power of Salem to put his own spin on haunted house fiction.

Here, as will be explored in other chapters throughout this book, the liminality contained within the haunted house motif—in working to separate the protagonist from the course of everyday life and mundane experience—provides the liminar with exceptional insights. In particular, the protagonist in this tale—an ardent seeker of groundbreaking scientific knowledge—is forced, ultimately under duress, to witness staggering revelations about the possible outcome of humanity's quest for such knowledge. Played out against a backdrop of known regional space, one with ongoing significance in terms of American history and culture, the Gothic trope of haunting here facilitates a liminal encounter that both challenges and upholds entrenched genre conventions.

Self-confessed as "a sort of hybrid betwixt the past and the future,"[129] Lovecraft found himself torn between the promise of progress and the threat of the loss of older modes of living. It has been shown that, at least to some extent, his views achieved a measure of congruity with other writers and thinkers of the first few decades of the twentieth century. The physical locale of Arkham, as a fictionalized version of Salem, plays an integral role as a liminal space in which aspects of history, culture and identity—pertaining to changing perceptions of humanity's place in the universe, as well as to more prosaic concerns about the fate of regional history and identity on a changing national stage—can be explored.

This, then, is a tale that uses the liminality of haunting to invoke an atmosphere of ambivalence and of fundamentally unresolved tension. In so doing, it indexes complex social forces at work in the early part of the twentieth century during, in the words of Niall Palmer, "an age which venerated its past but was simultaneously preoccupied with the 'now' and the 'new.'"[130] As a modernist reflection on this transitional period of American history, "The Dreams in the Witch House" exhibits both progressive and conservative tendencies. Pulling to the future while at the same time looking back to the past, the liminality of haunting here unleashes the underlying historical and ideological clashes of the time, clashes which Lovecraft depicts as ultimately irreconcilable.

Chapter Two

"Behind the barricades of silence"

Haunted Suburbia in A Stir of Echoes

Born in 1926, Richard Matheson produced horror fiction in the form of novels and short stories, as well as writing frequently for film and television, from the 1950s.[1] Breaking with tradition by setting his fiction in everyday situations rather than the more archaic, atmospheric scenarios favored by writers like Lovecraft up to and into the early part of the twentieth century, Matheson soon established himself as a key figure in the developing field of American Gothic. His innovative emphasis on the quotidian proved to be extremely influential on later practitioners of horror, and in a 1985 interview, Stephen King designated Matheson as the "guy who taught me [that] horror … could happen in the suburbs, on your street, maybe right next door."[2] For these reasons, his work is integral to this study. In eschewing the exotic in favor of the commonplace, his brand of Gothic plays out in familiar space, keeping pace with escalating post-war social shifts, and thus represents a decisive new direction for the haunted house motif.

As one of Matheson's early novels, A Stir of Echoes is set firmly during the height of the Cold War in mid twentieth-century America, a historical and cultural setting crucial to an understanding of the novel. The plot details an unusual episode in the otherwise unremarkable life of North American Aircraft publications employee Tom Wallace, who lives in Inglewood, California, with his wife, Anne, and their infant son, Richard.[3] A hypnosis performed on Tom by his brother-in-law, psychology major Phil, at a neighborhood get-together triggers a chain of supernatural events that unexpectedly propels the narrative into Gothic territory. The liminality of haunting creates a complex narrative arena in which conflicting attitudes towards American cultural change are played out. The novel's placement within a typical 1950s suburban environment is especially fitting and the incongruity of the depictions of this space is of vital importance to my argument.

Matheson has played a significant role in popular cultural treatments of horror for over half a century. Although his tales tend to contain scientific (or at least pseudoscientific) ideas and explanations, and may often be designated as science fiction, many fall much more comfortably into the category of horror and Gothic.[4] Peter Nicholls calls his works *romantic* science fiction, largely unconcerned with hard facts and thus more "mysterious, inexplicable, gothic, and menacing."[5] Less disposed to draw on gruesome scenes of physical violence and bodily decay or monstrosity than either Lovecraft or Stephen King, Matheson focuses instead on exploring how his characters respond when all their ostensible certainties come under threat. He declares that "to me, horror connotes blood and guts, while terror is a much more subtle art, a matter of stirring up primal fears."[6] Indeed, it has been noted that Matheson exploits the potential of the Gothic to undermine the supposed certainties by which people live their lives.[7] Nicholls identifies a "radical alienation from humanity,"[8] evoked by "vivid, lurid images of ordinary men standing their ground in a hostile universe"[9] as defining preoccupations in his fiction. Similarly, Keith Neilson points to the typical conceit of "the man in a trap," which also indicates Matheson's tendency to narrate his stories purely from the point of view of a lone or isolated male protagonist.[10] As such, his brand of Gothic works to unsettle readers by thrusting them into the troubled mindsets of individuals trapped in a world they no longer recognize.

As Matheson observed of his own fiction, "people have described my work as being the embodiment of paranoia."[11] Stefan Dziemianowicz takes a slightly different view, arguing instead that "A fragile dynamic exists between the personalities of Matheson's characters and the security of their surroundings. When that security gives way, it leads not to the paranoiac's smug assumption that the world is conspiring against them, but to feelings of insecurity about themselves that threatens [*sic*] their very identities."[12] This is a subtly different take which still emphasizes themes of anxiety and isolation while stressing that the vulnerability of Matheson's protagonists stems more from confusion about their changed circumstances than simple suspicion of the part that others might have played in their suffering. Dziemiano-wicz develops his argument by adding that the typical Matheson protagonist defines himself on the basis of his relationships with others, particularly his friends, family and romantic partners. When this normality starts to disintegrate, these characters feel threatened in the very core of what they have previously understood themselves to be.[13] This means that they are not only alienated, but are also then obliged to question aspects of themselves that they previously took for granted. The suggestion that a separation from the mainstream of daily life affords privileged opportunities for interrogative potential can readily be linked to liminality and easily detected in Matheson's novels about haunting.

A Stir of Echoes, despite being adapted for cinema as Stir of Echoes in 1999, is a text especially bereft of critical attention. In her 2009 study, Bernice M. Murphy includes it as an example of what she calls Suburban Gothic, which is characterized by "the lingering suspicion that even the most ordinary-looking neighbourhood, or house, or family, has some-thing to hide, and that no matter how calm and settled a place looks, it is only ever a moment away from dramatic (and generally sinister) inci-dent."[14] The trappings of earlier Gothic, like that of Lovecraft, made it seem far removed from the day-to-day experience of most Americans. Yet Matheson's Gothic, with its insistence on the contemporary, was of explicit relevance to the very time in which he wrote. Critics have ever stressed the mundanity of Matheson's settings and characters as the hall-mark of his fiction and his chief contribution to the horror genre. Dziemianowicz notes that "he is one of the first modern horror writers to evoke the ordinary specifically to undermine it, seeing the potential for horror behind its most fundamental relationships and beneath its most banal surface,"[15] and Stephen King extols his "mastery of terror against what appears to be a normal, everyday backdrop."[16] Thus the choice of an unremarkable house in a commonplace neighborhood, peo-pled with average men in average jobs who reside quietly with their fam-ilies until estranged from the usual courses of their lives by extraordinary events, can be seen as typical of Matheson's fiction: literal territory to which he returns time and again.

Tom Wallace is burdened with extrasensory powers as a result of his hypnosis, and chief among these is an unbidden access to the innermost thoughts and feelings of those around him. These abilities work to unearth a murder, the details of which are embedded in the very fabric of his community, which forms the narrative and thematic backbone of the novel. This crime, through which the past retains its hold on the present, is tied to the familiar physical space of an ordinary suburban neighborhood. For David A. Oakes, in Matheson's fiction, "the haunted castle manifests itself as a mundane location, such as an apartment building, a basement, or a home."[17] So the haunted house motif, the guiding focus of my study, here becomes updated with a move to a distinctive physical setting which is conspicuously contemporaneous with the late 1950s milieu of the novel's appearance.[18]

In keeping with other literary treatments of haunting examined here, *A Stir of Echoes* is defined by liminality. In this tale, the boundaries between the public and private spheres, between bland normality and shocking aberration, and between life and death all become blurred, even dismantled entirely. Protagonist Tom, when acting as a liminar, is obliged to contend with the collision of the disparate forces unleashed by this process. It has been observed that the liminal "can be a place of threat as well as of promise, and can produce and perpetuate conservative as well as progressive ideologies."[19] The liminality encountered here is certainly cast as threatening. Written entirely in the first-person from Tom's perspective, the novel immerses the reader in that state of disorientation and alienation Matheson so often metes out to his protagonists. The revelations of liminality isolate Tom immediately and unceasingly: enlightened though he is by his time apart from his normal existence, he struggles to cope with the insights brought by liminality and longs to return to the simplicity of his pre-liminal state.

As will be shown in later chapters on Stephen King, fictional haunted space can contain both menace and allure. In this novel, haunting is always associated with unhappiness and trepidation and therefore shown as unattractive. Crucially, however, its chief threat is shown to lie in its ability to disrupt, not to destroy, Tom's life. This anxiety about mere disruption is shared with other 1950s fictions, where even "the smallest deviation from the norm, from ritual and habit"[20] can be traumatic. Matheson uses haunting to critique aspects of the 1950s suburban setting in which it arises. Yet, at the novel's close, Tom is only too keen to overcome this disruption, even to overlook what it has revealed, so he can return to his former way of life. My argument centers on the tension released by the liminality of haunting: it works initially to problematize space, yet paradoxically renders that same reviled space as desirable. Finally, by working only to perpetuate the status quo, liminality here fails to effect change. In accordance with Leslie Fiedler's contention, discussed in the Introduction, that American Gothic is far more conservative than its European predecessor,[21] Matheson's novel ultimately sends a reactionary message.

"The World of Twists and Warps"— *Suburbia Reviled*

The corner of Southern Californian suburbia inhabited by the Wallace family forms the backdrop to the whole tale. Bearing in mind historian Kenneth T. Jackson's claim that "California became the symbol of the postwar suburban culture,"[22] this location seems a noteworthy one. It comes as no surprise that this domestic setting gives rise to troubles of a domestic nature, and this apparently-serene locale soon proves to be rife with marital discord and the dissatisfaction concomitant with a routinized existence. In focusing on such issues, the first part of this chapter will show how the liminal experience triggered by Tom's hypnosis, with the haunting at its heart, serves to depict this most archetypal of 1950s American living spaces as highly problematic.

The novel's opening instantly evokes the tranquility of middle-class American life in the post-war years.[23] Unlike the haunted spaces of Lovecraft's fiction, there are no florid descriptions of buildings or their environs here and the space depicted is unobtrusive almost to the point of invisibility. This lack indicates its very normality—it is so familiar, it needs no explanation. The simple scenario that instigates the narrative with Matheson's characteristic brevity,[24] Tom's habitual drive home from work, suggests that his is a lifestyle structured around that separation of living and working space which is definitive of suburbia.[25] As he moves into his residential space, references to such a culture quickly manifest themselves: "I nosed the Ford into the driveway and braked it in front of the garage. Across the street Frank Wanamaker's wife, Elizabeth, was sitting on their lawn pulling up weeds. She smiled faintly at me and raised one white-gloved hand."[26] This innocuous moment anchors the novel firmly to a quotidian setting peopled with the compliant house-wives and reliable male breadwinners associated with 1950s America.[27] The initial air of complacency is soon to be shaken by Tom's liminal encounter, which sees the incursion of a ghostly woman whose presence signals that this is a troubled space.

All the reader gets by way of scene-setting is that the Wallaces have inhabited their two-bedroom residence, rented from neighbors Mildred and Harry Sentas, for the last two months. The designation of their home as a tract house immediately marks it out as one of many identical dwellings in the kind of residential area that came to epitomize changes in living arrangements in the 1950s as white middle-class families left the cities for the promise of cleaner and safer suburban environments in which to raise their children.[28] Howard Davis explains the nature of tract housing with reference to those areas of land designated for mass building, a practice closely associated with "the large tract-house devel-opments in Levittown, in which construction was essentially based on an assembly-line method in which building workers moved from house to house,"[29] producing vast swathes of indistinguishable homes. Real estate developer William Levitt "virtually invented the post-war suburb," beginning with the Long Island Levittown in 1947 to which he gave his name, which comprised "17,400 Cape Cods, colonials, and ranch houses."[30] A succession of such designs, popularized by Levitt and made available to buyers throughout the continent, spelled the end of distinc-tive regional architecture.[31]

This ordinary space becomes liminal once subject to haunting. As with the introduction to the neighborhood, there is nothing too con-trived about the event at which the hypnotism takes place. It happens at a party given by Elsie and Ron, the Wallaces' neighbors, at which Anne and the Wanamakers are also present. The mundanity of the sit-uation is underscored by Tom's observation that "what happened that evening up to the point when it all began is not important ... the usual breaking up and re-gathering of small groups ... the drifting knots of conversation that take place at any get-together" (ASOE: 5). Phil is keen to showcase his knowledge of psychology by hypnotizing one of the guests. Being in possession of a more open and enquiring mind than some of his neighbors—Elsie is openly skeptical and Elizabeth is clearly uneasy at the potential for manipulation—Tom is dubious yet still amenable to Phil's experiment.[32] He shares the party-goers' subsequent surprise and delight at the success of the hypnotism, which is a pleasant diversion from a mediocre occasion. Later the protracted, quite understated, process of achieving his state of hypnosis can be seen as a kind of ritual inducing him to enter a liminal state.

During the night Tom is roused from his sleep and greeted by the sight of a ghostly woman "in her thirties, pale, her hair in black disarray" (*ASOE*: 25). He reveals this to Anne and Phil the following morning, though neither will countenance his assertion that "I saw a ghost last night" (28). Only the first of several such encounters with the female specter, this incident is also the first in a series of diverse supernatural experiences to which he is grudgingly subjected. That night marks Tom's introduction to a liminal experience that, beginning with his family's initially amused rejection of his claims, quickly isolates him from his community and sets him apart from his hitherto routinized and commonplace existence in this most average of living spaces. That the ghost is an ordinary woman—neither overtly sinister nor anachronistic—who emerges from the context of a routine neighborhood gathering suggests that suburbia itself is potentially troubling. Unlike the inherently Gothic figure of the witch[33] whom Lovecraft chooses to haunt his fiction, this specter is a strikingly modern one. As such, the underwhelming appearance of the ghost is symbolic of the horror latent in the similarly underwhelming mundanity of life in this prefabricated environment.

Critics have long forged a link between suburbia and the Gothic, as Kim Ian Michasiw avers,[34] so Matheson's choice of setting is perhaps unsurprising. After all, while the increase in marriage and birth rates helped drive the post-war housing expansion, the new Cold War mentality also had a part to play. Widespread anxieties about external threats to American society, such as nuclear attack or the more insidious potential for communists to infiltrate and forever change daily life, left citizens with an ill-defined sense of dread. Peter Nicholls notes that Matheson's early work is highly expressive of an era when "people felt threatened, and yet could not easily find a focus for this sense of threat."[35] Robin Wood observes that a fear of danger to society from without loomed large in 1950s popular culture: "The 50s science fiction cycles project horror onto either extraterrestrial invaders or mutations from the insect world…. *Them!*, for example … sets out to cope with the fear of nuclear energy and atomic experiment … fear of Communist infiltration also seems present."[36] The nature of the threat in many 1950s horror fictions often centered on a loss of individuality, which was typically perceived by critics as the inevitable outcome of living under a communist regime. As demonstrated by the rise of McCarthyism, fear that such a regime might conceivably take root in America and render its citizens as undifferentiated as members of a communist state was endemic.

Given these circumstances, suburbia worked to provide a type of safety net, fostering a "sense of uniformity, order, community, and safety"[37] in a Cold War America increasingly shaped by fears of its vulnerability to communist Russia.[38] Arguing that the "cold war made a profound contribution to suburban sprawl," Elaine Tyler May points to pressure put on Congress in the early 1950s by scientific and industrial groups which sought to keep citizens and industry away from city centers on the grounds that such places were potential targets for a nuclear attack. This resulted in such measures as the 1956 Interstate Highway Act and an increase in suburban housing.[39] *A Stir of Echoes* thus speaks to a time when living arrangements, at least in part, were determined by fear. Suburbia was intended as a sanctuary in a wider world fraught with hostility.[40]

Paranoia about invasion aside, so-called "cookie-cutter" housing had other implications for its inhabitants. These homes were integral to a new ethos of domestic consumerism. "In open-plan interiors arranged around the kitchen, the appliance acquired enormous visual prominence."[41] The interior design of these residences readily accommodated, even invited, a constant supply of the latest consumer goods, including washing machines and television sets, which stood as testament to modern technological advances and post-war American capitalism. Yet, as critics lamented, such changes fostered a uniformity of aspirations to a standardized and conventional lifestyle. The Coca-Cola Phil is drinking as Tom enters his home for the first time heralds a recurring theme of consumer culture.

Neighbor Elsie, undisputed mistress of both the marital home and of her browbeaten husband Ron, is repeatedly associated with consumer goods. Hers is a world bound up with the vagaries of fashion and structured by parties, comprising such domestic trappings as "raffia-covered glasses" (*ASOE*: 35) and endless rounds of "little glazed cakes" (18). These details render her an essentially materialistic figure. One of Tom's first liminal experiences is triggered by Elsie. Still shaken from his sighting of the ghostly woman the previous night, Tom is at home when Elsie calls to borrow some glassware with which to impress her next set of guests. Inadvertently accessing her thoughts, Tom is perturbed by the capacity for sexual aggression and manipulation he detects in her mind, censuring it as "an awful place" (38).[42] Elsie has already been cast as a typical shallow suburbanite. While the social and domestic image she has constructed of herself is made to seem unappealing enough, Tom's newfound abilities reveal that this masks an even less palatable side to her. Liminality thus heightens the sense of suburbia as intrinsically troubled.

For many, the pervasive effects of consumerism seemed to tear at the very fabric of society. America has had a long tradition of casting its identity in terms of the individualist spirit: "From its formative years, the United States was an experiment in government founded on the value of the individual; Americans considered their nation a "city on a hill," an example to the rest of the world, unburdened by class privilege and tradition-bound institutions."[43] The American national character is strongly bound up with notions of self-reliance and independence. In the 1950s, these were widely seen as integral to the democratic freedom enjoyed in the United States and a stark contrast to life in the Soviet Union. However, David Riesman's influential 1950 study *The Lonely Crowd* tracked changes discernible in the American character by the middle of the twentieth century.[44] He argued that society was shifting from being inner-directed, what might be called characteristic of "old American culture … an amalgam of our biblical, republican, and utilitarian individualistic types,"[45] to being other-directed. This latter term denotes a society increasingly shaped by the pressure to conform to social influences such as the peer group and the mass media. Americans were thus in danger of losing their celebrated individualistic streak.

This period saw a whole host of intellectuals become apprehensive about what was happening to America and to its citizens. In *The Power Elite* (1956), C. Wright Mills stressed the centrality of the belief of power being vested in the public, whereby public discussion would lead to public action, to America's established perception of itself as a democracy.[46] For Mills, the increased concentration of power in the hands of fewer individuals, as evidenced by the rise of large corporations and a mass media potentially working to manipulate whole swathes of the nation, meant that the hallmarks of American culture were now "more the features of a mass society than of a community of publics."[47] Decrying "the frustration of idea, of intellect, by the present organization of society,"[48] Mills delineated the ever more conformist members of this mass society as people who "do not transcend, even by discussion, much less by action, their more or less narrow lives."[49] Similarly, Norman Mailer's *The White Negro* (1957) evoked the nation's time-honored character traits to paint a bleak picture of changes wrought by the 1950s: "One is Hip or one is square ... one is a rebel or one conforms, one is a frontiersman in the Wild West of American night life, or else a Square cell, trapped in the totalitarian tissues of American society, doomed willy-nilly to conform if one is to succeed."[50] America was thus seen to be losing touch with its roots and transforming into a society that restricted the freedoms of its members.

While suburbia was an attractive prospect for families like the Wallaces, it clearly had another side to it that has long been criticized. Zoning practices on economic grounds led to class and racial segregation and gave rise to "homogenized environments marked by identical houses and similar lifestyles."[51] Writing as early as the beginning of the 1960s, Humphrey Carver comments, "The flight to the suburbs has taken us to a monotonous, standardized environment where everyone has much the same amount of money to do much the same things in the same ways."[52] Historian May similarly notes that suburban tracts "promoted homogeneity in neighborhoods, intensified racial segregation, encouraged conformity, and fostered a style of life based on traditional gender roles in the home."[53] Condemned by "nay-sayers quick to equate stylistic sameness with middle-class conventionality and intellectual conformity,"[54] suburbia arguably contributed to a shift away from the national character's individualist roots.

So the constraints of the physical environment in which an increasing majority of American citizens were spending their domestic and leisure time were believed to have a stifling effect on their creativity and intellectual freedom. This banality is evoked early on when Tom attributes his post-party restlessness to "coffee and conversation. Living in this neighborhood I was taking too much of the first and getting too little of the second" (*ASOE*: 23). Suburbia is shown to be intellectually and socially stultifying. Later, he offers a similar denouncement of suburban prioritization of style over substance when he peruses the "true confessions and screen romances which were Elsie's only mental fare. Once, when she'd brought herself a small, wrought-iron bookcase, she'd come over and asked if she could borrow some books to display that night at a party—books with pretty jackets, she'd specified" (105). Derided early on by Tom as "the poor man's Elsa Maxwell" (3),[55] Elsie is preoccupied with appearances to the detriment of any potential she might have for more meaningful emotional or intellectual activities. This episode clearly speaks to fears about intellectual degradation. It also resonates with the strong element of theatricality detected by sociologists in 1950s domestic life. As Lynn Spigel puts it, "Families transformed their homes into showcases for their neighbours."[56] Elsie's relegation of books to mere props at a social event is particularly interesting. Catherine Jurca notes the recurrent motif of books as items for display in previous suburban fictions, including Sinclair Lewis's *Babbitt* (1922) and James M. Cain's *Mildred Pierce* (1941).[57]

The flaws in the neighborhood demonstrate, then, that this supposed sanctuary begets its own set of problems. Over the course of the novel, it becomes evident that all the households are experiencing turmoil in one form or another. Superficial Elsie is also a poor mother and Ron seems to compound their familial inadequacy through his inability to stand up to his wife. Long desperate for a child, the pregnant Elizabeth repeatedly incurs her husband's displeasure as he rails against "marriage and kids and all the rest of it" (*ASOE*: 65), perceiving his status as a husband and a father as an infringement of his freedom rather than as a blessing. Only Tom and Anne, happily settled with their young son and a daughter on the way—the very embodiment of the growing young American suburban family[58]—are shown in a positive light.

Some of these problems are tangible from the outset of the novel when they seem fairly prosaic. However, through liminality, Tom becomes privy to previously-concealed information. He sees that the ostensible mundanity of his environment is a veneer concealing unpleasant truths. A few days after the party, during which time he reflects that "life had become a nightmare" (*ASOE*: 103), he comes to view the community which comprises his whole world from a horrifying new perspective: "The neighborhood was two creatures. One presented a clean, smiling countenance to the world and, beneath, maintained quite another one" (104). It is liminality which reveals such visions—represented by Matheson as insights into fundamental truths about his suburban home—to Tom. These truths include the thoughts, feelings and motivations behind the façade put up by his friends and neighbors, especially the women who, by simple virtue of their gender, are made to seem less knowable to Tom than his male neighbor and colleague Frank. Furthermore, liminality discloses a violent crime which reveals the precarious nature of the whole community.

Matheson's trademark sense of normality, and the way in which liminality works to strip that away, is exploited to great effect during one of the tale's grimmest moments. On the discovery of Frank's infidelity with a female colleague, a desperate Elizabeth shoots him with the Luger he keeps in the house. In an episode when the veneer of normality over the horror beneath seems precariously thin, Tom and Anne fetch Elizabeth home from hospital after she subsequently suffers a miscarriage. Frank survives, and the real tragedy is shown to be the loss of—she is told—the only child Elizabeth will ever be able to bear. Tom experiences the feelings of violent jealousy directed by the normally mild Elizabeth towards the still safely pregnant Anne. Referring to, and reversing, some of the time-honored clichés of Gothic fiction, Tom encapsulates Matheson's style and themes in noting that "the most hideous of moments, I discovered then, could take place in bright sunlight, in the most mundane of locations. Night is not a requirement; nor are thunderstorms, high winds or the rain lashed battlements of mad doctors. There were no monsters here; just three human beings" (179– 180). Once again, liminality gives Tom a glimpse of the turmoil beneath the exterior of one of the community's most upright members: "shy, quiet Elizabeth" (206).

Liminality amplifies issues of domestic conflict. Yet, through the woman's persistent haunting, it also reveals that Tom's own home is contaminated too—a possibility formerly unsuspected. This implies the existence of problems embedded deeply within 1950s American culture and which flourish even in the midst of contentment. *A Stir of Echoes* speaks to an era mindful of the impact of rapid social developments. As cited above, 1950s horror fictions are noted for their depiction of external threats. Readings such as Robin Wood's tend to portray such horror as conservative in its efforts to preserve the American status quo—a lifestyle rooted in individualism—from such perils. Yet fears about this loss of individualism have also been attributed to a very different source. Mark Jancovich describes the application of Fordist labor procedures to American society at the time, which gave rise to "a system of centrally ordered administration which relied on an elite of experts. It was their task to regulate social, political, economic and cultural life, and they did so through the use of scientific-technical rationality."[59] America in the 1950s then, clearly sought to reorganize its own society along cooperative lines.

It has often been claimed that the alien invasion narratives so common to the period—such as the takeover and dehumanization of the residents of a small California town by the "pods" in *Invasion of the Body Snatchers* (1956)—depict fears of the communist threat.[60] Jancovich maintains that they may actually depict a threat closer to home: "Many American critics claimed that in the Soviet Union people were all the same; that they were forced to deny personal feelings and characteristics, and to become mere functionaries of the social whole. It should also be noted, however, that ... it was common in the 1950s for Americans to claim that the effects of scientific-technical rationality upon their own society was producing the same features within America itself."[61] Horror texts of the era accordingly showed a new concern with the changing nature of contemporary life and its impact on the American character, as detected by sociological studies like those of Riesman and Mills. Science fiction writers of the time addressed such issues in their work too.[62] Indeed, Jancovich places Matheson alongside authors such as Ray Bradbury, whose stories also express unease about conformity.[63] The free-floating sense of fear about irrevocable decline in American society thus might be said to stem as much from developments within America as from those beyond its borders.

In a similar vein to Riesman's study, William H. Whyte's *The Organization Man* (1956) argued that the new corporate culture, which nurtured the kind of ideals internalized by other-directed individuals, was reinforced by suburban living.[64] As the natural environment of the "organization man," Whyte described post-war suburbs as "communities made in his image."[65] This threat to American society, created by itself and from within, caused many citizens to become increasingly uneasy and even fearful.[66] A *Stir of Echoes*, with its depictions of consumer culture and standardized living arrangements, reflects such anxieties throughout. In *Invasion of the Body Snatchers*, in which those who fall asleep are taken over by the pods and lose their humanity, sleep can be seen as symbolic of succumbing to conformity. Tellingly, sleep also plays a key role in this novel. Tom's introduction to both the liminal state and to the haunting occurs on a night when—unexpectedly and disconcertingly for him—he is unable to sleep. Liminality disturbs his complacency.

The liminality of haunting, unsettling Tom night after night, hints at horror concealed within the community and culminates in the discovery of the identity and then the body of the ghostly woman. She is Helen Driscoll,[67] sister of Mildred Sentas the Wallaces' landlady and next-door neighbor. Elizabeth, present at the detection of the corpse, finally loses her tenuous grip on her composure and reveals that it was she who bludgeoned Helen to death because of her sexual involvement with a number of married men, including Mildred's husband, Harry, and her own husband, Frank. The perpetrator of the crime is revealed to be a character who has sought to conform to the standards of her time and place: "to have a baby and be loved" (*ASOE*: 207). Her failure to achieve this goal, coupled with her inability to cope with that failure, lead to a wider tragedy which scars the whole neighborhood.

The novel's link to the Gothic tradition is reinforced with Tom's exhumation of Helen's body from under their family home to finally dispel her restless spirit. Exploring his hunch that she might be buried beneath the house, he receives ghostly validation on moving towards a mound of earth that looks likely to conceal her: "Swallowing, I crawled toward the mound; and, as I did, the doubt began to fade in me. Because it seemed as if I heard someone speak a word in my mind and the word was *yes* [original emphasis]" (200). This episode has its roots in early Gothic literature, and its concern with "the *return* of the past, of the repressed and denied, the buried secret that subverts and corrodes the present, whatever the culture does not want to know or admit, will not or dare not tell itself [original emphasis]."[68] Certainly, the discovery, then the unearthing, of the hastily-concealed corpse that proves Helen was murdered is a clearly Gothic effect which brings home the troubled nature of this living space.

Up to now, this chapter has shown how liminality and haunting work to problematize suburbia, placing Matheson in the ranks of those writers who saw it as detrimental to American life. While the novel as a whole demonstrates anxiety about the changing nature of American society, the horror buried beneath the ordinary tract house reveals the unpleasant realities—the stress caused by the pressure to conform to social standards and the misery induced in those who fail to do so—that lie beneath the civilized surface. Culture works to repress these truths, and they are only discovered here as an outcome of Tom's liminal experience. It is both inevitable and necessary that the troubles in the community, which have found their expression in supernatural activity, be exposed, confronted, and thus overcome. Liminality provides this closure. The next section considers how, despite these revelations, liminality ultimately leads Tom to embrace this suburban lifestyle.

"This Peaceful Neighborhood"— Suburbia Idealized

Tom's liminal experience in his typical 1950s American home, over a lonely week when his abilities set him apart from his everyday life, can be seen as a revelatory one. The Gothic trope of haunting reveals the problems to which that domestic space gives rise. Unlike the fifties fictions alluded to by Robin Wood, Matheson's tale sees horror emerging from the community itself and hence locates it not outside of society but within its very heart. Despite this reflection on how America might be damaging its own way of life, the ultimate outcome of this enlightening liminal process is still a conservative one. Whereas Murphy maintains that, in this novel, "nothing can ever be the same again—'order' can never be fully restored,"[69] I would stress that order actually *is* restored. Tom is so threatened by the lessons of liminality that, rather than evincing any lasting sense of awareness as a result of his experience, he seeks only to turn his back on the whole episode.

Earlier, it was shown how liminality worked to expose the dual nature of the neighborhood, likened by a repulsed Tom to "Jekyll and Hyde" (*ASOE*: 104). The discovery of such a dichotomy works both ways, however: while the "clean, smiling countenance" (104) might be masking a dark heart, the façade persists nonetheless. Phil and Anne are both quick to reject the potential existence of a ghost. They have different rationales for this: Anne is an average citizen blinkered by her unquestioning acceptance of "normality" and Phil represents the rationality of a scientific worldview which excludes such a supernatural possibility. Close as they are to liminar Tom, neither of them ever gains much insight into the true nature of the community and there is no firm suggestion that anyone else does either. For the likes of these characters, the mask never really slips. That Tom comes to see normality as an illusion need not, and does not, detract from the fact that this is a potent illusion which existed before liminality revealed it as such and which continues to exist afterwards.

The novel does much to endorse this illusion, which is repeatedly shown as a blessing rather than a curse. Such a view has clear echoes of Lovecraft's cosmicist perception that humanity might be better off oblivious to the horrors potentially lurking in a wider hostile universe, as evidenced in his oft-quoted opening paragraph to "The Call of Cthulhu" (1928): "We live on a placid island of ignorance in the midst of black seas of infinity, and it was not meant that we should voyage far."[70] The abilities unleashed by liminality, including the sighting of the ghost, make daily life unbearably challenging. As Murphy observes, Tom tries hard to disregard the insights it brings by "undertaking mundane, comfortingly routine tasks like mowing the lawn."[71] Indeed, he comes to appreciate secrecy as an inevitable fact of harmonious communal living, since "what a terrible world it would be if ... everyone knew what everyone else was thinking. What a terrible breakdown of society. There could *be* no society when every man was an open book to his neighbors [original emphasis]" (*ASOE*: 166). However damaging the concealment of truth is shown to be here, the novel still works to imply that suburban culture's suppression of these truths is actually desirable.

Though Tom is sporadically intrigued by his glimpses of the underbelly of his world, the overriding impression the novel gives—tied as it is to his first-person narration—of his reaction to the liminality and haunting is undoubtedly a negative one ranging from simple disquiet to outright terror. Besides the damage to his own peace of mind, he is also concerned that his role as a husband and father is compromised by his condition. The risk to the stability of his family is summed up by the pregnant Anne's lament: "I got a friend in here needs a daddy.... Not some character in a padded cell" (41). Unsurprisingly, desirous as he is of restoring the harmony they once enjoyed, he seeks assistance with his quandary. After several days of disturbances—haunting, uncontrollable access to the thoughts of those around him and prescience of events both personal and public, including the death of Anne's mother and a terrible train crash—Tom visits family friend and psychiatrist Alan Porter to find an explanation. This seems a natural course of action for an everyman in an era declared by 1957's *Life* magazine as the "age of psychology and psychoanalysis,"[72] and when "people were quick to seek professional help. When the experts spoke, postwar Americans listened."[73]

Tom and Porter conclude, as the former has previously suspected, that Tom's mind has been freed from what might be considered normal human constraints on communicative reach and ability after Phil's attempt to extract him from hypnosis failed to take full effect:

> "Your mind is free now," he'd said to me. "There's nothing binding it. It's free, absolutely free." It's something he'd said a hundred times before to hypnotized subjects. As I understand it, it's a command designed to prevent the subject's mind from retaining any suggestions inadvertently given which might later prove harmful. As I say, Phil had used it a hundred times; he verified that later. Yet, for some reason, with me it had backfired [*ASOE*: 55].

Much to Tom's relief, the "authoritative" (145) Porter confirms his suspicions that his mind interpreted this comment all too literally. The psychiatrist's diagnosis is that the hypnotism has tapped into latent yet natural abilities—telepathic powers that preceded the advent of verbal communication—and he attributes the ghost to these. He theorizes that such abilities were once widespread and likely to persist in many people in the modern world, commenting that they are "not so much lost, I think, ... as repressed. I believe they still exist in us, faint echoes of their former vitality" (148), providing a partial explanation for the novel's title.

Keith Neilson readily accepts the "scientific" explanations offered up here: "Finally a psychiatrist gives Tom a lucid explanation of his condition and another round of hypnosis; Tom immediately gains confidence and control over his talents, stabilizes his marriage, [and] solves the 'ghost' problem."[74] However, Porter's intervention does not adequately explain or alleviate Tom's condition: he fails to account for the haunting and certainly does not free him of it. Any suggestion that this might have been the case is readily undermined the following evening when Harry Sentas visits the Wallaces' home to carry out some maintenance work. Utilizing the vocal cords of Tom's young son, Richard, to declare her identity as Helen Driscoll, the ghostly woman addresses Sentas, whom she believes to be guilty of her murder, in a distorted version of her own voice to which he responds with uneasy recognition. Tom's frequent insistence that he has seen a ghost, shored up by the discovery of the corpse beneath the place it haunts, confirms that this is a tale of haunting. So desperate is he to minimize this disruption and reinstate order in his life that he seeks professional assistance. Its failure to fix matters is no small cause for concern. Anne, despairing that Porter has failed to remedy the problem, sobs, "I thought it was over, I thought it was over" (*ASOE*: 163) on realizing that the powers endure. Although Porter is able to reassure Tom, the continued liminal experience still comes between the latter and his wife and, periodically, threatens to overwhelm him.

Even though the tract house inhabited by the Wallace family functions as the prime physical area affected by the ghost, the violence instilled in their home by its recent history seems to have infected the wider neighborhood. Matheson conveys this through the rhetoric of haunting. Tellingly, Tom feels extensive psychic disturbance on visiting the home of the unhappily married Wanamakers for dinner a few days after the party: "That house was haunted too. I felt it strongly. Haunted by despairs, by the ghosts of a thousand cruel words and acts, by the phantom residue of unresolved angers" (62). This remark shows the wider effects of those phenomena characterized as "haunting." Elizabeth may be unaware of the supernatural form taken by her victim until the novel's climax, but the rage, guilt and misery surrounding the incident, engendered by the pressures of 1950s suburban life and lying beneath its surface, taint her life and those of people around her even so.

It was noted earlier that the exhumation of Helen Driscoll's corpse, coupled with Elizabeth's confession, brings a measure of closure to the tale which Tom finds only too welcome. However, putting aside the mystery of the haunting, liminality reveals many other issues which he studiously avoids confronting. In his corporate environment, he is aware for the first time that his colleagues have inner lives which they routinely conceal from one another. It quickly becomes apparent that Tom's immediate neighbors have problems, the extent of which goes undetected until he enters liminality, but he only gradually realizes that such issues are not confined to the borders of his own street. He learns about "the bus driver up the block who was an alcoholic who spent half his weekends in jail; about the housewife on the next street who slept with high school boys while her salesman husband was on the road" (104). In an incident with a troubled babysitter who attempts to snatch Richard, Tom's ability reveals that the teen is likely suffering from the absence of her mother. Yet his instinct is not to address this issue but rather to remove the threat to his own household and then to ignore it altogether: "I don't want to see you in our neighborhood after tonight" (87), he tells her. Liminality shows the potential for further events just as harmful as those that Tom's powers eventually drive him to uncover. While the haunting is addressed, there is a clear implication that other horrors may be occurring all around the community and on a regular basis.

A Stir of Echoes provides a number of examples of repressed events and feelings throughout, such as Elsie's sexual desire and Elizabeth's frustrated yearning to succeed in her role as a wife and mother. Repressed emotions, not acted upon but still strongly felt, also leave their mark. The aftermath of Elizabeth's miscarriage is one of the novel's most traumatic events, depicted through a horrifying account of the despair it brings and her reaction to it. She doesn't act upon, or articulate (even to herself), her distress, and her feelings and desires are completely repressed. Even when she confesses to the murder and exhibits her latent aggression at the novel's climax, the horror of this incident is not brought fully to light. So the Gothic drive to expose repressed horrors fails to expose all horrific events in this novel; rather, it suggests that others are brewing beneath the surface and very likely to go undetected. Tom's struggle to "blank [his] mind" (104) to this reveals the strength of his inclination to return to his former settled way of life.

As mentioned above, liminality and haunting are linked to sleep disruption from the outset. The association of the revelations brought by these experiences with sleep—or lack thereof—continues throughout the novel as Tom is variously unable to sleep, roused from his sleep or painfully aware that others around him sleep peacefully while he remains wakeful. Discussing films which feature such a possession, Vivian Sobchack comments that "there is a definite emotional appeal to the idea of being 'taken-over.'"[75] She asserts that this attraction lies in the possibility of a life without dangerous extremes of emotion and which demands very little of the individual. This appeal is plainly demonstrated here as the disruption of liminality, with all the discomfiting intensities of emotion it both reveals and instigates, is shown to threaten the harmony previously enjoyed by Tom and the entire Wallace family.

Desperate to dispel anything out of the ordinary in the early stages of his liminal experience, Tom paints a compelling image of the power of perceived normality in noting that "sunlight ... a tasty breakfast, a sunny-countenanced wife, a happy, laughing baby son, the first day of a week's work [array] a potent force against belief in all things that have no form or logic" (*ASOE*: 43). Given the appeal of such a scene, redolent as it is of popular images of suburban family life in the fifties, it is hardly surprising that he seeks a return to the pre-liminal state. For, despite its revelations, liminality is too disruptive a force—especially when the alternative is a tranquil and happy family life. Embracing Anne's early resistance to his ability, on the grounds that it "throws our whole life out of balance" (55), Tom eventually rejects its radical potential. Taking responsibility for laying bare the problems inherent in his community is not in his best interest. His doing what effectively amounts to regaining his capacity for undisturbed slumber, characterized by a blissful ignorance of the mundane horrors that surround him and his family, means much the same thing as succumbing to conformity, mindlessly accepting the routinized lifestyle which liminality has briefly problematized for him.

His propensity for regressing to his former state of torpor is reinforced by the surprisingly brief coda with which Matheson concludes his disturbing tale. In this short paragraph, Tom recalls the tussle that marked the confrontation with Elizabeth and addresses Anne's subsequent anxious inquiry as to whether he was still experiencing his powers:

But I wasn't. I don't know what happened—unless that head wound joggled something in my brain. Or maybe I'd only had the power limitedly—or for a specific purpose. At any rate it's gone. But I can always say I batted a thousand in my predictions. Because, in late September, Anne went to the hospital and, after delivery, I visited her and she asked me in a sweet little doped-up voice, "Was it a girl?" I kissed her and grinned. "What else?" I said [211].

Focused as it is on the restoration of a peaceful family life, this summary barely acknowledges—much less reflects upon—the traumatic, yet enlightening, events of the recent past. Certainly, no sense that any permanent change has been effected in Tom emerges here. With the emphasis laid on the primacy of the family unit, and on the bright future connoted by the advent of a daughter, this summation leaves no room for dwelling on wider social issues.

Tom makes the transition from ignorance to knowledge in evolving, albeit temporarily, to an altered state of perception and communication that represents the kind of progress and even status change which characterizes the liminar. Although he does not retain his paranormal abilities, they ensure that Helen's murder is brought to light and the related disturbances cease because of this. However transitory, the experiences give him a deeper appreciation of what he has by providing a greater insight into the changing world around him. It is through liminality and the device of haunting that Matheson explores the extent to which imperfections exist beneath the surface of 1950s suburban life. Yet this heightened awareness is presented as threatening. Rather than seeking to embrace its potential to reveal hidden horrors, Tom wishes to escape it and effectively chooses a return to the dormancy of a less enlightened lifestyle—a return to his former life in an ostensibly "peaceful neighborhood of quiet, little houses basking in the sun" (104).

Conclusion

Buildings blighted by spectral presences have an ancestry that can be traced back to the haunted castle of early European Gothic literature. Tom's puzzled declaration about the apparent haunting in his modern home—"It doesn't make sense. Why should a place like this be haunted? It's only a couple of years old" (*ASOE*: 97) indicates the extent to which haunting is traditionally associated with certain types of physical space.

Yet haunted spaces continue to be utilized by horror authors into the twentieth century. The liminality inherent in the haunted house motif provides a narrative space for acting out anxieties about culture and cultural change. It is characteristic of Matheson to make use of contemporary settings, thus transplanting the haunted house motif—apparently absurdly—to 1950s American suburbia with all the safety and modernity that context implies on the surface. Matheson's fiction has typically sought to undercut the perceived link between haunting and antiquity, and Tom's observation, as well as the question it raises, also points to Gothic's ability to adapt to and address changing social circumstances. Haunted spaces need not be ancient; they are haunted because they are troubled by violent pasts, however recent, and inhabited by restless spirits that must be understood and confronted to be dispelled.

Liminality lets the protagonist, and by implication the reader, see beneath the surface of such a world and witness something of the kind of troubles that lie within. The traumatic, though eventually enlightening, events in and around the Wallace home prove crucial to solving the neighborhood's biggest secret. It is through the collision of normally separate spheres, and the liminal experience provided by their intersection, that the vital knowledge required to bring Helen's murder to light and restore some measure of peace to the troubled neighborhood is attained. Keith Neilson's summation of the relatively positive resolution as "too fast and easy, denying the novel the final impact of *I Am Legend* or *The Shrinking Man*,"[76] indicates that these other novels both result in radical and irreversible changes in the lives of their isolated male protagonists. Arguably, though, Neilson's view of the ending of *A Stir of Echoes* seems somewhat dismissive when viewed through the lens of liminality. For this would emphasize that such an outcome can only follow a challenging and alienating time of learning, and Tom's liminal experience certainly does not shrink from revealing the full extent to which his suburban environment is a troubled place.

What Neilson overlooks, and what has been crucial to my argument, is the fact that the novel's ending offers only the appearance of tranquility. The Wallaces certainly have reason to be happy; Tom especially so, given his firsthand insight into the misery of his neighbors and his realization that a similar degree of suffering is surely set to continue beneath the surface of other communities like his own. Neilson sees the tale's end as simplistic in its buoyancy. The glib, self-absorbed nature of the conclusion, which essentially works to gloss over Tom's liminal experience and underscore instead his own family's potential for future happiness, has already been discussed. Yet liminality has shown the ordinariness of the suburban community to be a veneer over the darker, more complex world beneath. This upbeat insistence on a bright new future can be nothing more than an attempt to reconstruct this fragile façade.

Despite the enlightening nature of the liminal process, then, it is not shown to effect ultimate change here. Once the ghost is identified and exorcized, the boundaries violated by liminality are reinstated and life is essentially restored to its former unthinking composure. Tom's anxiety about the conformist tendencies of the time in which he finds himself living, with all the radical questioning of post-war American society it brings, seems quite sincere. As will be discussed in later chapters, Stephen King's fiction also draws on Gothic tropes of haunting to address many of these same anxieties about 1950s culture some twenty years after the decade's passing. King tenders a more overt critique of that era's less palatable qualities. Yet Matheson was, of course, writing during the 1950s. So, for author and protagonist alike, the seismic changes of the 1960s are still some years away and Tom is in no position to perceive change as truly desirable, much less as actually attainable.

Because Tom is desperate to have his eyes closed to the revelations of liminality, there is no move here towards a permanently-enlightened, post-liminal state. Life for him will continue to be as normal as it ever was, as no abiding lesson has really been learned. Further, his status as a first-person narrator means that his perceptions are, in essence, the views espoused by the narrative as a whole. It is perhaps inevitable, as everyman Tom is so firmly ensconced within his social milieu, that a return to quiescence should be the final outcome of this tale. Therefore, although Matheson's novel certainly has radical implications in suggesting that 1950s American society should look within to find the causes of its problems, and should question the pressures it engenders in itself, its message is ultimately a conservative one. While *A Stir of Echoes* does work to critique suburbia, it also works to idealize it and, in doing so, ushers its protagonist back to normative behavior rather than having him reject it.

CHAPTER THREE

"A ghost in his life?"

The Legacy of the 1950s Marriage
in Earthbound

The preceding analysis of *A Stir of Echoes* showed how Matheson provides a fictional space in which Tom Wallace, once isolated by his extrasensory abilities, reluctantly encounters challenging and conflicting views of the society from which he finds himself set apart. Much of Tom's distress stems from the rift that develops between him and his wife, and it is his commitment to his family that eventually persuades him to close his eyes to the unpalatable truth about his community. Likewise, *Earthbound* (1982; 1989) reinforces the centrality of marriage and family to its male protagonist's sense of security and self. In the wake of his infidelity, David Cooper and his wife, Ellen, retreat to their honeymoon destination of Logan Beach in an attempt to repair their marriage of twenty-one years. Yet this place is not the haven they remember. Their time there is plagued by Marianna, the sexually voracious "earthbound" spirit of the title. Once again, haunting provides a time and space apart in which the protagonist is forced to confront aspects of history and culture, here with a particular focus on America's changing perceptions of marriage and gender relations.

Matheson's conservatism is as notable here as it is in the much earlier *A Stir of Echoes*. In each of the novels the liminality provoked by haunting works to critique the conventional view of family life ingrained in post-war America, and both narratives seek to contain the radical impulses they unearth by moving finally to endorse an essentially conservative stance. In tracing the progression of the genre throughout the twentieth century, it can be seen that Fiedler's observations about the deep-rooted conservatism of American Gothic are borne out once again.

The haunted house motif thus facilitates an exploration of the inevitable disquiet which accompanies social transformation, and the contradictory drives contained within the motif point towards the intractability of these issues.

As is also the case with *A Stir of Echoes*, *Earthbound* is a novel which has received minimal critical analysis. It represents a sustained and detailed engagement with David's reflections on self-identity, aging and sexuality, all of which center chiefly on his anxiety about the breakdown of his marriage, and Matheson's use of haunting to engage with these themes ensures the tale is of particular interest to this study. In contrast to *A Stir of Echoes*, this novel is written in the third-person. Although, as it is effectively conveyed exclusively from David's perspective, it still provides what amounts to a subjective account of "the proving ground of the familiar world turned hostile"[1] comparable to that supplied by Tom Wallace. David's encounters with Marianna—the ghostly young woman who haunts their holiday cottage—both heighten his turmoil over these issues and throw his previous beliefs about Ellen, and even about himself, into doubt. *Earthbound* first appeared in 1982, at which time it was "heavily edited without Matheson's approval."[2] In 1989 another publisher put out an edition of the novel which he deemed acceptable and which will therefore be used in this chapter.[3] So, although I will be citing a text with a publication date from the late 1980s, it is essentially an early eighties novel. Appearing at this time, two decades after the setting of *A Stir of Echoes*, *Earthbound* indexes pre- and post-countercultural shifts in America's attitudes towards, and expectations about, sexuality, intimacy and marriage. The 1980s context is of special interest, as the election of Ronald Reagan to the White House ushered in an era with a renewed fervor for those allegedly "traditional" family values long associated with the 1950s.

Taking the return of Ellen and David to their honeymoon locale as its starting point, a journey to a space replete with meaning, *Earthbound* shows the significance of space to identity and narratives of self. Underscored by the kind of domestic setting so distinctive of Matheson's fiction, the haunting here releases the protagonist from his usual frame of reference and forces him to re-evaluate who he is and how he relates to those closest to him. In doing this, the liminal experience prompted by the ghostly events draws attention to conflicting views about marriage and the individual. Stefan Dziemianowicz notes that, for Matheson, the "intimacy of marriage represents a sacred trust."[4] Marriage here is certainly cast as a desirable source of stability, yet the novel also repeatedly asserts that nothing in life can go untouched. This marriage was formed in the same post-war era that saw Tom Wallace turn to his own young family as the sole refuge in a hostile world. As this union has aged, society has changed and the experience of David and Ellen reflects these wider shifts. Haunting here thus foregrounds the tensions inbuilt within Americans' beliefs about this pervasive cultural tradition. This chapter explores the legacy of the ideal of 1950s marriage and how it was challenged by the countercultural years only to resurface, under the leadership of Reagan, in the penultimate decade of the twentieth century.

"We'll Always Love Each Other"— The 1950s Marriage

Historian Kristin Celello begins her study of marriage and divorce with the assertion that "Americans demonstrated great faith in marriage" throughout the twentieth century.[5] This attitude can undoubtedly be detected in *Earthbound*, where marriage represents a force for stability in a seemingly unstable world. Though a novel of the eighties, *Earthbound* deals with a union forged in the 1950s and is the product of an author who began writing at that very time. When David struggles to reconcile with Ellen, it becomes clear that what he is trying to preserve is a relationship grounded in memories of their youth and shaped by that post-war culture. Marianna's haunting reveals his investment in this way of life and causes him to reappraise his marriage in terms of how well it conforms to 1950s social mores and expectations. This drive for long-term commitment is at odds with the liberalized America of the 1960s and 1970s, although very much in keeping with the more conservative Reaganite era. Liminality tenders a fictional space in which various historical milieus—and the ideologies which underpin them—run up against one another, thus revealing the contradictions inherent within culture. Even in post-countercultural America, *Earthbound* upholds the idealized vision of gender relations and family life associated with the fifties context from which the events it depicts originally emerged.

The novel plays out over the four consecutive days David and Ellen spend at Logan Beach. It begins with their arrival at the holiday cottage in a scene which reveals much about what this trip means to them. As they reflect on their last stay, we learn that they are obliged to lodge here because their original honeymoon home was destroyed by a hurricane. Despite this disappointment, they have still chosen to return to the spot where their married life began. This visit soon stirs up memories of a long shared history: "dear God, *twenty-one years ago* [original emphasis],"[6] David calculates. Ellen comments on her sudden feeling of "'terminal nostalgia'" (*E*: 4) which instantly marks out this locale as one of special and lasting significance. Such happy reminiscences hint at a positive outlook for the couple in spite of their recent troubles. Almost painfully aware of his wife's reaction to this emotionally loaded situation, David takes heart from a mannerism rooted in his memories of the bond between them: "Something in her voice—a vestige of the eager, childlike quality he'd always loved—made him smile" (6). His reassurance to her that "It's going to work out fine, El," (10) serves to underscore the notion that the preservation of this marriage is fundamental to their well-being. Dwelling as it does on both the future and the past, this crucial moment foreshadows the liminal power of the haunted cottage to stage a confrontation between different times and the shifts in values they bring.

The importance of place to a sense of identity, and the privileged status of dwelling places,[7] has already been noted in the Introduction. It has also been observed that a key Gothic trope is the disturbance of such personal, familiar, and thus seemingly safe places.[8] As the previous chapter showed, Matheson is keenly aware of the importance of these literary dynamics. Yet here he chooses to remove his protagonist from where he feels most immediately at ease—the Coopers' "comfortable hillside home" (*E*: 7)—in order to undermine his sense of security from the novel's onset. David's decision to return to what he describes as their "honeymoon haven" (4), back to somewhere ostensibly even more cosseted than the family residence, reinforces the notion that place is linked to identity and suggests that he feels somehow able to tackle his troubled relationship history by literally revisiting old territory.

David and Ellen were married in 1960, during what family historian Stephanie Coontz describes as the "long decade of the 1950s, stretching from 1947 to the early 1960s in the United States."[9] The end of the Second

World War ushered in a time of peace and prosperity that wrought significant changes in the lives of many American citizens. Not least among these changes was the shift in attitudes towards marriage and family. Factors including post-war affluence—as evidenced by the rapid spread of affordable housing and the boom in domestic consumer goods—and the Cold War push to keep America united and self-disciplined in the face of the communist threat led to the decade's distinctive emphasis on nurturing "white middle-class nuclear families."[10] Couples married young, channeled their energies into raising families and intended to stay together. In common with many of their peers, at a time when "the age of marriage dropped sharply,"[11] David and Ellen wed at the respective ages of twenty-five and twenty-one and lost no time in starting a family of their own.[12]

As a result of these social changes, which propelled almost 60 percent of the population into the middle-class income bracket by the heart of the decade,[13] the 1950s supplied "the first chance many people had to try to live out the romanticized dream of a private family, happily ensconced in its own nest."[14] This was an era when Americans redefined the institution of marriage as one characterized by a high degree of spousal intimacy and a commitment to prescribed gender relations: "Never had married couples been so independent of extended family ties and community groups. And never before had so many people agreed that only one kind of family was 'normal.' The cultural consensus that everyone should marry and form a male breadwinner family was like a steamroller that crushed every alternative view."[15] A firm sense that this dynamic has structured David's relationship with Ellen emerges as the novel progresses. Several allusions are made to his career as a screenwriter while Ellen—like Anne in *A Stir of Echoes*—is defined purely by her role as a wife and mother. Although they never appear as characters in their own right, frequent mention is made of their children, Mark and Linda, particularly as their daughter is shortly due to give birth to their first grandchild. From its inception, it seems that the Cooper family has conformed to the idealized 1950s mold.

Once established these marriages were meant to be stable and permanent, meeting the various needs of both spouses within the context of a committed relationship. Indeed, Coontz observes that the view that "marriage should provide both partners with sexual gratification, personal intimacy, and self-fulfillment was taken to new heights in that decade."[16] Divorce, though still considered unavoidable in some few instances, was not taken lightly and divorce rates began to fall.[17] The emphasis was very much on keeping couples together by encouraging them to accept some degree of marital friction as inevitable and to take responsibility by working to resolve any problems.[18] Expert help for such couples was not hard to come by and Celello notes that marriage counseling became increasingly prominent in the 1950s.[19] As she describes, "marriage experts found a broad audience for their advice about how to save marriages. They judged any marriage that did not end in divorce to be a success, and they urged couples to strive for this goal."[20]

Though David and Ellen evidently still share a deep emotional attachment, by the time of the novel's commencement it seems chiefly to be their desire for commitment—in conjunction with their entrenched familial responsibilities—which is keeping them together. Given the socio-historical context in which they married, the sense of duty that underpins their relationship hardly seems surprising. Coontz discerns the social pressures at work in the fifties that resulted in a widespread and tenacious compliance with the nuclear family ideal: "Although men and women aspired to personal fulfillment in marriage, most were willing to stay together even if they did not get it."[21] Even in the unhappy aftermath of an affair, this estranged couple strives to preserve their longstanding union—an arrangement about to be replicated as their young daughter starts a family of her own. With the arrival of the ghostly Marianna, whose presence unites and juxtaposes two divergent moments in twentieth-century American culture, the liminal experience of haunting calls attention to the Coopers' anxiety about these expectations.

This "second honeymoon" (*E*: 5) represents an opportunity to salvage their relationship. Marriage historian Elizabeth Abbott explains that, in the early part of the nineteenth century, a minority of newlyweds had a honeymoon—a trend which introduced "implications of privacy and withdrawing from the world."[22] Similarly, Coontz observes that "after 1850 … the honeymoon increasingly became a time for couples to get away from others"[23] and quotes an 1870s wedding guide which recommended a "honeymoon of repose, exempted from the claims of society."[24] Barry Curtis avers that "susceptibility to haunting is usually indicated or promoted by a withdrawal from society."[25] With its insistence on the inherent liminality of the haunted house motif, this study repeatedly demonstrates that haunting is indeed associated with precisely such a withdrawal. *Earthbound* is unusual insofar as its protagonists deliberately choose to place themselves in a situation which society deems as a desirable period of seclusion.[26] Echoing the language of liminality, these descriptions of the honeymoon apply to David and Ellen's efforts to devote time to making their marriage work, while also foreshadowing the haunting that sets them unequivocally apart from everyday experience.

Despite some early obstacles, like Ellen's rebuttal of David's sexual advances on the first night, they work hard to regain the atmosphere of intimacy that has eluded them for so long. The next day they quickly resort to recreating past memories, and learn "with relief, that the seafood restaurant they remembered from their honeymoon was still in operation. There, they'd ordered the same meal they had enjoyed then.... There had even been the same white wine with which they'd toasted one another again" (*E*: 60). Once more, a cherished place—in this instance one miraculously untouched by the passing years—has the power to provide a sense of security as, in this "location associated with their happier past," (60) the prospect of renewing their bond seems stronger. Such efforts to recapture their youth form a kind of retreat into the fantasy—what Paul Grainge refers to as the "Rockwellian nostalgia"[27]—of the idealized 1950s. This impulse has real resonance within eighties America, as Reagan's presidency relied on "a large degree of mythic invocation,"[28] looking back—before the perceived disorder of the 1960s and 1970s—to the nation's past to find inspiration for its future.

By the time they come to share this evening, with its overtly nostalgic emphasis on rekindling their romance, David has twice encountered Marianna. As with Helen Driscoll of *A Stir of Echoes*, so congruent is she with her surroundings that he will not accept that she is a ghost until very late in the novel. Unable to sleep on the first night, Ellen takes a walk while her equally wakeful husband marvels at the view of the beach from the artist's studio between the cottage's first and second floors. He is startled by an entrancing young woman, "the most beautiful woman he'd ever seen in his life, her shoulder-length hair jet black, her features perfect, carved as if from ivory" (*E*: 20), who says she is seeking the artist who stayed in the cottage the previous summer. Her appearance and her presence in the cottage both seem completely natural and plausible. The verisimilitude of this ghost implies the extent to which troubles can lie within the context of everyday domesticity. This meeting signals the onset of David's virtually unrelenting immersion into the liminality of haunting that isolates him from Ellen and causes him to question the nature of their relationship and even of himself. As blatantly attracted to David as he is to her, Marianna represents an illicit fantasy. She is a temporary distraction from his role as a responsible "family man" and yet, as such, she ultimately acts as a reminder of the hold that function has exerted over him since he first came to assume it.

One especially troubling aspect of the marriage is the loss of sexual intimacy. For David, at least, this issue seems to be a priority on this vacation and he reflects to himself that romantic activities like the dinner and dancing he and Ellen enjoy on that second evening are "natural forerunners to lovemaking" (72). As a traditional date, stemming from the early days of their relationship, this episode further evokes the 1950s marital model. Indeed, the Coopers' attitudes towards sex and sexuality seem generally redolent of 1950s social mores. This is manifest in how Matheson presents their clearly demarcated gender roles. David fixates on wooing his wife all evening, castigating himself beforehand with an anxious "don't let me fail her now" (59) and complimenting both her appearance and her effect on him lavishly throughout: "You look marvelous ... like a billion dollars. In gold" (59). Desperate to arouse desire in her, his internal lament that he has to "win back her interest" (72) on their return to the cottage implies that he is the instigator in their sexual relationship.

Ellen, meanwhile, prepares by subjecting herself to a painstaking and elaborate ritual through which she is transformed into the epitome of 1950s femininity. Celello notes, "Historians have clearly identified sexual availability and responsiveness as an important duty of the postwar wife"[29] in phraseology that signals an uncontested expectation of the wife's essential passivity at that time. That Ellen should work—and has worked frequently in the past—at the subtle seduction of her husband is implicit here. Marianna, in contrast, is enticingly proactive in this regard and David succumbs to her sexual overtures during the first full day at Logan Beach. Exhausted by this, he sleeps the day away and awakens to observe:

Ellen was seated at the lamp-lit dressing table, legs crossed, fastening her stocking to a garter strap. He stared at her in puzzlement. Beneath the open robe she wore her black merry widow. He watched in stolid curiosity as she leaned forward to pull on black, high-heeled shoes.... He hadn't seen her in the merry widow for years; she didn't like to wear it because it was so binding ... her hair had been set ... her nails were painted, too; she hadn't done that in years. She looked strikingly trim and luxuriant sitting there, her waist drawn in, hips full and rounded, breasts molded tautly, long legs sheathed in dark silk, face made up with care.... "You look marvelous." He ran his gaze across her figure [E: 57–59].

It is evident that she has labored for some time to perfect this look—a look with which David was once familiar.

This is a striking scene in which Ellen compels David's gaze through the calculated employment of the trappings of 1950s constructions of femininity, e.g. highly sexualized and restrictive underwear in conjunction with the overt use of cosmetics and other contrivances such as hairstyling. Elaine Tyler May observes the part played by fifties fashion in eroticizing the female form and establishing gender relations: "Female sexuality was ... contained in stays and girdles that pinched waists and padded brassieres that made women appear to have large breasts."[30] There is a clear indication here that Ellen is long-rehearsed in the 1950s wifely art of performing desire. The element of performance is laid bare by her riposte to David's insinuation that they should dispense with dinner altogether: "You have to play the game," (E: 59) she says. On this basis, the fact that her costume is intrinsic to this facet of their marriage is also of interest. Further to this, there is a strong implication that her jettisoning of this routine in later years has not only been missed by her husband, but may also have contributed to his infidelities.

Compared to Ellen's artfully constructed appearance, Marianna's natural allure is palpable: "She wore a pale white skirt and sweater set.... Her feet were bare and flaked with sand" (20). Conditioned by the confines of her 1950s marriage, Ellen has learned to anticipate and reciprocate her husband's sexual desires and seems to regulate her own sexuality accordingly. In contrast, the spectral Marianna, who exudes an innate and uninhibited eroticism, is in no way controlled by such a socially-sanctioned arrangement. Anthony Giddens observes that "the image of the sexually voracious woman, of course, has long existed alongside that of female passivity."[31] The disparity between the contained sexuality of the wife and the uncontained sexuality of this beguiling young woman reflects an enduring tendency to dichotomize women along precisely these lines. That David finds her so immediately and overwhelmingly tantalizing, even in the context of a situation he has contrived for the purpose of reconciling with his wife, designates Marianna's predatory brand of sexuality as a threat to the sanctity of the 1950s marriage. This issue of so-called problematic female sexuality, singled out as it was for scrutiny in the 1980s, will be explored in greater depth in the second part of this chapter.

One result of the haunting is thus to reveal the contrast between the prescribed nature of David's marriage and the enticing spontaneity symbolized by Marianna. However, another very marked effect of this experience is how it serves to remind him of the centrality of the marriage to his life. David's view of this relationship is partly shaped by his clinging to fifties values. Although he is instantly infatuated with Marianna, embarking on a sexual relationship with her all too readily, his time with her is punctuated by frequent references to his dutiful nature. When they first meet, and she blandly inquires if his wife is angry with him, he is immediately defensive about this invasion of the privacy of their domestic sphere: "He felt inclinded [sic] to snap: What business is it of yours?" (E: 25). Two days later, once she starts to take greater hold of him, David forces himself to reject her despite the anguish he feels. His language emphasizes his commitment, even once Ellen has told him she believes they have no future as a couple: "I'm leaving, Marianna. I'm going home with my wife…. My responsibility is to my marriage" (108), he asserts. This insistence on the value of responsibility is reminiscent of the 1950s ideal—a commitment to marriage in the face of adversity— and Marianna effectively reminds David of this.

Yet, though David rediscovers the value of his marriage through the liminality of haunting, a strong impression remains that this is due to his adhering to the fixed patterns of the past rather than reflecting on how things have changed. The haunting experience here is characterized by many twists and turns. Due partly to Marianna's influence, partly to their own troubled history, David and Ellen swing from the point of reconciliation to the point of separation and back again. Having dismissed this seductive ghost, David makes a breakthrough with Ellen and they decide to return home to make a fresh start. Though this seems a positive step, David's appraisal of the situation is naïve and simplistic: "Little Ellen Audrey, he thought. He patted her clothes as he put them in the suitcase. She was good for him. It was appalling to consider that he might have left her for Marianna. What a nightmare that would have been" (116). Again, this view of their relationship harks back to the fifties version of demarcated gender roles by infantilizing Ellen and casting her in terms of how she helps him. Coupled with his subsequent and nostalgic assessment of Ellen as "his child bride" (119), this is further evidence of how the haunting reveals his propensity for viewing their union along fifties lines.

David makes no real attempt to reflect on the profound issues to which Marianna's presence has drawn his attention and of which Ellen has also become mindful. Implicit in the above discussion of his orchestration of their conjugal relations is a critique of David's devotion to traditional gender roles. Although it is perhaps unremarkable that a literal recreation of their honeymoon should lead to a revival of past patterns of behavior—and even that these should be enjoyed—there are signs that these patterns have come to seem outmoded. For instance, Matheson makes Ellen's disinclination for adopting clichéd feminine attire all too apparent. To some extent then, despite *Earthbound*'s promotion of fifties values, the novel also implies that these standards have become untenable with the passage of time. A contradiction emerges here insofar as Matheson's novel sees David both castigated and commended for maintaining the old-fashioned views which have shaped his marriage.

The first part of this chapter has demonstrated the extent to which post-war ideologies about marriage, sex and gender roles have become ingrained in twentieth-century American culture. Through haunting, it can be seen that David's own marriage has developed—and continues to be conducted—largely on the basis of such values and Marianna represents a temptation that must be resisted if the goal of a successful marriage is to be sustained. Yet liminality here not only prompts a confrontation with this aspect of David's personal past, but also releases wider historical forces that he seems loath to acknowledge, let alone accommodate. His retrogressive urges, accentuated by his endeavors to recreate his honeymoon, seem to stand in opposition to the changes in gender relations and attitudes towards sexuality set in motion by the countercultural shifts of the 1960s and 1970s. In addition to her role as a figure of sexual fantasy, then, the assertive Marianna also posits a direct challenge to David's conservative outlook, and her influence necessitates a re-examination of how he handles his relationship with Ellen. However, while haunting drives these issues to the fore, the novel ultimately seeks to contain them. The next section will therefore examine how *Earthbound* portrays these changing views on sex and marriage as potential threats to earlier modes of behavior.

"A Little Terminal Nostalgia"—
The Backward Turn of the 1980s

Earthbound first appeared in the early 1980s and David's backward-looking stance resonates with wider societal impulses discernible in America at this time. Mary Caputi contends that the neoconservative movement that flourished under the presidency of Ronald Reagan all through that decade saw "1950s America [as] a spiritual place housed in our past ... an idealized locale created by a longing in the present."[32] Likewise, Graham Thompson classes the Reagan administration as one dominated by a morally conservative outlook that valorized ostensibly traditional notions such as "family values."[33] *Earthbound* does address—though retrospectively—the post-war socio-historical context discussed in the analysis of *A Stir of Echoes*. Yet, it is also evident that it speaks to the cultural moment at which it emerged—the onset of the 1980s. Further, although this era was more conservative than the time that preceded it—because its pronounced conservatism was, in many ways, a response to the liberalism of those recent years—the eighties was complicated by a sense that the 1960s and 1970s had unleashed social forces that could no longer be ignored, much less controlled. The thwarted nostalgic impulses of the Coopers—as evidenced by their recourse to a 1950s-style cultural fantasy—can be seen to echo those of the wider nation.

Nostalgic thinking is typically seen to be distinguished by a sense of loss. Gil Troy suggests that "the great liberation movements of the 1960s had left many Americans feeling unmoored," especially in light of trends like the decline in family stability and the erosion of once firmly entrenched social roles.[34] The feeling that the nation had somehow lost its former vitality became endemic by the late 1970s. In Caputi's words, neoconservatism yearned for what it perceived as that "simpler, clearer American identity, which two decades of hang-loose liberals had, in its opinion, nearly destroyed."[35] America needed rebuilding because of this perceived breakdown of society, and Reagan was deemed by many to be the right man for this momentous task. As Troy notes, his election resulted in what was broadly seen as "morning in America—the great party known as the 1980s, when the stock market soared, patriotism surged ... and America thrived."[36] The beginning of *Earthbound*, with its melancholy dwelling on the developments wrought by the passage of the last two decades, echoes the mood of a nation unhappily preoccupied with its past. The destruction of the cottage in which David and Ellen shared their honeymoon appears symbolic of a wider sense of national loss with the 1950s at its heart.

A distinct break with established attitudes towards sexuality and marriage, engendered by the counterculture and thus welcomed by some more than others, was very much in evidence by the eighties. One predictable outcome of these new sensibilities, which proved a source of great concern for many, was the steep rise in divorce rates. These "more than doubled between 1966 and 1979"[37] and peaked around the end of the 1970s.[38] A 2007 study, *Alone Together: How Marriage in America Is Changing*, paints a similar picture: "The divorce rate increased dramatically in the United States in the 1960s and 1970s, then crested at a historically high level in the early 1980s."[39] Yet, in keeping with newly modified opinions on marriage, many gradually began to espouse the view that divorce could actually be a positive step. By 1968, national polls revealed—for the first time—that an increasing number of Americans felt that obtaining a divorce should be a less taxing process.[40] As divorce became more prevalent, even among middle-aged empty-nesters who married during the fifties, marriage counselors strove to help couples through their separations; the notion of divorce as an opportunity for personal development began to take hold.[41]

David's experience of haunting certainly throws the cultural shifts reflected in his own marriage into sharp relief. During their stay he and Ellen both reflect on the state of their relationship and on the possibility of divorce. Almost as soon as they set foot in the cottage, they are confronted by a near-ghostly likeness of their own coupledom. On opening a door on the upstairs landing, David stands "twitching at the shadowy image of himself and Ellen in the bathroom cabinet mirror" (*E*: 9), in a tableau that neatly conveys the atrophy of their marriage. This impression is only intensified by the significance of the location and reinforces Matheson's wider agenda of engaging with the past to shed light on the present, utilizing meaningful space in order to do so. Since this is a supernatural tale, he also employs the Gothic device of haunting to accomplish this task. Marianna's function is to highlight social changes and dramatize the extent to which David and Ellen are affected by them. However, as this chapter argues, the liminal experience incited by her haunting powers throws up conflicting attitudes towards those evolving gender roles and relations which the novel struggles to keep in check.

As indicated above, Americans' attitudes towards marriage underwent something of a revolution during the latter half of the twentieth century. Integral to this was a shift in perceptions about how individuals related to wider society. Ronald Inglehart and Pippa Norris perceive that the post-war prosperity that came to highly developed industrial nations—including the United States—enabled citizens to prioritize "quality-of-life issues, individual autonomy and self-expression,"[42] when basics like housing became taken for granted. Coontz also argues that, between the 1950s and the 1970s, Americans began to value self-fulfillment and emotional gratification over compliance with social roles—however ingrained these roles might once have been.[43] Professionals lent the weight of their expertise to these tendencies. The Human Potential Movement of the late sixties, stemming from 1950s humanistic psychology, advocated various forms of therapy through which individuals could nurture their latent potential in ongoing quests for self-fulfillment.[44] Giddens recognizes the legacy of this impulse when he remarks, "The self today is for everyone a reflexive project ... a project carried on amid a profusion of reflexive resources: therapy and self-help manuals of all kinds."[45] Such practices spelled "the erosion of the traditional two-parent nuclear family" and the rise of "liberalizing patterns of sexual behavior, marriage, and divorce."[46] The very conditions that permitted the fifties breadwinner home to flourish may well also have precipitated its downfall.

The new therapeutic approach stressed the importance of individuality to social relationships, rather than foregrounding those notions of obligation that underpinned the 1950s marriage ideal.[47] Marriage study *Alone Together* reveals that: "Individualism ... became especially pronounced during the 1960s and 1970s. Since then people have become inordinately preoccupied with the unrestricted pursuit of personal happiness. Because people no longer wish to be hampered with obligations to others, commitment to traditional institutions that require these obligations, such as marriage, has eroded ... marital commitment lasts only as long as people are happy and feel that their needs are being met."[48] When the belief that marriage should give both spouses happiness—which seemed to find its expression in the fifties vision of gender relations and family life—habitually proved to be erroneous, relationship dissatisfaction became widespread.[49] The authors of *Habits of the Heart: Individualism and Commitment in American Life* (first published in the mid 1980s) discovered from surveys that, while love and devotion were still highly sought after by 1980, fewer Americans believed the marriages that embodied those ideals could last a lifetime.[50] As they suggest: "If love and marriage are seen primarily in terms of psychological gratification, they may fail to fulfill their older social function of providing people with stable, committed relationships that tie them into the larger society."[51] With more Americans inclined to value happiness over responsibility, it is perhaps unsurprising that lifelong marriages diminished in favor of other kinds of relationships. Indeed, Giddens proposes that the term "relationship"—with its connotations of intimacy, sexuality and a measure of loyalty—was becoming a substitute for the term "marriage" by the 1990s.[52]

In this respect, it is striking that the original publisher of *Earthbound* was Playboy Paperbacks. With its pledge to "liberate its readers from repressive codes of sexual behavior,"[53] of which marriage might be taken as emblematic, *Playboy* can be seen as a harbinger of the sexually permissive spirit which held sway in the 1960s and 1970s. Regardless of David's resolve to defend his troubled marriage, Marianna acts as a catalyst for his personal quest for emotional and sexual gratification. After their first meeting he searches the beach for her home, eventually struggling to recall the original purpose of the trip: "You're here to make up with Ellen. Stop forgetting that, he thought" (*E*: 36). Looking back later on their tempestuous fling, he sees Marianna as "nothing less than the ultimate objective of this search: an exotic wanton who expected no emotional responsibility, who wanted and encouraged only self-indulgence" (118). As the novel moves to its climax and he fights to save Ellen and escape the haunted cottage, he is forced to confront this aspect of himself—the urges that threaten his marriage. Local resident Grace Brentwood, who has previously warned David of Marianna's malign influence, tells him, "You've been acting as a medium. The body you've been—making love to, as you so quaintly put it, has consisted, in every detail, of the cells in your own body" (142). Hearing this, he fixates on "the sickening notion that he may have been in essence, making love to his own flesh. If it were true, it meant that he had consummated, in literal terms, what, emotionally, he'd been doing all these years—holding personal gratification above all else" (143). In Dziemianowicz's words, Marianna is "an externalization of David's lust."[54] The liminality she unleashes lays bare the conflict within him—that between honoring his commitment to his wife and obtaining individual satisfaction—which echoes the discord inherent in late twentieth-century American culture.

In the same way that David's quandary speaks to its socio-historical context, Matheson's rendering of gender roles also indexes the tensions inherent in 1980s sensibilities. Not only does the novel depict the effects of social change on gender roles, it also—at least to some extent—seems to accept them over previous modes of behavior. Since the time of their marriage, born as it was of post-war society, the women's movements of the sixties and seventies have come to leave their mark. Though only forty-two, Ellen will soon be a grandmother and her time at Logan Beach reveals that her fifties role as a dutiful wife and mother—now effectively concluded—has left her suddenly bereft of any personal agency or a firm sense of her own identity: "I feel … extraneous, somehow. As if I've served my purpose and it doesn't really matter what I want anymore" (*E*: 111). It is made clear that she is unhappy with her lot at this stage in the marriage and her dissatisfaction is symbolic of the plight in which many American women found themselves in the middle years of the twentieth century and which second wave feminism sought to redress.

The novel's handling of female sexuality smacks heavily of the contested legacy of social change. Ellen's despondent self-appraisal reveals the inadequacy of the social role thrust upon her, as a woman, in the post-war era. The liminality of haunting also problematizes the treatment of her sexuality. As evidenced by the scene discussed earlier, when David is engrossed by the transformation she submits herself to for their evening together, she works hard to capture his interest in a way that he finds acceptable. Even as she chooses to re-enact this ritual, Ellen indicates her physical discomfort with it in a phrase which strongly connotes that containment of sexuality associated with female fashions of the 1950s: "Oh; this merry widow ... they ought to call it the Iron Maiden" (67). Two days later she confronts her husband with her pent-up aggression about his desire for her to dress this way, accusing him of: "one night not caring how I looked and the next night wanting me to look like a whore ... Black Merry Widows? Black demi-bras? Black garter belts? Black silk stockings? Black high heeled shoes? What do you *think* they made me look like [original emphasis]?" (136–137) she demands of him. Though David is shocked at this outburst, it is undeniable that he has long been a party to the regulation of his wife's sexual behavior. So her utilization of these uncomfortable accouterments for the purpose of attracting her husband eventually becomes subject to heavy criticism and, crucially, from Ellen herself. With their connotations of female sexual objectification, these items make her look and by implication feel "like a whore" (136), and thus she comes to rail against them.

Yet the haunting reveals that, though he is repeatedly drawn to this type of accommodating female sexual behavior, David's attraction to the sexually independent Marianna is very nearly as strong. It is blatantly clear that he finds her dominance and the rapacity of her sexual appetites both unprecedented and thrilling. She is "animated and demanding" (50) in "bestowing on him the kind of headlong wantonness that he'd imagined only in his most covert of fancies" (51). The dynamic of this experience differs markedly from that of his marriage, shaped largely as it has been by his proclivities. Marianna's assertiveness with regard to acknowledging and fulfilling her own desires is highly evocative of the female sexual liberation movement—due in part to changing attitudes, as well as to increased access to contraception and to legal abortions[55]— that took place in America in the decades following David's youthful marriage.

All these aspects of the novel—Ellen's frustration with the confines of fifties gender roles, David's routine sexual objectification of his wife and Marianna's more liberated approach to sex—suggest that Matheson is entirely cognizant of these social shifts and, at least to some degree, supportive of them. However, despite the fact that these insights denounce those 1950s patriarchal practices targeted by feminism, there are contradictory impulses at work in *Earthbound* that undermine this sense of critique. One pointed example of this occurs only shortly after Ellen admits she feels she has little to show for her years of marriage. She quickly glosses over her personal sense of loss, and all the issues it raises, by expressing a willing desire to return to this life simply on the basis that her compliance fulfills David's needs: "I won't leave you. Not if you need me, never if you need me" (*E*: 112). Interestingly, then, the haunting in this novel insists on privileging the fifties marriage ideal while simultaneously stressing its shortcomings. When viewed against the backdrop of the Reaganite context, though, it seems congruent that these traditional standards of social behavior are shown as obsolete while still being desirable.

Matheson's depiction of Marianna is as conflicted as that of Ellen in what it reveals about attitudes towards women and sex. Immediately drawn to her physical charms, David soon becomes infatuated with the enticing young ghost, and his obsession betrays an anxiety about the threat posed to men by untrammelled female sexuality: "It was almost unbelievable that any woman could be so lovely. He stared at her, imprisoned by her beauty" (26). Building on this sense of menace, as alluring as her forcefulness may be, it quickly comes to be demonized and Marianna is thus cast as a monstrous figure. Barbara Creed points to ongoing academic debates centering on such ambivalent male attitudes towards female sexuality.[56] In this vein, the following passage reveals that, however tantalizing, the overt sexuality of this female specter also leads David to see her as dangerous and ultimately repellent: "Marianna licked his lips tempestuously. She raked her teeth across his cheek, her breath like spilling fire on his skin ... she pulled him savagely against herself.... Her hands were clutching at his head like talons of steel ... her exquisite face gone bestial with demented sensuality" (*E*: 51). His ambivalence towards her is thus reflective of entrenched views on women, whereby "femininity is typically framed in terms of being sexually desirable rather than sexually desiring whereas masculinity connotes sexual aggression and prowess."[57]

Just as Ellen's complaints about her marriage are soon retracted, the potentially more progressive version of womanhood embodied by Marianna is readily undermined. Bernice M. Murphy detects a "strain of latent misogyny" in both *I Am Legend* and *A Stir of Echoes*,[58] and this stance is also in evidence here, in a tale which rests on a deep-seated anxiety about how women relate to sex. My reading, however, goes beyond Murphy's in linking this misogynistic streak directly to Matheson's use of haunting, which works to stage a liminal clash of competing historical and ideological forces. Very much at odds with 1950s ideologies of gender traits and sexual roles, Marianna seems rather to be a product of the women's movement which followed that time. Placed within the early 1980s context of *Earthbound*, her character seems redolent of the unease about feminism contemporaneous with that era discussed by the likes of Susan Faludi.[59] Ultimately, she is unfavorably compared with the non-threatening and controlled sexuality represented by Ellen, and the contrast between the two women serves to draw David back to his marriage. In spite of its recognition of problematic social mores, then, *Earthbound* betrays an affinity with the antipathy to feminism so rife in Reagan's conservative 1980s.

The Coopers seek to mend their union by returning to the place—and, by implication, the time—that it began. This regressive impulse, motivated as it is by nostalgia for the loss of their past life together, seems a naïve attempt to stifle the effects of social strictures which prompted Ellen's discontent and David's infidelity. In keeping with this nostalgic impetus, the ghost of Marianna proves to be a focal point for David's anxiety about aging. Time and again, he ponders that she makes him feel younger, "like a bedazzled school boy" (*E*: 21) and "a nervous boy" (49), and he is mindful of "his adolescent eagerness" (35) for her company. This opportunity to revisit his youth, however illusory, proves as compelling for him as the prospect of reliving his honeymoon with Ellen. Yet, despite the couple's attempt to evade the complexity of their present through a literal return to the innocence of their honeymoon days, liminality works to unleash precisely those historical forces from which they seek to escape. Building on this, going back can be seen as a typically Gothic impulse to confront the past and the liminality of haunting certainly brings the problems contained within history to light, even if the novel has its protagonists gloss over the issues rather than resolve them. Once more, the liminality of haunting engenders a literary encounter with intractable cultural complexities which defy any easy resolution.

I therefore argue that, with its narrative and thematic emphasis on the reclamation of an idealized past, *Earthbound* engages with the preoccupations of the late twentieth-century context in which it emerged. It is a tale of haunting which shares Reagan's early 1980s vision of turning back the clock to the perceived state of strength and tranquility that was America in the 1950s. Thompson describes the eighties backlash against liberal politics which led to a reassertion of conservative values and manifested in a proliferation of "pro-life, religious and family orientated organizations like ... Concerned Women for America (1979) and the Family Research Council (1983)."[60] This movement sought a return to a time prior to what it saw as the upheaval and destruction brought about by the countercultural years, particularly with regard to issues such as the changing place of women in society.[61] Yet, as has been shown, contradictions abound here, and the novel promotes this nostalgic impulse while also suggesting that recapturing this bygone era might not be possible or even wholly desirable. Matheson plainly recognizes all these concerns—the legacy of the fifties, the influence of the women's movement and the sexual liberation of the sixties and seventies. However, at the last, the novel keeps these progressive forces in check by placing them firmly within that conservative Reaganite framework.

This struggle to somehow avoid the forces instigated by the seismic shifts of the counterculture is especially pronounced in the manner through which Matheson chooses to conclude his novel. It is eventually revealed that Marianna is the younger sister of Grace Brentwood. Now in her late sixties, Grace explains that, in life, her sister "thought of nothing but carnality [and] had an endless succession of lovers" (*E*: 140). One of these men was Grace's own fiancé, who drowned while on a sailing trip with Marianna. To punish Marianna, whose fleshly appetites cause her to become "an earthbound spirit" (98) after she takes her own life in the cottage, Grace repeatedly lets the property but then chases away male tenants in order to frustrate her sibling. The epilogue sees David blissfully reunited with Ellen, while also divulging that—in returning to the cottage to save the Coopers—Grace has become possessed by her sister, who relishes the chance to have a physical body of her own again. This ending works to displace all the socio-historical pressures released by the liminality of haunting onto those female characters who have failed to comply with fifties expectations about gender roles: Grace and Marianna Brentwood. One woman is a nymphomaniac who destroyed her own sister's chance at marriage, and the other is now a spiteful old maid incapable of forgiving the theft of her mate. As such, they conform to pervasive stereotypes about unmarried women and underscore the perceived desirability of 1950s ideologies of sex and gender. Despite David's own transgressions, he is ultimately free—to embrace his fifties marriage in a fashion that sits comfortably with Reaganite values, no less—while the problematic Brentwood sisters are left, in isolation, to contend with the issues raised by the haunting.

Conclusion

The chapter on *A Stir of Echoes* identified Matheson's preoccupation with the psychological and emotional terror born of estrangement, typically played out in the quotidian spaces of late twentieth-century America and delineated through tales of male protagonists who find their unexceptional lives somehow thrown into disarray. Following David Cooper's endeavors to save his marriage, set in an unremarkable vacation cottage, *Earthbound* offers one such portrayal of the conflicts buried in the most ordinary of lives. Indeed, back in the normality of the "neat, clean, modern house" (*E:* 34) which is the family home in California, David comes to question whether the events at Logan Beach took place at all: "A ghost in his life?" (179) he skeptically asks himself. Yet the act that drives the novel, that of returning to meaningful space, inevitably elicits an encounter with the past, and the device of haunting brings this past vividly into the novel's present. Once more, the haunted house motif sees Gothic conventions at work—even in apparently incongruous physical surroundings—to draw attention to the ideological conflicts prompted by the march of time.

This analysis has worked to show how the legacy of such prescribed social roles plays out in Matheson's later haunted fiction. It also recognizes the inconsistencies—emblematic of the complexities inherent within culture—woven into the fabric of both fictions. Through *Earth-bound's* depiction of a pre-countercultural couple whose lives are challenged by means of their liminal experience, Matheson explores the social changes which occurred in the intervening years between their marriage and their second honeymoon. Returning at the outset of the eighties to the place where they celebrated their youthful union—formed in the optimism of the post-war years—David and Ellen are obliged to contend with the various ways in which time has exposed the fissures in the fifties marriage ideal, and concomitant gender roles, to which they have clung for so long.

Tackling this broad sweep of history as it does, the overall thrust of the novel replicates the unavoidable instabilities and incoherencies of such profound ideological shifts. As a result, 1950s views on sex, marriage and gender are both upheld and critiqued here through haunting. The ghostly Marianna serves as an emanation of those shifts in attitudes towards sex and sexuality in general, and female behavior in particular, while the atmosphere of the haunted cottage throws up diverse issues surrounding David and Ellen's perceptions of their relationship and their own roles within it. At a time when marriage was increasingly seen as optional, yet also viewed by many Americans as both "more important than ever" and "more fragile and difficult to maintain than ever,"[62] the predicament in which this fictional couple finds itself is an all too familiar one.

As with Tom Wallace, the liminality of haunting encountered by David Cooper highlights the shortcomings of established social practice, yet in the end provides no way to transcend them. Many Americans, while mindful of the value of lessons learned about challenging the status quo in the sixties and seventies, still felt the pull of conservatism in the prosperous and consumerist eighties. Troy argues that, throughout the decade, "the baby boomers continued the great reconciliation between the sixties and the eighties, seeking to encase new lifestyles within traditional frameworks."[63] This struggle is in evidence throughout *Earthbound*, as Matheson strives to recognize—even to openly censure—the limitations of fifties social mores while simultaneously perpetuating stereotypes and ultimately endorsing those same lifestyle patterns. In David's own assessment, the haunting here proves to be "a destructive yet enlightening episode" (*E*: 114). In terms of liminality, while the haunting certainly uncovers issues, the revelations it brings seem destructive enough to render them insurmountable. Simultaneously staging a retreat to the idealized fifties and insinuating that this is a cultural fantasy which is no longer tenable in the post countercultural years, the liminality of *Earthbound* offers an insight into—though no solution to—the conflicting forces at work in eighties America.

CHAPTER FOUR

"Protecting the hotel was his job. He was the caretaker"

Masculinity, Class and Capitalism
in The Shining

Stephen King, born in Portland, Maine, in 1947, has been a steady and extraordinarily prolific writer of novels and short-story anthologies, as well screenplays for film and television, since the 1960s.[1] Nearly half a century on, he is as remarkable for his longevity as for his huge popularity as a horror writer.[2] Inspired by H. P. Lovecraft, who in King's own words "opened the way for me,"[3] King was also creatively stimulated by Richard Matheson's practice of situating horror within the context of everyday life. This influence can be detected in much of King's fiction, which tends to be grounded—however fantastic a particular narrative may become—in "familiar settings and realistic characters"[4] drawn from his own experience in small-town America. King offers a fresh direction for haunted fiction in adapting the haunted house motif to encompass new spaces, beyond the traditional haunted house of Lovecraft or even the more mundane dwellings utilized by Matheson. Yet they are still the kinds of spaces that reflect precisely this drive to explore situations that constitute daily life for millions of Americans.

The first in a long line of best-sellers from King, and adapted by Stanley Kubrick into the 1980 film of the same name, *The Shining* (1977) has loomed large on the American popular cultural landscape for more than three decades. Both novel and film have attracted a good degree of critical attention and previous criticism has demonstrated a diverse array of focuses. Several scholars have provided psychoanalytical readings of both King's novel and Kubrick's adaptation.[5] Several have considered the impact of authors such as Edgar Allan Poe, Emile Zola and

Frank Norris on the novel.[6] Others have explored its treatment of the American Dream.[7] These readings largely focus on realistic elements, for example the representation of women or of child psychology, thereby often ignoring the more supernatural elements of the story. My chapter focuses on haunting and the way it connects with the novel's Gothic depictions of masculinity, class and capitalism.[8] *The Shining* forms a type of reflection on the state of the American nation. Published in 1977 in the wake of the bicentennial celebrations, its location is Colorado, founded in 1876 as the Centennial State—apposite times and places for an examination of American history and culture.

The main protagonist is a young writer, Jack Torrance, desperate to reconcile his responsibility to support his wife and young son with his personal ambition to achieve literary success. Out of this necessity, he relocates his family to the luxurious Overlook Hotel in Colorado's Rocky Mountains so he can take on the post of winter caretaker. The Overlook is eventually revealed to be haunted, the malevolent supernatural forces which normally lie there dormant being triggered by the psychic abilities of Jack's son Danny—the "shining" of the title. As a place of leisure for America's wealthy and successful, the hotel has a lineage entrenched in a long history of American capitalism. Yet the novel reveals that such success goes hand-in-glove with corruption; thus this history has far-reaching ethical and social implications. King therefore unites the personal and the political as Jack's own desires and needs are run up against, and affected by, the hotel's history. Once more Fiedler's remarks about the political leanings of American Gothic can be brought to bear, though King works here to contest established notions pertaining to class and gender and thus offers a more progressive variant on the genre.

On one level the novel is about the downfall of a family, as themes of economic and domestic hardship are in evidence from the outset. King himself stated, in a 1980 interview, "I discovered about halfway through that I wasn't writing a haunted-house story, that I was writing about a family coming apart."[9] Yet other, sometimes contradictory, concerns emerge as King's narrative progresses, and the liminality inherent in haunting is integral to these. Haunted both by the hotel's troubled history and by his own difficult past, Jack finds his creative capacities diverted by, and ultimately his very agency swallowed up in, the haunted space he occupies. Against the backdrop of 1970s America, *The Shining* plays out a drama of conflict between the wealthy world, represented by the hotel, and its new menial employee who comes from lower down the social hierarchy. A man long motivated by literary aspirations, once at the Overlook, Jack finds his desire for advancement twisted and exploited by the forces this haunted space represents.

Since his early days as a writer, King has been politically-minded and his views have manifested in his fiction. In a 1980 interview, he acknowledged that some of his first novels helped him work through the resentment towards the government he developed during his college years:

> It's my own political pilgrimage: I've always lived in Maine. I come from Anglo-Saxon stock. We're all Republicans. Dinosaurs walked the earth, my people were Republicans.... I voted for Nixon in '68. I was convinced that people who burned their draft cards were yellow-bellies. My idea was, "Let's bomb 'em into the Stone Age." I went to college from 1966 to 1970, and it was an accretion of the facts—teaching, seminars, and little by little I came around. It's like someone who converts.... And the marches and everything else followed.[10]

King's time at the University of Maine saw him turn away from his conservative roots and adopt a more liberal position. His political realignment can be seen as typical of students at the time, who were calling for wider social and political change during the counterculture. For Sharon Monteith, this movement was characterized by "a disillusion with a national or 'official' culture as signified by government, the military and 'the establishment'—in all its forms from stifling parents to party politics. It also contained optimism about the idea of renewing that same culture by reinvigorating as well as condemning the status quo."[11] Along with many of his peers, King came to feel a deep frustration with the state of the nation and a concomitant dissatisfaction with authority figures, the counterculture arguably representing "another revolt of the sons against the fathers."[12] In Gothic terms, his outlook might therefore broadly be seen as one of unhappiness with the impact of the past on the present.

Referring to the perceived failure of the counterculture to achieve its goals, King remarked in his memoir, *On Writing* (2000), that "I don't want to speak too disparagingly of my generation (actually I do, we had a chance to change the world and opted for the Home Shopping Network instead)."[13] Yet his "political pilgrimage" saw him into adulthood and, as the next chapter will show, into the malaise of the 1970s. This process helped shape some of the key thematic concerns of *The Shining*. In considering the nature of literary criticism, Pierre Macherey describes the quest for those ideological circumstances which affect the writer and act as the "conditions of its possibility"[14] for any literary work and thus "shape the meaning."[15] The seismic events of the 1960s and 1970s might be seen as precisely such conditions for King's novel, ones which found resonance with the reading public of the time.

Situated on the edges of civilized space, haunted by its history of opulence and violence, the Overlook is both situated *in* a liminal place and, indeed, acts *as* a liminal place. It has clear potential for Gothic revelation. As this study maintains throughout, fictional haunted spaces and haunted experiences, essentially liminal in their nature and function, provide the opportunity to interrogate aspects of American place and culture in terms of their socio-historical significance. Haunting gives rise to liminal experiences and spaces in which opposing forces and apparently discontinuous temporal zones meet. In the world of the hotel, this means conflict along class and gender lines. King uses the haunting powers of the Overlook to stir up and dramatize themes including the demands made by the shifting definitions of masculinity in America, as well as the constraints imposed by class and the exploitation inherent within corporate capitalism, his portrayals reflecting the contradictions embedded in culture itself.

In this liminal arena, the drama of Jack's own past is played out along with that of his present, which is increasingly shaped by the haunting he experiences rather than by his own goals and efforts. Ultimately, the Overlook—an instrument of American capitalism—ensures that his creative and family identities are eradicated and the family is destroyed. Obsessed by the history that surrounds him in this place, Jack eventually resolves to be a part of it by acting as its chronicler. Fredric Jameson has explained notions of history in the following way: "In the modern world, and therefore in modern literature as well, there are many experiences ... where an individual or a character is faced not with an interpersonal relationship, with an ethical choice, but rather with a relationship to some determining force vaster than the self or any individual, that is, with society itself, or with politics and the movement of history."[16] Such a stance places individuals in the context of wider circumstances that they are powerless to control or perhaps even to comprehend. History in this sense goes beyond the lived experience of the individual. It becomes a systemic force, and Jack's time at the Overlook builds towards his being crushed by the vast sweep of history that haunted space represents. For Joseph Grixti, the Overlook's haunted clock works to "throw reality into its own fatal dimensions of time."[17] Given its liminal powers, I would ascribe this property to the entire hotel. It is a portal into a history that initially repels Jack but in which he later seeks to partake. Once the historical eras contained there begin to merge, the ensuing liminal situation in which Jack is placed assails him with an overwhelming array of forces which pressure him and vie for his attention. These issues are never resolved, to which the Overlook's explosion at the novel's climax stands testament.

Focusing on three key incidents, this chapter will explore how Jack's experience of haunting speaks to the themes above. The liminality inherent in King's use of the haunted house motif in this novel, I argue here, is a literary strategy for enacting and exploring the traumas and tensions not just of the period, but of America two hundred years after its founding. So, the convention of haunting gives Gothic fictions access to historical and ideological materials in a manner denied to more formal narrative strategies. With its emphasis on the simultaneous persistence of past eras into the present day, haunting here serves to dramatize the conflicts at the heart of American masculinity in the late twentieth century.

"Where the action is"—The Basement

The Shining begins as Jack obtains the caretaker position courtesy of his well-connected former drinking companion, Al Shockley. An unskilled job, this represents no part in the career plans of a young man whose early adulthood saw him acquire a college degree, publish many short stories and secure a teaching position at prestigious New England preparatory school, Stovington Academy. Yet the first few weeks at the resort see Jack settle into his routine maintenance tasks with relative ease, even with pleasure. He descends to the basement on one of his regular trips to tend the dilapidated boiler and, on a whim, decides to explore further. The basement, a space to which Jack is compelled to return time and again, seems symbolic of his new station. Containing a repressed history awaiting exposure, it is also a space vital to instigating the supernatural events which play out over the course of the novel. For the first of my three haunting episodes, I have chosen to focus on the events that take place in the basement in the chapter entitled "The Scrapbook." However, before discussing the haunting, I need first to consider how Jack came to be—symbolically and literally—in the basement, as the reasons for this are a key part of my analytic focus on masculinity, class and capitalism.

To put Jack's humbled status into context, it is necessary to examine the changes in his personal and professional circumstances prior to the maintenance job. His situation speaks to wider issues of masculinity in America. As Barbara Ehrenreich describes, "The American economy, by the early twentieth century, was based on the principle of the family wage: a male worker should be paid enough to support a family."[18] The Torrances' Boulder home provides a spatial metaphor for the plight in which the family finds itself after Jack is dismissed for assaulting a student. His wife, Wendy, reflects, "The high hopes they had begun with came down to this unpleasant apartment building in a city they didn't know."[19] In a society predicated on the male breadwinner role, where supporting one's wife and children had become "the hallmark of manhood,"[20] the caretaker post seems their last hope for security. Already vulnerable, the family is primed for a breakdown. Once subjected to the powerful liminal forces of the Overlook, these concerns become heightened and the dangers more pronounced.

Historically then, an individual's sense of masculine identity has been closely tied to his employment and role within the family. Jack certainly feels his masculinity is weakened once he loses his status as a reliable breadwinner and his role as chief provider of family stability subsequently comes under threat. Sara Martín Alegre detects "an evident anxiety about parenthood on the side of baby-boomers"[21] in King's novels; this is unmistakable here. At Stovington, Jack's nascent alcoholism irrevocably altered the course of the family's life when he broke Danny's arm in a violent act of discipline. Reflection on this time stirs images and emotions centering on his shortcomings as a husband and father: "Jack would stumble into their leased house with dawn seeping into the sky and find Wendy and the baby asleep on the couch…. He would look at them and the self-loathing would back up his throat in a bitter wave" (*TS*: 37). Failure as a provider is not Jack's only concern. Determined to make his name as a writer, he spends his spare hours writing and publishing and proves to be "something of a catch for Stovington, a slowly blooming American writer perhaps" (38). Though he later quits, his drinking impairs his productivity as well as his home life, and his dismissal places both aspects of his life and identity in jeopardy.

From the nation's early days, American masculinity has been bound up with the image of the self-made man, "a model of manhood that derives identity entirely from a man's activities in the public sphere, measured by accumulated wealth and status."[22] Having squandered his hard-earned teaching post, Jack becomes reliant on his wealthy friend and this sudden dependency diminishes his masculinity further. The loss of his job, with the attendant loss of prestige and potential for career advancement as a writer, introduces a class dimension to his predicament. Because of his family he is driven to accept Shockley's offer of menial labor, which undermines his masculine identity even as the workings of the hotel reinforce his disadvantaged social and economic position. The novel commences *in medias res* as the interview takes place and the prospective caretaker's view of manager Stuart Ullman is made clear right from the opening line: "Jack Torrance thought: *Officious little prick* [original emphasis]" (*TS*: 3). Jack dislikes Ullman because he is bureaucratic and pompous, affecting an air of superiority to which Jack feels he is far from entitled. Yet Ullman has his own resentments. Shockley, a major shareholder in the Overlook, has decreed that Jack shall be employed there. So Ullman is forced to ignore his qualms and bow to his superior's wishes, even though Shockley "is not a hotel man" (5). All his frontline experience is overruled at the whim of the shareholder; a slight which he feels compelled to air in the interview. The novel bristles with hierarchical conflict from that point on. Liminality heightens this conflict, pressurizing Jack until both he and the hotel are destroyed at the novel's climax.

So Jack enters a corporate world, defined by hierarchy, which contrasts sharply with his plans for life as a self-made author because he now finds himself in a subservient position. His boss, Ullman, represents the ultimate corporation man. Extolling the Overlook's reputation and material attributes, he takes pride in his role as its steward and basks in the reflected glory of the building to which he has dedicated his life. Departing for his winter job, he despondently owns that "the place in Florida is a dump.... The Overlook is my real job. Take good care of it for me, Mr. Torrance" (99). His position is perhaps best summarized in his declaration: "I only want what's best for the Overlook. It is a great hotel. I want it to stay that way" (10). Though he is well paid, it seems unlikely that the monetary rewards truly enrich his life, as his whole being is structured by work. In retrospect, once the hotel is revealed as haunted, the reader is left to ponder the insidious effects that inhabiting—and working to sustain—such a place might have had on him. Existing solely to serve the interests of the ruling class, Ullman is an instrument of a capitalist system that exploits his labor without offering him a real stake in the hotel he preserves.

This organization relies on hierarchy to succeed and to generate its profits. Such a system is inherently exploitative, hiding unpleasant secrets and fostering resentment. Indeed, Sharon A. Russell observes that capitalism attracts evil to the Overlook.[23] Even before the haunting begins, its basement is a site for sordid revelations. After the interview, Jack is schooled there by Watson—the summer caretaker—in the maintenance requirements. Ullman, who "treated the cellar as another country—a nasty underdeveloped one at that" (*TS*: 183), feels his managerial role sets him apart from such activities. Watson teaches Jack about more than just the boiler. He undercuts the sales-speak and paints an unflattering picture of the manager: "It's like some people just come here to throw up and they hire a guy like Ullman to clean up the messes" (22). Ullman has worked hard to protect the Overlook's good name and obscured a catalogue of horrors in doing so. Delbert Grady, Jack's alcoholic predecessor, murdered his wife and daughters before committing suicide. In Watson's words, Ullman "split a gut tryin to keep it out of the papers" (21). Watson's contempt for his boss endears him to Jack, who identifies to some extent with his summer counterpart. There is a clear sense of antipathy, directed from those lower in the hierarchy to those directly above, right through the novel.

Despite his lowly status, Jack sees a chance to regain what he has lost, including his masculine identity. Personally motivated by artistic rather than fiscal goals, he is unaffected by Ullman's desire to preserve the hotel for its own sake. However, a strong element of the haunting influence that the place comes to have over him is its appeal to his creativity. Jack might identify with Watson rather than the manager, but he has no intention of remaining at the bottom of this hierarchy for long. Rather, he intends to take advantage of a menial job that leaves his mind free for writing. Once the family is settled, he feels able to resume this and rejoices that his play—which he has struggled with for months—"was going very well" (104). Making the link between his work and the family's happiness, Wendy also takes his renewed enthusiasm as a good sign: "Jack had not been writing so steadily since the second year of their marriage … his writing made her immensely hopeful" (120). The Overlook seems to offer him success on two fronts, as it enables him to provide materially for his family while also giving him the opportunity to meet his own artistic needs.

So the caretaker work helps Jack to reassert his masculinity. The basement seems likely to help his writing further when he finds a scrapbook down there. This tome suggests a chance for an exposé based on the hotel's dark side. Ullman previously recounted the official version of the Overlook's history, replete with names of prestigious guests and details of the opulence that attracted them over the years. In keeping with America's tradition of grand hotels, visitors included many high-flyers from industry and politics: "Vanderbilts have stayed here, and Rockefellers, and Astors, and Du Ponts. Four Presidents have stayed in the Presidential Suite. Wilson, Harding, Roosevelt, and Nixon" (6).[24] Old desk registers commemorate visits by such luminaries of the entertainment industry as Clark Gable, Jean Harlow and Carole Lombard. Luxury is a given, as all the guest rooms benefit from stunning views, and the grounds contain what is said to be "the finest roque court in America" (7),[25] installed by millionaire Horace Derwent in the 1940s. In short, the Overlook appears to boast a laudable pedigree.

The story of the Overlook's ownership, passing from its original builder to an aggressive entrepreneur and then to corporate control, indicates shifts in capitalism from before the turn of the century down to the time of the novel. The industrial and economic growth of the Gilded Age nurtured "'barons of industry' who engaged in unrestrained and unregulated laissez-faire capitalism and thereby accumulated immense fortunes, often at the expense of their workers."[26] This led to "a great disparity between the few who were extraordinarily wealthy and the masses who were extremely poor and who found themselves dependent on the rich for their very existence."[27] As Jeffrey Louis Decker argues, the promise of the Gilded Age, "that the opportunity to amass personal wealth was an American birthright,"[28] was restricted by the turn of the century to the privileged few because corporate structure, newly-introduced to the business world, meant reduced opportunities for class mobility.[29] The Overlook, boasting the company of Vanderbilts, Rockefellers and Astors, is a showcase for capitalism's success stories from this prosperous era. Yet the system meant that some accrued vast material wealth while those lower in the social hierarchy gained little for their labors.

Reading the scrapbook, which details the hotel's history in quasi-documentary form, Jack becomes immersed in the story of the Overlook. This story is microcosmic of the development of American capitalism from the Gilded Age to Jack's own era, and through this device the novel shows him becoming immersed in the movement of history—Jameson's "determining force"—that threatens to consume him. After the Second World War, American business became increasingly corporate as tycoons such as the Gilded Age robber barons "were supplemented by a complex arrangement of corporate- and state-sponsored hierarchies that, worst of all, lacked genuine public accountability."[30] The scrapbook reveals that Derwent, who acquired the Overlook during this era, was an industrialist with ruthless business instincts. Earning patents in aviation and munitions in the 1920s and 1930s, he became a Hollywood player in the 1940s. Many critics have likened him to Howard Hughes, "the most famous representative of the faceless corporate head and the new class of entrepreneurs."[31] As discussed earlier in relation to the fiction of Matheson, the rise of corporate culture and its impact on the American character began to be explored in studies at that time such as David Riesman's *The Lonely Crowd* (1949). By the time of *The Shining*, corporate capitalism was more globally prominent than ever. Historian Howard Zinn notes that, by the early 1970s, "American corporations were active all over the world on a scale never seen before."[32]

The basement thus yields a compelling insight into the Overlook's past, suggesting that big business and politics are rife with sleaze—Derwent had holdings in several Las Vegas casinos and was purportedly involved in bootlegging, smuggling and prostitution. Struggling to make the Overlook pay, he sold it in 1952 and it passed from one corporation to another, though by 1963 it emerged that he was the latest corporation's controlling shareholder. The hotel's new status as an exclusive business-men's club was exposed as a sham when an insider revealed it was fre-quented by gambling moguls "linked in the past to both suspected and convicted underworld kingpins" (*TS*: 161). The gangland-style killing of mafia crime lord Vito the Chopper took place in the august chambers of the Presidential Suite, and the bodies of his murdered bodyguards were found outside the door. As Karen A. Hohne states of Jack's discov-ery, "The unofficial story he puts together from the scrapbook gives the lie to the official version—the fine old hotel is actually a charnel house produced by corruption in high places."[33]

Initially, this revelation seems rather innocuous. However, it is the point at which Jack begins to understand what the Overlook represents, in capitalist terms, and finds himself drawn to it. Here, opposing forces start to make themselves manifest. Though scornful of Ullman, as he still sees himself as a man of independent literary talents, Jack soon starts to take on the mindset of a responsible employee. In this liminal arena, the conflicting demands unleashed by the "rich history of death and scandal surrounding the hotel"[34] pull him in various directions. When he picks up the scrapbook, out falls a card bearing the words *"Horace M. Derwent Requests the Pleasure of Your Company at a Masked Ball to Celebrate the Grand Opening of THE OVERLOOK HOTEL"* (*TS*: 155). Entering a brief reverie, Jack envisages the wealth on display at this event and casts it in terms of patriarchy and material success, imagin-ing "the richest men in America and their women." Yet this becomes more than mere history. The inclusive phraseology of *"Your Com-pany,"* coupled with his response to the invitation—"he grabbed it in mid-air before it could fall to the stone floor" (155)—renders this as the moment when the haunted Overlook reaches out to Jack and he recip-rocates.

This episode reveals contradictory impulses in Jack's character. Partly stemming from the demands of masculinity and partly from pres-sures pertaining to class, these contradictions—all of which become crys-tallized for him upon his arrival at the Overlook—have their roots in twentieth-century American politics and ideology. A newly-disenfranchised

Jack, faced with the prospect of the loss of his writing career, suddenly has the information necessary to compile a damning and potentially lucrative indictment of the privileged classes—both the owning classes, like Derwent, and the managing classes, represented by Ullman, who serve the interests of the former—and at whose mercy Jack now finds himself. Yet, despite this rebellious inclination to tell the Overlook's "hell of a story" (163), he is quickly drawn into the very capitalist dynamic he despises. He thus finds himself torn between different ideas about manhood and between different attitudes towards capitalism.

Although the scrapbook provides Jack with material for a potential book, it also serves another purpose. Confronted by clippings that show the hotel in a state of disrepair after Derwent's time, Jack is as distressed as one might imagine Ullman would be. It is at this point that he appears to internalize a sense of allegiance towards it: "He promised himself he would take care of the place, very good care. It seemed that before today he had never really understood the breadth of his responsibility to the Overlook. It was almost like having a responsibility to history" (159). So he resolves to write a book detailing the Overlook's untold story. However, there is an ambiguity about this episode. Later, Jack clearly articulates that this is an opportunity for him to regain his authorial status, regardless of the ramifications for the hotel's reputation. But at the time, as he ponders the project, his practical decision becomes confused by his growing sense that the Overlook must be protected.

This haunting by history commences without Jack, or the reader, being aware of what is happening. Liminality pervades this haunting scene. As he wanders beneath the hotel, he senses that history lies in between: "buried between the entries in these ledgers and account books and room-service chits where you couldn't quite see it" (154). Nothing supernatural has overtly manifested yet, but, humbled by his recent circumstances and tempted by the promise of the Overlook, he is susceptible and, in time, will literally see its hidden history for himself.[35] Thus the liminality unleashed by the haunting in the basement, emblematic as it is of the corrupt and exploitative hierarchy on which the Overlook depends, puts Jack into direct contact with the forces of history. The contradictions contained therein pull him in different directions.

"Shall we go or shall we stay?"— The Snowmobile

The chapter entitled "The Snowmobile" is underpinned by increased domestic tension and portrays Jack's loss of agency. His masculine identity, tied to his work, has been undermined. Nevertheless his future hopes, which hinge on the repetition of his early publication success, remain alive. Haunting causes Jack to feel committed to the hotel, although his desire to claim writerly authority over his situation persists. The tension triggered by the contradictory demands of being a responsible employee and trying to become an independent man starts to make itself felt. By now, as each family member has experienced the hotel's power, Jack promises they will leave on the snowmobile once the weather permits, although he wants to stay.

Commenting on anxieties about masculinity that emerged in the 1950s, Michael S. Kimmel observes that the conflict between being a good employee and being a self-reliant individual—the two extremes of manhood embedded in American culture—posed such unanswerable questions as: "How could men remain responsible breadwinners and not turn into docile drudges.... How could men let their hearts run free with a wife and kids to support?"[36] Such cultural reappraisals meant that, by the late 1970s, "adult manhood was no longer burdened with the automatic expectation of marriage and breadwinning,"[37] though traditional male values would still exert their influence. Jack identifies strongly with the breadwinner role yet is clearly frustrated by its constraints. His desire to stay stems partly from his drive to support the family and his lack of job opportunities. He sees the Overlook as the best chance they have—he can finish his play, return to Stovington and "be able to handle his responsibilities much better" (*TS*: 270). Incensed by Wendy's disregard for their hardship, he feels he has to fight his family to help them, perhaps asserting his masculine power within the domestic sphere all the more strongly because of his lack of power outside it.

But a confused sense that the hotel is offering him a more personal salvation also persists in Jack: "*He might be able to find peace here. At last. If they would only let him*" (270). This implies that his private happiness is separate from that of his family, even if he cannot consciously own this fact. Ostensibly, his writing acts as a barometer for Jack and the Torrances' general well-being: when he writes, he and the family are stable, and when he stops things disintegrate. Yet the family and the writing are arguably in opposition to one another, vying for his time and energies. The breaking of Danny's arm years ago illustrates this. When the child took his father's beer and poured it over the draft manuscript of his play, a "slow, red cloud of rage had eclipsed Jack's reason" (16), leading to an act that Wendy would never be able to forgive. Tellingly, this violent outburst—disturbing because it shows what Jack is capable of prior to any supernatural influence—is prompted by his son's impinging on his creative output. Further, it is his most prized achievement—the acceptance of his story by *Esquire*—that sets in motion his estrangement from his family. The binge with which he marks the occasion commences with Wendy urging him not to go out because he is too drunk and concludes with him accidentally dropping Danny, and Wendy spending the first of many nights on the couch.

Through haunting, the Overlook incites these conflicting impulses in Jack. In addition to the threat to his masculinity from his reduced employment status, he is repeatedly torn between his role as a family man and his personal ambition. Out in the equipment shed in an attempt to get the snowmobile running, Jack is delighted when unable to locate the vehicle's battery, though his pleasure turns to anger once it is found. A sense of the conflict within him emerges as the scene progresses. Jack runs a gauntlet of overwhelming emotions and impulses—from bitterness at having to leave and fear of being unable to do so, to resentment of Danny's shining ability and protectiveness towards his family. Outside of the hotel, in a rare moment of clarity, he perceives that the Overlook possesses active and aggressive forces and is trying to keep them there, which motivates him to install the battery. Yet an admission creeps into his thoughts, parenthesized and italicized for emphasis, which causes him to regret this: "(*Except he still didn't really want to go*)" (281). Convinced that he has no alternative to this post, no agency over his fate, he sabotages the snowmobile so they have no choice but to remain.

Jack is thus able to shore up his masculinity by fending off financial ruin and keeping his personal dreams alive. Yet his writing aspirations cause conflict with people other than Wendy when he calls Ullman to declare his intent to write about the Overlook. Though it seems at odds with his new-found loyalty to the place, Jack suspects soon afterwards that he made this provocative move unconsciously in order to get fired and thus remove the family from the hotel before they could become snowed in. The manager angrily denounces Jack's plan in a heated exchange laced with the rhetoric of class and hierarchy: "You are an employee of the hotel, no different from a busboy or a kitchen pot scrubber" (180), he warns his newest and lowliest recruit, though he is a mere employee himself. He contacts Shockley, who calls Jack to forbid such a book. Their conversation reiterates Jack's lowly status within this system and points to his lack of agency. Acceptable to Al as a teacher and an up-and-coming author, he will not be tolerated if his literary ambitions threaten his powerful friend's business interests. Further, this scene underscores Jack's contradictory attitudes about the hotel and all that it represents. Though authoring a candid history of the place might help him make his name as a writer, in situating him as its critic rather than as a dedicated employee, such an act would inevitably conflict with his nascent sense of identity as the Overlook's servant.

This dispute highlights the friends' social disparity. It also reveals the extent to which both men have been bound by their alcoholism but placed very differently because of their class. Jack tells Al: "You don't have to take some rich friend's charity.... The fact that you were one step from a brown-bag lush goes pretty much unmentioned, doesn't it?" (187–188). The moneyed Al—who exploits Jack's companionship for leisure purposes—can "afford" to be alcoholic, but their drinking costs Jack dearly. Alcoholism has been a major factor in his reduced circumstances and the Overlook fatally exploits his vulnerability. Labor historian Stephen Meyer has noted the prevalence of alcohol use and abuse among manual laborers. This was particularly pronounced among men whose working days were highly routinized: "For mass production workers in the automobile plants, alcohol numbed the body's senses and reduced the tedium, fatigue, and monotony of their work. Especially when they worked in isolated work areas, men sometimes drank on the job."[38] Jack was sober before he came to the hotel, but working in the basement triggers his alcoholism. This association, especially when considered in light of his predecessor's alcoholism, symbolically aligns him with the tradition of manual workers drinking to escape the pressures of routine, here exacerbated by isolation.

Earlier, mention was made of the ambiguity surrounding Jack's decision to write a book—is it for his benefit or the hotel's? This project certainly diverts his precious creative energies away from the play that has been central both to his sense of worth and to the Torrances' lives for so long. His placement in the Overlook's hierarchy has enabled him to learn its secrets and nurtured a fledgling desire to expose the deficiencies of his celebrated workplace and his social superiors. Hence tension develops between subservience and independence. Further, Jack's authorial goal is dependent on an agency which is clearly prohibited by his menial status. Subject to the Overlook's escalating haunting, including a nightmarish episode where the CB radio transmits the voice of his dead father urging him to kill his family because they're "trying to hold you back" (*TS*: 227), Jack's inner turmoil intensifies and his power is diminished. So liminality subjects him to forces from his own past and from a wider history. Such experiences, reinforced by Al's censure, give him a different view of history—one grounded in his disadvantaged social position and initially motivated by revenge: "If Al Shockley had connections with the Derwent empire, then God help him" (190).

Jack's refusal to abandon his project seems constructive. However, over the weeks that follow, this task threatens to consume rather than to empower him:

> His eyes had begun to get heavy as he leafed through packets of milk bills, a hundred to a packet, seemingly tens of thousands all together. Yet he gave each one a cursory glance, afraid that by not being thorough he might miss exactly the piece of Overlookiana he needed to make the mystic connection that he was sure must be here somewhere. He felt like a man with a power cord in one hand, groping around a dark and unfamiliar room for a socket. If he could find it he would be rewarded with a view of wonders [221].

He seeks ardently to be part of the history the hotel represents. In its basement, shortly after his initial decision to write an exposé, he is momentarily overwhelmed by a feeling of its immensity: "He could almost feel the weight of the Overlook bearing down on him from above" (159).[39] It is the sheer weight of history, as Jameson has described, unleashed here by the liminality of haunting, that so oppresses him.

The incident with the snowmobile, a vehicle that represents agency and the chance to traverse the wilderness and reach the safety of civilization, brings these events into sharp focus. It causes Jack's loss of agency in the face of a powerful supernatural force to become starkly apparent. As he wrestles with the possibility of leaving the Overlook, all these issues—his role as father and husband, his teaching job, his alcoholism, his writing aspirations, his sense that the hotel is haunted—all pass through his mind. And the writing project is a strong factor in his compulsion to remain: "Perhaps the Overlook, large and rambling Samuel Johnson that it was, had picked him to be its Boswell" (282), a link that suggests the harnessing of his talents by the potent (and anthropomorphized) haunted hotel. But soon there are other reasons for Jack to stay at the Overlook, too.

"Time had been canceled"—The Ballroom

The final haunting scene on which I wish to focus takes place over two consecutive chapters entitled "Drinks on the House" and "Conversations at the Party." After the snowmobile incident, Jack is able to restore harmony for a time. But the Overlook is gaining strength through absorbing Danny's shining. As Jack identifies with it rather than with his family, the problems intensify. Danny encounters a ghost that physically harms him; Jack, insisting that he must have imagined this, slaps him. The family deteriorates as Danny has a horrifying premonition of impending violence and Wendy arms herself through fear of Jack. Further embroiled in what he sees as research, Jack slips away from the present and towards the Overlook's past. For Mary Jane Dickerson, he "has allowed himself to enter the Overlook's history, to become a character in its story rather than to maintain his integrity as artist."[40] This is true up to a point, as Jack is undoubtedly drawn into the hotel. But I would argue that he lacks the agency Dickerson imputes to him. Originally, his experience in the basement made the prospect of a book seem like an opportunity for him. Now, however, this project seems to be sucking him inexorably into the service of the Overlook.

As these haunting chapters commence, Jack further anthropomorphizes the hotel and theorizes that his caretaking efforts on its behalf will be noted and, more importantly given his hardship and toil, rewarded. The liminality of the Overlook's haunting powers seems to collapse the hierarchies imposed in its reality, giving him direct access to its history—an alluring history in which he believes he can participate:

"All the hotel's eras were together now, all but this current one, the Torrance Era. And this would be together with the rest very soon now. That was good. That was very good" (*TS*: 342). Abandoning his intended project of critiquing the hotel and, by implication, the capitalist system with which it is entangled, Jack instead becomes subject to that very system. Ascending eagerly from his customary realm of the basement towards the higher-status rooms reserved for the guests, he moves with "the hurrying steps of a man who has come home from a long and bitter war" (333). Once he stands on the threshold of these elite chambers, the haunting gains clarity: "He could hear the Overlook Hotel coming to life…. It was as if another Overlook now lay scant inches beyond this one, separated from the real world (if there is such a thing as a 'real world,' Jack thought) but gradually coming into balance with it" (342).

This is the most sustained sequence of haunting in the novel, book-ended by Jack's decisive move into the Colorado Lounge bar and the macabre vision, played out by the ballroom's ornate timepiece, of a clockwork father obliterating his son with a mallet. For Jack, this occurs as a process of intoxication. It has already been shown that he enters a kind of liminal state when he drinks, and that it is partly through the trappings of alcoholism that the Overlook has sought to ensnare him. Yet here the consumption of alcohol—which must be ghostly, as no alcohol remains on the premises—is aligned with the likes of Al Shockley rather than Delbert Grady because it is tinged with the promise of material status and success. The seemingly convivial atmosphere and the prospect of a longed-for drink draw Jack into the bustling bar. The subservience of Lloyd the spectral bartender and the glamour of the ghostly crowd, which fulfills the promise of the scrapbook invitation, help to keep him there. Here, in addition to his status as an employee, he becomes assimilated into the ruling class through his fervent adoption of their leisure practices.

Once ensconced at the party, Jack is manipulated more openly and strives to comply with what is requested of him. Despite his distaste for Ullman's devotion to the Overlook, despite his scorn for Shockley's unmerited position of privilege, Jack comes to absorb the manager's attitude and to covet the shareholder's wealth. He relishes mingling with the rich and powerful and even comes to hanker after a permanent position within the business hierarchy. He speaks with Grady, who echoes the castigatory sentiments ostensibly expressed by Jack's father in the ghostly radio transmission and insinuates that—if willing to "discipline" his family—a clever and accomplished man like Jack could readily improve his material and social standing: "Think how much further you yourself could go in the Overlook's organizational structure. Perhaps ... in time ... to the very top" [original ellipses] (353).

Jack's feeling, long-held and now apparently about to be validated, that he is deserving of recognition resonates with 1970s corporate culture. Commenting on how attitudes towards achievement in the workplace changed from the 1950s, Christopher Lasch observes that, in the 1970s, devotion to the organization is no longer enough, as an ambitious corporate employee will instead attain promotion by "convincing his associates that he possesses the attributes of a 'winner.'"[41] Jack insists that he is keen for advancement, as he does later when he implores Grady to release him from the pantry in which Wendy and Danny fearfully imprison him, but this will clearly come at a price. Lasch also detects a shift in expectations about domesticity—whereas a wife formerly was seen as integral to an "organization man's" career, the executives of the 1970s were warned of the conflict inherent between matrimony and corporate advancement.[42] Jack will have to rethink his own domestic situation if he wants to advance in this corporation.

There are other tensions at work in this scene, however, and the liminality of haunting provides contact with a domestic patriarchal past as well as a corporate one. The Overlook's eras are coming into alignment and Jack's own eras are coalescing too. Before coming to the hotel, he was troubled by personal and professional failure. As well as being haunted by his adult past, Jack is perpetually disturbed by his chaotic childhood, when his father's "abusive example of family terror"[43] seemed to sow the seeds for his young son's hot temper. He has been pondering his relationship with his father over the last few weeks and a sense of empathy with the punitive patriarch of his youth asserts itself in this scene. Jack's failure as a breadwinner has meant letting his dependents down, but it has also meant a failure in his own authority. In the same way that it pulls Jack between the extremes of good employee and self-made man, the Overlook stirs up the contradictory demands of fatherhood, especially the tension between being a nurturer and a disciplinarian.

The ballroom scene forces Jack to confront the fissures in his own past as well as those in the varied definitions of masculinity that appear throughout America in the twentieth century. Ehrenreich observes that, for critics such as Philip Wylie, 1950s culture was steeped in a consumerism that chiefly benefited women. In some senses, then, "the corporate work world was actually a refuge—perhaps men's last indoor refuge—in a matriarchal society."[44] Beleaguered by memories of his 1950s upbringing, Jack now struggles to reassert his masculine identity through earlier models of manhood. His response to Grady's urges that he control his family seems rooted in a fear that his authority has been usurped, so he grasps at the Overlook's promise that he will regain his rightful role as head of the family and achieve success.

It soon becomes apparent that the Overlook wants Danny and Wendy disposed of entirely, not merely subdued, as it plans to acquire the boy's psychic powers for itself. The ghostly revels, overseen by Derwent, are undercut by signs that all is not as glamorous as it seems. Connotations of death and decay abound, as with the vision of Lloyd as "plague-raddled" (*TS*: 346) and the funereal scent of lilies. Grady, Vito the Chopper and the woman who committed suicide in Room 217 are all reminders of a troubled history which suggests that all might not go as well as promised for the present caretaker. Although wary of these portents, when exhorted by the party-goers to "drink your drink," Jack advances further into a liminal zone of inebriation and haunting and, on downing his martini, "he [feels] fine" (346). The ballroom clock's inexplicably bloody enactment of a mechanical father bludgeoning his son leaves no doubt as to the nature of the "discipline" intended by the Overlook. Jack is horrified by this but clearly internalizes its lessons. As the haunting ceases, he collapses into a stupor, and when Wendy rouses him he immediately falls into the pattern of aggressive violence, attacking his family with a roque mallet, that moves the novel towards the climactic explosion of the hotel with Jack still inside. So the ghostly promise of social advancement proves to be a hollow one. Although he finally turns the mallet on himself rather than on his son, Jack is too enmeshed in the Overlook to extricate himself, too far gone to leave the liminal state and learn from his time there, and his family is left alone.

Conclusion

Some weeks into their time at the Overlook, realizing that their stay there is harming rather than helping him, Wendy and Danny convey their concerns to Jack. Wendy remarks "The place seemed good for you. You were away from all the pressures that made you so unhappy at Stovington. You were your own boss, working with your hands so you could save your brain—all of your brain—for your evenings writing. Then … I don't know just when … the place began to seem bad for you. Spending all that time down in the cellar, sifting through those old papers, all that old history" (*TS*: 245). Her observations indicate that, despite the promise of a fresh start, Jack is still subject to wider ideological forces in the form of the constraints of the workplace and the contradictory demands inherent in masculinity. Yet they also point to the corrosive influence of the Overlook Hotel which—as Jameson observes of Kubrick's cinematic version—is haunted "simply by History, by the American past."[45] Hotels are public spaces, "inhabited by a multiplicity of people both simultaneously and linearly,"[46] and the haunted house motif here permits an exploration of the tensions contained within this crowded space. Symbolic of the capitalist enterprise of which it is a part, the sentient Overlook embodies the ultimate faceless corporation. Jack's initial location in the basement underscores his disadvantaged position, both within this organization and within American society. His haunting experiences in this liminal place tempt him with dreams of success, though the snowmobile incident sees him confront his lack of power and yield to the hotel. Finally, the ghostly ball—once its trappings of glamour and hints of his advancement fall away—exposes the domestic abuse of Jack's childhood and lays bare the aggressive demands of capitalism.

Politicized as a young adult by the counterculture, King uses *The Shining*—as one of his earliest novels—to engage with his resentment towards deep-seated inequalities within American society. The haunted hotel that dominates the tale is entrenched in a capitalist system of greed and inequity which, though it stretches back into American history, seems especially conspicuous in the context of the bicentennial. Despite the drive for celebration, this was a time when the nation was taking stock of what it stood for. The widespread feeling that "there was something fundamentally wrong with the country"—ignited by the counter-culture movement in the 1960s—was to endure for the remainder of the seventies.[47] King's initial foray into haunted fiction represents a departure from the conservative tendencies discernible in Matheson's ghostly tales. Though he chooses to follow Matheson's lead in adapting the haunted house motif to a recognizable setting, King's handling of liminality is markedly different. Matheson's protagonists succeed in managing the ideological contradictions they encounter via haunting by recognizing challenges to the social order without being fundamentally changed by them. The doomed Jack, who is incapable of extricating himself from the liminal state, has no such prospect. As is the case with Lovecraft's protagonist, given the context of thorny issues that besets him, Jack's predicament seems reflective of King's sense that no clear resolution is possible.

Jack's neglect of the boiler causes it to explode and destroy the hotel. It seems unlikely, however, that the evil for which it stands can be extinguished, as Shockley continues to intervene in the remaining Torrances' lives and Ullman is presumably still entrenched in the corporate hotel business. Both money and bureaucracy endure to sustain a system that Jack sees as unjust and yet—in identifying with it and being destroyed by it—to which he finally succumbs. His dispensability to the Overlook underscores his wider position; his life insurance policy makes him a better provider for his dependents after his demise. Ultimately, the impossibility of his planned exposé is finally established. While researching, the threat of the boiler's failure makes him reflect that such an incident would "destroy the secrets, burn the clues, it's a mystery no living hand will ever solve" (*TS*: 329). The Overlook defies both exposure and, at least in spirit, final destruction.

CHAPTER FIVE

"Going places with the Young in Heart"
Haunted by Nostalgia and the Past in Christine

The previous chapter on *The Shining* demonstrated the haunting power of the Overlook Hotel, a building that mirrors twentieth-century American history, to first enthrall and then entrap protagonist Jack Torrance. Similarly, *Christine* is a novel concerned with the past. Its characters evoke history in various ways, whether to control it, to warn against it, or to mourn its passing. The narrative deals with the relationship between the eponymous Christine, a Plymouth Fury made in 1958, and teenager Arnie Cunningham, who acquires her some twenty years later. Initially, the car appears to have a salutary effect on its young owner. Yet it soon becomes evident that there is a price to pay for this: Christine, *"like some kind of horrible vampire,"*[1] consumes Arnie's energies and resources. Her influence gradually transforms him into an aggressive cynic, undermining his family life before destroying it altogether. Gothic tropes offer an innovative form of access to the past the novel depicts. I argue that the liminality of haunting, which sees the past and present coexist, creates a uniquely complex narrative space. This space allows a direct engagement with history, and with all the cultural associations that history brings, as well as with the conflicts to which competing ideologies inevitably give rise.

Existing criticism on King's novel tends to focus on one of two broad areas: either asserting that the predatory vehicle represents a fear of technology, or scrutinizing the specifically female nature of Christine's threat. For Jonathan P. Davis, *Christine* shows the dangers in "Americans' subordination of their humanness in favor of surrounding themselves

124

in technology's immediate gratifications."[2] James Egan, Tony Magistrale, Donald R. Knight and Mary Findley all make similar observations about King's fictive enactments of the dark side of technological progress.[3] Magistrale sees the seductive yet deadly car as "built upon the fundamental masculine distrust of femininity."[4] Edward Madden notes the equation of cars with females (observed by Norman Mailer in a 1950s essay[5]) and decries the "objectifying misogyny and its corollary homophobia endemic to American culture—that is, both the commodification of female sexuality circulated among men and the homosocial desires and homosexual panic that structure such an exchange."[6] Andrew Schopp also detects *Christine*'s misogyny,[7] and Sylvia Kelso avers that the feminized automobile is a "gynophobic" monster rooted in the union between American males and their cars.[8]

No ordinary car, this vehicle possesses the power to grant access to the late 1950s of its manufacture. Christine is described as a vampiric entity, yet she is also increasingly characterized by Arnie, and by others who encounter her abilities, in terms of her connection to the past. She functions as a "time traveller" (*C*: 207) and comes to be understood as "a hellish haunted house that rolled on Goodyear rubber" (433). With these features in mind, and in keeping with my wider focus on the haunted house motif, my argument focuses on how the car operates as a ghost, rather than as a vampire, and I therefore aim to interrogate what aspects of the past she evokes and why these are of significance to the particular historical moments in which the novel is set and was written.

As this book has discussed, work on the liminal designates it as a borderland or threshold territory, a transitional area between more clearly-defined concepts such as childhood and adulthood, living and dead, past and present. The liminal spaces of fictional hauntings are arenas in which normally distinct realms interact, forcing protagonists to contend with the interplay of historical forces released therein. Turner's account of liminality, as the zone between steps in a status sequence,[9] highlights its links to progression—one enters the liminal state in order to leave it at a higher stage of personal or cultural development. Yet some critics have noted that "the liminal can be a place of threat as well as of promise, and can produce and perpetuate conservative as well as progressive ideologies."[10] Liminality might reveal social circumstances that cannot be transcended, and transition may be denied to some who find themselves within it.

The liminal spaces of King's Gothic fictions tend to inhibit rather than facilitate progress. In emphasizing conflict and shying away from narrative resolution, King's liminality shows the complexity of the historical and ideological themes with which his fictions contend. Lovecraft's use of haunting exudes a similar turbulence about the issues his fiction portrays while Matheson takes a different tack. Another novel which resurrects the 1950s from a vantage point late in the twentieth century, *Earthbound*—despite conveying a degree of discomfiture with romanticized visions of this time—proves in the end to be conservative in striving to uphold precisely such a nostalgic stance. To return to Fiedler's conception of American Gothic as a politically conservative form, it can be seen that King—though not entirely impervious to the nostalgic impulse—is ultimately critical of tendencies to wallow in such idealized versions of the past.

In *Christine*, as in *The Shining*, King uses haunting to literally show how the past can linger into the present. The novel provides a late twentieth-century critique of America's understandings of, and attitudes towards, its own recent past. A rites of passage tale, bound up with Gothic re-enactments of the 1950s, *Christine* taps into and interrogates the effect of the wider nostalgic turn taken by American culture in the early 1980s of the novel's publication. Through the liminality of haunting it vividly portrays diverse, and sometimes incompatible, views of the past, revealing as it does so something of that past's continued relationship with the present.

"The Good Old Days"—The Lure of the Past

Christine dramatizes, in various ways, a longing for the past. The characters evince a sense of loss associated with the passage of time, whether due to personal experiences of growing up and growing old or to the societal changes time inevitably brings. Although the main protagonist is seventeen-year-old Arnie, much of his tale is recounted in the first-person by his best friend, Dennis Guilder. When juxtaposed with Dennis, a self-assured character blessed with athletic ability and a succession of girlfriends, Arnie is found wanting. Plagued by acne and socially inept, he epitomizes the tortured adolescent. His situation alters when he discovers—or, rather, *meets*—Christine in the novel's first pages. A 1950s vehicle, "one of the long ones with the big fins" (*C*: 8), Christine is a relic two decades old by the tale's 1978 setting. Hailed by Arnie as a "beauty" (8) and an "antique" (16), she symbolizes a bygone era with particular resonance in American popular memory. The haunted Christine permits literal access to that past and her union with Arnie unleashes liminal forces that blur the boundaries between past and present. In evoking the 1950s, she speaks to the nostalgic tendencies many critics have detected in the popular culture of 1970s and 1980s America, though she both echoes and critiques this nostalgia. King couches his tale of a ghostly car within a narrative preoccupied generally with history and the passing of time.

As a retelling of events some years distant, once Dennis has graduated from college and started a career, *Christine* meets the same criteria as those cinematic texts designated by Lesley Speed as nostalgic.[11] These films are defined by such features as a past setting, an adult—typically first-person—narrator and an emphasis on the protagonist's move towards maturity.[12] Speed cites Rob Reiner's *Stand by Me* (1986), adapted from King's novella "The Body" (1982), as one such example. As a coming-of-age tale, *Christine* exhibits all these traits. Writing in the 1980s, Fredric Jameson detects a pronounced rise in nostalgia films. His oft-cited arguments cast nostalgia as part of wider trends in late capitalist society. He sees the prevalence of such cinema as symptomatic of "the waning of our historicity, of our lived possibility of experiencing history in some active way."[13] By this he means that an authentic engagement with history has become diminished in favor of an artificial, ultimately apolitical, version of history—one more concerned with surface and style than with the realities of the past that mere images of it evoke. So Jameson sees nostalgia as a negative impulse, one that replaces the genuine with the ersatz to the detriment of any meaningful engagement with the politics of either past or present.

Yet other critics have defined nostalgia in less pessimistic ways. As Paul Grainge remarks, "There has been a renewed tendency in recent social, historical, and cultural theory to write against the idea that nostalgia is a bankrupt, and politically regressive, disease."[14] Philip Drake describes a number of divergent impulses that might all be termed nostalgic. He comments that, while nostalgia can be defined as yearning for a lost time, it might also be concerned more broadly with "conveying a knowing and reflexive relationship with the past."[15] Further, the term might be applied to those portrayals of history that emphasize the attraction of certain versions of the past while simultaneously reinforcing their artificiality, i.e., nostalgia can combine a sense of longing with the insight that such longing is likely to be misguided. It is therefore vital not to simply equate nostalgia with longing. The more nuanced definition above, which allows for yearning alongside critique, seems applicable to King's stance in *Christine*. I will consider first his treatment of longing before turning attention to the social critique he couches in the vocabulary and conventions of horror.

As the sole first-person narrator, the privileged voice here belongs to Dennis. The prologue makes it clear that his account is not of the events as they unfold but a set of reminiscences about his 1970s high school years. Unlike Arnie, Dennis navigates the liminal zone of adolescence—even overcomes the obstacles posed by the liminality of the haunting both boys face—to become the kind of mature narrator identified in Speed's analysis. Reflecting back on his experiences, he comments on the benefits of hindsight in speaking of the "heights of wisdom I've attained in my twenty-two years" (*C*: 1). Peppered with wistful observations such as "six is an optimum age" (14) and recollections of childhood memories, Dennis's account is filtered through the lens of nostalgia in the simple sense of longing. He looks back fondly on his early days, recalling the time he spent with Arnie and thus mourning the loss of this treasured friendship. Suddenly aware of his childhood coming to an end, he recalls that he felt a "fierce nostalgia-in-advance" (75) with the advent of his senior year at high school. Despite the incursions of Christine then, Dennis looks back on his past with genuine affection.

Although the reader has privileged access to Dennis, he is not the only character with whom such wistfulness for the past is associated. There is a strong sense of intergenerational conflict in *Christine* that works on a personal—as well as on a social—level, and this is often commingled with yearning, notably a yearning for the transience of youth. Arnie's parents, Michael and Regina, still entrenched in a lifestyle of protest that began in their 1960s youth, exert an infantilizing level of control over their son that stems from an inability to accept their own advancing years. Arnie explains their behavior with his grim assertion that "part of being a parent is trying to kill your kids…. Because as soon as you have a kid, you know for sure that you're going to die" (26–27). It is almost as though keeping Arnie a child for as long as possible will somehow negate this process for them. Further, besides Dennis, several characters indulge in more knowing reminiscences about their lost youth. A certain melancholy about aging, and the loss that entails, thus pervades the novel.

A sense of looking back fondly to childhood is very much in evidence then, yet the era to which *Christine* harks back is not the time of Dennis's childhood but of King's. In other words, the haunting is not concerned with the past of the novel's narrator—the 1970s—but rather with that of its author—the 1950s. In a 1984 interview with *Starburst* magazine, King reveals the meaning *Christine* has for him: "I grew up in the 50s. That's my generation…. The car is a symbol for the technological age, or for the end of innocence, when it plays such a part in adolescence and growing up."[16] History, in terms of the individual and of society, is thus central to this text. Svetlana Boym avers that nostalgia acts as an "intermediary between collective and individual memory"[17] and her claim is certainly borne out by *Christine*, which combines the personal with the cultural. As will be discussed, the turn to the 1950s is a significant one for the early 1980s context in which the novel appeared. I argue that the liminal effect of the Gothic trope of haunting further heightens this nostalgic turn.

Set in the decade that produced *Happy Days* (1974–1984) and *Grease* (1978), laced with lyrics from mainly rock and roll music about cars, *Christine* provides a "compendium of the 1970s as 1950s retro culture."[18] King clearly has *Happy Days* in mind as Arnie's name is an amalgam of the show's lead character, Richie Cunningham, and its key setting, a hangout known as Arnold's.[19] As these texts bear out, the 1950s is a decade imbued for many with an aura of enchantment. Mary Caputi observes, "For Americans, the 1950s bristle with an array of ideological connotations."[20] These are epitomized by the "Norman Rockwell vision of American life … the happy families and safe neighborhoods, the homespun quality of simple American virtues, the innocence and predictability of it all."[21] Jameson also argues that "for Americans at least, the 1950s remain the privileged lost object of desire—not merely the stability and prosperity of a pax Americana but also the first naïve innocence of the countercultural impulses of early rock and roll and youth gangs."[22] He summarizes this era, as it has come to be represented thus: "Main Street, U.S.A.; Marilyn Monroe; a world of neighbors and PTAs; small retail chain stores (the produce trucked in from the outside); favorite television programs; mild flirtations with the housewife next door; game shows and contests; sputniks distantly revolving overhead, mere blinking lights in the firma-ment, hard to distinguish from airliners or flying saucers."[23] From the outset, Christine is a striking visual reminder of this supposedly golden age.

King uses the car to physically conjure up this era. While Arnie is occupied with Roland D. LeBay, from whom he buys Christine, Dennis's inspection of her brings the phrase *"The good old days"* (*C*: 34) to his mind. Sitting behind her wheel triggers the first of many haunting episodes; her liminal interior supplies him with a tantalizing glimpse of precisely this past:

> And for just a moment it seemed that *everything* changed [original emphasis]. That ugly snarl of cracks in the windshield was gone—or seemed to be. The little swatch of LeBay's lawn that I could see was not yellowed, balding, and crabgrassy but a dark, rich, newly cut green. The sidewalk beyond it was freshly cemented, not a crack in sight. I saw (or thought I did, or dreamed I did) a '57 Cadillac motor by out front. That GM high-stepper was a dark minty green, not a speck of rust on her, big gangster whitewall tires, and hubcaps as deeply reflective as mirrors. A Cadillac the size of a boat, and why not? Gas was almost as cheap as tap-water [35].

With its depiction of suburban order and affluence, this brief scene encapsulates the nostalgic, longing view of the American 1950s described by Caputi and Jameson. Even without the haunting, Christine insists on re-enacting this past. Once renovated by Arnie (via supernatural means, as it turns out), her retro interior—complemented by a radio that favors "WDIL, the AM station from Pittsburgh that plays only oldies" (190–191)—provides her 1970s passengers with a sensory immersion in what Joseph Reino calls the "American pseudo–Eden"[24] of her 1958 heyday. The recurrent inclusion, as chapter headings, of lyrics from these very oldies serves to heighten the sense of longing for that time.

A vehicle of this particular vintage is a natural focal point for depictions of idyllic suburban life and post-war prosperity, given the large part cars played in 1950s culture. Car ownership increased and motels and drive-ins flourished.[25] Indeed, Arnold's diner in *Happy Days* was of the drive-in variety. Cars themselves reached new heights of extravagance,[26] as the "tail-fin craze" demonstrated.[27] Originating with the 1948 Cadillac, this design feature became widely imitated in the industry by the mid 1950s and reached its gaudiest proportions in 1959.[28] In her discussion of the 1950s American romance with the automobile, Karal Ann Marling notes the rise of the Motorama. These events, which ran from 1949 to 1961, were a combination of art show and advertising and functioned chiefly to showcase new vehicles to an eager public.[29] LeBay's informal sales-pitch reveals something of such traditions: "'This here is the best car I ever owned. Bought her in September 1957. Back then, that's when you got your new model year, in September. All summer long they'd show you pictures of cars under hoods and cars under tarps until you were fair dyin t'know what they looked like underneath. Not like now.' His voice dripped contempt for the debased times he had lived to see" (*C*: 10). LeBay is thus openly yearning in his recollections of a lost time when cars were held in such esteem.

American consumers saw cars as "objects that were symbols of their desires, reflections of themselves, expressions of their fantasies."[30] Advertisements in the 1950s promoted images of glamorous, increasingly oversized vehicles which boasted opulence and convenience. In Dennis's first encounter with her haunting power, Christine herself exemplifies such imagery: "For a moment the torn upholstery seemed to be gone. The seat covers were whole and smelling pleasantly of vinyl ... or maybe that smell was real leather. The worn places were gone from the steering wheel; the chrome winked pleasantly in the summer evening light falling through the garage door" (*C*: 34–35). This sense of luxury and comfort was reinforced in the 1950s themselves in advertising for cars of a variety of makes and budgets. One 1958 ad for Cadillac extols the vehicle's "beauty and elegance,"[31] while a Studebaker advert from the same year specifically touts the latest model's "color-correlated, deeply cushioned upholstery."[32] A 1956 Plymouth ad emphasizes the vehicle's large size,[33] and a 1957 promotion promises "floating luxury."[34] Cars pledged youth and vitality—a 1959 Plymouth ad casts the new model as "refreshingly youthful,"[35] and several 1956 Plymouth ads used the slogan "The car that's *going places with the Young in Heart*,"[36] which forges a clear link between the product, mobility and youth. Family values were also upheld as advertising "wrapped up family life, suburbia, and new cars in one neat and appealing package."[37] With the promise of both self-fulfillment and domestic bliss, the automobile thus embodies two equally enticing, yet potentially conflicting, facets of American life.

As King's comment regarding cars and adolescence above implies, this vehicle has other connotations besides the peace and plenty of the post-war years. Much of the narrative is concerned with Arnie's attempts to gain independence and assert a sense of self distinct from that imposed upon him by others. The automobile has long been a symbol of agency and freedom for Americans, and Christine initially seems no different in that respect. Peter J. Ling observes that, from the Progressive Era, cars "gave a sense of independence, and permitted wilful individualism,"[38] and James J. Flink notes that they "remained an important symbol of individualism, personal freedom, and mobility" into the 1970s.[39] Mastery of cars, along with the subsequent attainment of all they have come to symbolize, has often been seen as fundamental to adolescence and is arguably the "most important puberty rite in the United States."[40] Cars are important status symbols for American high school students.[41] A vehicle of his own gives Arnie the autonomy he craves.

A decisive link between cars and teens was forged in the 1950s and has endured, not least in the idealized depictions of that decade propagated by the likes of *Happy Days*. Timothy Shary singles out the automobile as a key component in the development of the teen genre in 1950s cinema: "Teenagers began buying (or at least driving) cars too, which gave them new senses of independence and mobility. Now teens no longer had to stay within the confines of their hometown and congregate around a single hangout…. The drive-in theatre also became a more prominent site for youth, where they could show off their cars [and] enjoy a show."[42] Shary highlights the significance of cars to puberty, a relationship that finds its expression time and again in American popular culture. Likewise, Speed observes the continued pervasiveness of transitional spaces, such as malls, parks and diners, in this genre.[43] Their appeal lies in their distance from "the constraints of the family and school"[44] and the car, "where social controls are assumed and felt to be less present,"[45] is vital to their accessibility. Besides bringing to mind the 1950s then, Christine acts as a catalyst for Arnie's immersion in a stylized teen culture of chasing girls—he acquires the attractive Leigh after first acquiring Christine—and the assertion of his burgeoning masculinity.

By invoking teens, suburbia and rock and roll, *Christine* showcases key aspects of an idealized, consumerist version of 1950s American life. The yearning component of this nostalgia, appearing as it does in King's 1983 novel, is no mere coincidence. In her study of the cultural turn to the 1950s, Caputi argues that Americans of the 1970s and 1980s became disillusioned with the uncertainties of late twentieth-century life and therefore looked back with longing to what seemed a simpler time. She ascribes the 1970s rise in neoconservatism, which exhibited retrogressive tendencies, in part to the destabilizing countercultural shifts of the 1960s and 1970s.[46] For many, Caputi argues, the Carter presidency (1977–1981) exacerbated national feelings of failure: "Carter represented the soft-hearted liberal par excellence, whose good intentions and kind manner offered a vision of the presidency that differed from that of his predecessors.... His administration has thus come to be associated not with flexing our collective muscles but with controlling them, not with whetting our imperialist appetite but with curbing it."[47] Carter avoided the overt reference to American exceptionalism so often used by presidents to instill a sense of destiny and strength.[48] Arguably, this style of leadership was a key component of America's "crisis in confidence" in the late 1970s.[49]

Some of these anxieties are palpable in Dennis's early encounters with the car. Not only does Christine seductively embody an earlier era of automotive bliss, in doing so she also lays bare the inadequacies of the time she has come to inhabit:

> The car's wheel was wide and red—a confident wheel. I looked at that amazing speedometer again, that speedometer which was calibrated not to 70 or 80 but all the way up to 120 miles an hour.... No big red 55 on the speedometer, either. Back then, gas went for 29.9 a gallon, maybe less if a price-war happened to be going on in your town. The Arab oil-embargoes and the double-nickel speed limit had still been fifteen years away. *The good old days* [original emphasis] I thought, and had to smile a little [*C*: 34].

Christine, with her unabashed size and strength, is a relic from a time when America felt the same way about itself. In the 1950s, gas was cheap, the interstate network was expanding and automobiles reflected this. Yet the 1970s and 1980s presented a different picture. On January 1, 1974, a nationwide 55-mph speed limit was enforced by President Nixon—an unpopular step taken on the basis of the prospect of a fuel shortage and a long-term energy crisis.[50] These anxieties were compounded when OAPEC,[51] in response to American support for Arab-Israeli conflict in late 1973, imposed oil embargoes on the USA and the Netherlands.[52] Christine thus accentuates the sense of malaise Americans came to feel in the 1970s.

By the time of King's novel, as symbolized by the automobile, the nation's perceptions of itself were changing. Once Arnie's renovation of Christine begins, Dennis contemplates her anew and marvels at the incongruity of this machine, with "tailfins that seemed a thousand miles long. A dinosaur from the dark ditty-bop days of the 50s when all the oil millionaires were from Texas and the Yankee dollar was kicking the shit out of the Japanese yen instead of the other way around" (C: 162). His observations point to anxieties about declines in American industry since Christine's time, a time when fuel still seemed plentiful and the U.S. economy was booming. Late in the tale, Dennis takes a ride in Christine through the ghostly Libertyville of the 1950s with Arnie at the wheel. He sees a wide array of those American-made cars which dominated this bygone era: "Long portholed Buicks. A DeSoto Firelite station wagon with a body-long blue inset that looked like a check-mark. A '57 Dodge Lancer four-door hardtop. Ford Fairlanes with their distinctive taillights, each like a big colon lying on its side. Pontiacs in which the grille had not yet been split. Ramblers, Packards, a few bullet-nosed Studebakers, and once, fantastical and new, an Edsel" (435–436). The American automobile industry was on a downturn by the late 1950s— the unsuccessful 1958 Edsel marked a cultural move away from huge vehicles[53]—and by 1980 Japan was the foremost automobile manufacturer in the world.[54] The excess of vintage American cars featured here emphasizes the change in the nation's fortunes.

Little wonder then, given these anxieties, that Carter was followed by Reagan, an altogether more confident and heroic-seeming figure whose presidential persona was augmented by his Hollywood appeal.

Caputi stresses that Reagan worked to "ostentatiously reassert American military strength, and, importantly, resuscitate the rhetoric of the Cold War—the rhetoric of the 1950s."[55] With an inaugural address that urged Americans to "*go back* to our former identity, search the past for forgotten meanings, and re-create a former, more innocent version of ourselves [original emphasis]"[56] Reagan clearly represented a nostalgic turn in the sense of harking back to a lost golden age.

It has been shown that Christine readily evokes this vanished era. Through LeBay—who dies shortly after selling her—she is also associated with a darker vision of this time, namely the insularity and aggressive militarism of the Cold War. This automobile is a liminal space in which incongruous attitudes towards the 1950s, as an era both idealized and condemned, are played out. Emblematic as he is of the prejudice and discrimination endemic in the fifties, LeBay represents a more sinister brand of longing. Blatantly sexist and racist, on their first meeting he makes apparent to the boys his "contempt for the debased times he had lived to see" (*C*: 10). Tom Engelhardt observes that America has defined itself in terms of a victory culture since its early frontier days of Indian warfare.[57] Arguing that this culture came to an end during the Cold War years, culminating in the conclusion of the Vietnam War in 1975, he remarks: "It is hardly surprising that, after 1975, the basic impulse of America's political and military leaders (as well as of many other Americans) was not to forge a new relationship to the world but to reconstruct a lost identity of triumph."[58] The reactionary LeBay, exuding an embittered sense of longing, stands in for the neoconservative tendencies of the post–Vietnam era. Not merely wistful for a golden age of material abundance, his longing for the past is fueled by hostility towards what he sees as a culturally degenerate present, the inevitable outcome of an increasingly liberal countercultural society.

Thus far, this chapter has focused on the passing of time as a form of loss—the individual loss of youth and the loss of a self-assured postwar America secure in its material wealth and consumer choice. King underscores this tale of transitions by centering much of the narrative on a character type with its roots in 1950s America,[59] a teenager trying to make his way in the world. Allied as they are with the transitional time of adolescence, cars provide liminal spaces in both a physical and a cultural sense. Christine, however, is a liminal space in more ways than one—as she is haunted, her interior literally bridges the gap between past and present as well as between youth and maturity in the usual manner of a teenager's first car. This retrogressive tendency, symbolized by her backwards-running odometer which expunges time rather than recording its progress, will be explored in the next section.

"Horrid Dead Hands"—The Past as Threat

King's novel exhibits nostalgia in the sense of craving. Drake's argument, introduced earlier, suggests, however, that nostalgia is often entangled with ambivalence about the past. As he puts it, nostalgia can be "emblematic of an engrossing but ultimately fabricated approximation of the past."[60] Such ambivalence is played out in this novel. However, rather than seeing the acknowledgment that nostalgic views of the past might rely on fabrication as indicative of a total lack of engagement with history, I argue that *Christine* provides a comment on the effects of nostalgia in late twentieth-century American culture. Yet King's take is paradoxical, as he both condemns and celebrates the past. Having shown nostalgia as longing at work here, this second section will focus on how the past acts as a source of anxiety for many of the characters, which the full impact of the car's haunting power works to reveal.

Like *The Shining*, *Christine* is steeped in specific historical references and preoccupied with a broader process of reflecting on the past. Though the reader is made privy to little of their work, Arnie's parents, Michael and Regina, as a history professor and an English literature professor respectively, share Jack Torrance's inclination towards the study of history. Regina, by far the more dominant of the two, has her subject "refined and calibrated like a blip on a radar screen" (*C*: 19). In a conflation of academic with parental discipline, she and her husband seek to manage history in the same anxious way that they manage their son. Perhaps unsurprisingly, given his experience of haunting, Dennis reveals in the epilogue that he has made history his chosen profession. History thus becomes an uneasy attempt to understand the world, as well as to exert a measure of control over aspects of it, for these characters.

It is Christine through which anxiety about the past is conveyed most acutely. Despite its positive associations, the car unsettles Dennis from the first. And Christine's interior soon reveals a less palatable sensory environment than the pleasingly retro one described in the previous section. She emits "a rotten, thick smell ... as if, at some time, something had crawled into the car and died there" (205–206). This lends her classic status a sinister aspect. Further, though initially quirky, her preference for rock and roll becomes an ominous ritual: "Sometimes all that Christine's radio would pick up was WDIL. It didn't matter what buttons you pushed or how much you fooled with the FM converter under the dashboard; it was WDIL or nothing" (276). These features form the backdrop to one of the novel's most vivid episodes of horror. Leigh, who feels an instinctive loathing for the car, almost chokes to death inside it. Once glamorous, its age comes to suggest both decrepitude and threat as it is slowly revealed as something akin to a dilapidated haunted house.

The Plymouth's ability to provide her passengers with access to the past culminates with a chilling incident late in the tale. Dennis accepts a lift from Arnie in Christine and sees for himself how the 1950s have endured. As in the Overlook Hotel, the liminality of the haunted car scrambles chronology to ghastly, unsettling effect. Indeed, it is primarily the simultaneity of eras which seems so shocking: "We went back in time, I have said, but did we? The present-day streets of Libertyville were still there, but they were like a thin overlay of film—it was as if the Libertyville of the late 1970s had been drawn on Saran Wrap and laid over a time that was somehow more real, and I could feel that time reaching its dead hands out toward us, trying to catch us and draw us in forever" (435). This passage illustrates that *Christine* is bound up with the wider nostalgic turn of the 1970s identified by the likes of Jameson and Caputi. The boys' hometown becomes a horrifying palimpsest as, through the Gothic trope of haunting, its 1950s past is revealed to still be occupying the same physical space as that of its present. This past, to which any return is felt by Dennis to be a threat, rather than a blessing, is still so apparently vital as to render the passage of time almost negligible.

Here, the liminal properties of the haunted car show the lingering spirit of the 1950s as a source of unmitigated horror. Far from promising a return to a simpler, happier time, this version of the past is a voracious and deadly trap. So Christine sets in motion two different versions of her glory days. In this scene, the car shows a past suffocating in its omnipresence as Dennis's anxiety that this "pre–60s" time is "more real" (435) than his own reinforces. In depicting the nostalgic turn of the time in which his novel appeared in the form of an ominous haunting, King denounces it as a regressive and stultifying tendency. Although he offers no specific examples, John Sears also detects a critique of "reactionary nostalgia"[61] at work in *Christine*, and I argue that this scene best epitomizes this tendency. In the novel's haunted spaces the past is literally re-enacted, yet it is a past which holds different meanings for different people. The liminality of haunting allows diverse, sometimes conflicting, visions of the 1950s to coalesce. Specifically here, it provides a narrative space that speaks to King's conflicted state over late twentieth-century attitudes toward the past.

It gradually transpires that the car is possessed by LeBay and, through it, so is its new owner. Having been identified so closely with her first owner in life, Christine seems the natural place for his spirit to take refuge after death. In life and after death, LeBay is defined by his status as a military man almost as much as by his fixation with the car he anthropomorphizes. An Army man from his 1920s youth, he served in World War II and Korea. Introducing himself proudly to the boys as "U.S. Army, retired," (C: 9), he launches directly into wartime reminiscences. Later, Dennis scathingly reflects on the older man's bluster and inflects the phrase "the good old days" to load it with cynicism. He pictures LeBay "coming home from the VFW hall after a night of drinking boilermakers and telling stories about the Battle of the Bulge or Pork Chop Hill. The good old days, when a man could see Europe, the Pacific, and the mysterious East from behind the sight of a bazooka" (33). After his death, LeBay haunts his car in an "Army uniform that was spotted and splotched with blue-gray patches of graveyard mould" (262) and in a suit festooned with medals (335). The recurring martial aspect of his haunting, coupled with his scorn for the America of the 1970s, provides a Gothic enactment of the cultural anxiety detected by Engelhardt.

Roland D. LeBay's vision of the 1950s is one on which many would look back with trepidation. As a "Cold Warrior"[62] figure, he represents an aggressively militaristic past lamenting the downfall of a more confident era. His perspective of how the past relates to the present is one shared by 1970s neoconservatism. Regina and Michael, still "into doing good" (C: 18) from the days of their countercultural youth, would find this vision repugnant. So Christine sets free a past which the likes of Arnie's liberal parents hoped would be eradicated by the social changes of the 1960s and 1970s. As a ghostly Cold Warrior, LeBay thus represents a Gothic return of that which was anticipated to have been repressed.

I join with Linda C. Badley, who sees LeBay as a "classic case of arrested development."[63] His brother George describes him as a violent bully consumed by his loathing of "the shitters" (*C*: 98), meaning anyone who provoked his ire. The embodiment of extreme hostility, although a lifelong Army man, he is defined by his isolation—remembered without affection by other members of Libertyville American Legion—and was unable to progress through the ranks because of his misanthropy. Preferring machines to people, his sole ambition was to own a new car: Christine. Emotionally stunted, he allowed his family—his future—to be destroyed. He held no affection for his young daughter who choked to death in Christine, or for his wife who committed suicide in the vehicle shortly after. George conveys that LeBay's obsession with Christine apparently led to his placing the dying girl, "as some kind of a human sacrifice" (453), within the car, where the spirits of both females linger. LeBay's complicity with his car in these deaths is a grim enactment of the tension between cars as family spaces, as opposed to spaces of individual gratification. His failure to embrace an unselfish life is vividly depicted by the corpse-like form of his ghost.

LeBay's aggressive brand of conservatism permeates the vehicle and Arnie comes to absorb it. Motivated by the older man's childish impulses, the teen becomes coarse and cynical, ever combative and unable to reciprocate the affections of family and friends. He remains mired in the liminal state, powerless to transcend the haunting or progress through adolescence, up to the time when Christine's rampages lead him into a fatal crash. Arnie's endeavors to control his life make his premature death all the more poignant. As Tom Newhouse notes, his "short-lived transition from outsider to social participant"[64] is a mere illusion. Like Jack Torrance, Arnie's accessing of the past through haunted space seems to offer him agency, although any real power is ultimately denied to them both. Flashes of the real Arnie—as opposed to the version of him perverted by LeBay—are occasionally apparent, as when he shyly confides to Dennis his delight in courting Leigh. Such episodes, combined with his efforts to assert independence, indicate that his ultimate goal is to progress to maturity. Unlike the eternally juvenile LeBay, Arnie desires to be accepted by his peers—to nurture friendships, form romantic attachments and be accepted as an adult. The 1950s Plymouth adverts promised progress, with claims like "when you drive a PLYMOUTH suddenly it's 1960"[65] and "Plymouth leaps three full years ahead—the *only* car that dares to break the time barrier!"[66] One such progressive slogan—"The car that's *going places with the Young in Heart*"[67]—is ironic given Christine's regressive impulses. King thus uses this aspect of her haunting to depict reactionary nostalgic tendencies as harmful, as they effectively work to halt Arnie's maturation.

The car, with the freedom and youth that it symbolizes, attracts LeBay, who cares nothing for Arnie's future and seeks a return to his own past. Christine enables this through permitting him to possess the teen. However, her malevolent will and haunting powers seem to elude LeBay's control. As a portal into a wider history that inevitably exceeds his own narrow vision of the past, she unleashes aspects of the 1950s which he seems unlikely to have intended or approved. Delineating Arnie's doomed quest for independence, Badley observes that he "reverts, at first into a slightly tougher, older self (and to the horror of his conscientious vegetarian ex-hippie parents): a greaser, the 'jd monster.'"[68] As a latter-day juvenile delinquent, the figure which dominated teen film from the mid–1950s,[69] Arnie actually comes to represent yet another aspect of the 1950s. Suggestive of the troubled element of that era's youth, seen at the time as a "threat to the social order,"[70] Arnie becomes—also through Christine—an image of the 1950s LeBay would regard with disquiet.

Michael and Regina clearly struggle with this also. They find Arnie's regression unbearable; the changes Christine wreaks in him tear the family apart. He loses all interest in planning for a future beyond spending time with Leigh and with his car. His parents watch in horror as their bright, formerly diligent son jeopardizes his—*their*—plans for a college education and all it promises to bring. The juvenile delinquents of the 1950s, so appealing in their rebelliousness to the youth of that era, can be seen as precursors to the Woodstock generation of the following decade.[71] Yet despite their countercultural past, which was similarly characterized by a youthful resistance to authority, Arnie's parents are unable to cope with the newfound rebellion of their own child, which is rooted in the nascent countercultural drives Jameson associates with the 1950s. These diverse historical impulses are set in motion through the liminality of haunting. It is through the haunted house motif that the inconsistencies in King's attitudes towards them are revealed.

For example, although *Christine* critiques the longing, nostalgic views of the 1950s that emerged in the decades after, there are nonetheless signs that King has a yen for aspects of that time. The contrast between the boys' families, which in many ways drives the narrative, illustrates this. The Cunningham home, with its 1970s liberal ethos and dual income, is fundamentally flawed. Schopp decries it as a "monstrous perversion of the ideal family."[72] He argues that, because she exerts her will over that of her permanently-cowed husband, it is the castrating Regina with her masculine wielding of power—rather than Christine or LeBay—who truly endangers Arnie.[73] By contrast the more traditional Guilder family, with Dennis's father at its head, is a harmonious and nurturing environment which produces two well-balanced children. So, even as *Christine* warns against longing for the 1950s, it seems to uphold certain elements of that era. Despite her forcefulness, I would argue that Regina's threat is minor in comparison with that posed by LeBay and exercised through his car. Yet King undoubtedly makes this liberated 1970s woman seem monstrous and, ultimately, the Cunninghams' progressive liberalism fails their son.

Writing on post–World War II cultural trends, Lawrence Grossberg argues that this was a time when America started to move from infancy to authority. Like a teen, the nation was coming to terms with its changing status and therefore with a new identity. As he puts it, America was "the kid among nations who had suddenly grown up and become the leader."[74] Developments of this nature have been detected in American culture throughout the middle part of the twentieth century. For example, in discussing *Christine*, Michael R. Collings casts the 1950s as just such a time. He asserts that "the America of the late seventies perceived itself as mature. It had, after all, successfully negotiated the turmoil of the sixties ... and it had begun looking back on the 1950s as a time of adolescence preparatory to entry into adulthood."[75] While the bicentennial was certainly a milestone year, it is debatable that the sixties had been "successfully negotiated," as observations about 1970s malaise and the rise of a backwards-looking neoconservatism imply otherwise.

Rather, the 1970s was a time when America was still struggling to establish how best to define itself.

Building on this, I argue that the arrested development inflicted on Arnie, as discussed above, mirrors the stultifying effect that being haunted by the 1950s has for late twentieth-century American culture. Many have decried the era, with its pronounced consumerism, as one characterized by an unhealthy conformity. With widespread prejudices along race, class and gender lines as yet unchallenged by the 1960s, the 1950s were not a golden age for all Americans. Overall, the turn to this decade dramatized in *Christine* is poisonous, stunting and deadly. It ensnares people in a past that prevents progress or maturation of any kind. Earlier, it was noted that cars are linked to adolescence and development because they connote freedom. Yet, as David Laird observes of cars in modern American fiction, freedom may have negative implications if it leads to evading social responsibility as opposed to merely being temporarily excused from it.[76] Here, the liminality of haunting ensnares Arnie and removes him from society altogether.

Conclusion

As a late twentieth-century Gothic tale, bound up with history and centered on the haunting powers of a vintage car, *Christine* works to stage the diverse views of the 1950s that had emerged by the late–1970s and early–1980s context in which the story is told. Dennis, a reflective narrator in the mold of King's author protagonists such as Gordie Lachance of "The Body" (1982) and Bill Denborough of *IT* (1986), describes the powers exerted by a haunted space that conjures up an era with profound continued significance for Americans in the latter part of the twentieth century. He recounts the story of a friend who, in trying to assert his independence, reaches out to a potent symbol of agency and progress in American culture—the automobile. Christine, as a liminal arena for the historical forces of the era that she calls to mind, unleashes varied aspects of that past. Her new owner, Arnie, is caught up in these forces and, trapped by her haunting power, remains in the liminal state.

Christine is obviously concerned with adolescence and with the part played by cars in American youth culture. However, as with other haunted tales discussed in this study, the novel also represents a working through of wider cultural issues with deep historical roots. Its characters, contending with the legacy of the past, reveal the extent to which haunting can be both a personal and a cultural experience. Utilizing some of the conventions of nostalgia texts, *Christine* dramatizes the effects of nostalgia as longing. Beyond this, and in keeping with developing academic understandings of the nature and uses of nostalgia, it can also be seen that King's novel casts such longing as a deadly force, one injurious to progress.

With regard to the former impulse, *Christine* indexes—through such literary devices as a nostalgic narrator and the haunted Christine herself—the ostensibly peaceful and prosperous post-war era towards which American culture has come to look back, fondly, upon as a golden age. Born in 1947, King was a child of the 1950s. It hardly seems surprising therefore—especially given his propensity, following the lead of Richard Matheson, for setting his horror firmly in the context of everyday experience—that *Christine* conveys affection for the time in which he himself was growing up. Though a young man rather than a child during this decade, Matheson uses his tales of haunting to reveal a similar fondness for the fifties as well as a yearning for them, as in *Earthbound*, towards the close of the twentieth century.

However, beyond her ability to summon up this potent period, Christine also encapsulates late 1970s and 1980s debates about this point in American history. Besides the popular perception of a happy and settled age, characterized by material wealth and underpinned by traditional family values, the fifties also came to be construed as a stifling time of constraint, riddled with conformism and hampered by convention. Though fresh from a conservative, small-town upbringing, King's time at college in the late 1960s gave him a sense of political awareness that stayed with him into adulthood and translated into a "strong undercurrent of liberal social values throughout his work."[77] Because of this, *Christine* also exhibits an anxiety about harking back to the very time from which the counterculture movement sought to move away.

Here, as elsewhere, the liminality of haunting affords a portal into the politics of the times it portrays, as King—like Lovecraft—uses his haunted spaces to convey intensely-competing attitudes towards this emotionally-charged era. Through Christine, even while upholding certain elements of the privileged past of her prime, King critiques nostalgic tendencies. The incursion of the past into the present, facilitated by the haunted car and reinforced by the specter of her dead owner, is associated with regression, destruction and even death. As such, the haunting of *Christine* illustrates that looking back—however tempting—may not only be misguided, it may also be harmful.

CHAPTER SIX

"It's my house, isn't it?"

Memory, Identity and Haunting
in Bag of Bones

Rich in historical referencing and lavish in its local detailing, *Bag of Bones* (1998) presents an in-depth study of the underbelly of small-town Maine life. Of crucial importance to this study is the way in which this later King novel, which has received only scant attention from scholars, uses the device of a haunted house to consider how the past lingers to inform and shape the present. As the novel progresses, the protagonist's experiences bring to light the brutal rape of an African American woman, Sara Tidwell, and the subsequent murder of her and her son some hundred years before. So themes common to American Gothic forms—shared responsibility and collective guilt over slavery and race—are brought to the fore.

The house and its environs here act as liminal space; caught between past and present, the living and the dead, they provide a transitional area in which traumatic memories are continually thrust back upon the community responsible until they are finally re-lived and relieved. The key Gothic theme that "the sins of the father are visited on the offspring"[1] is certainly borne out by the events of this narrative. Haunting here functions to transmit memory and shape identity, and there is a clear sense of the collective: collective aggression, collective guilt and a collective punishment which is not only shared by the guilty community itself but also passed down to its descendants. One of those ghosts who, in the words of Lois Parkinson Zamora, act as "reminders of communal crimes, crises, cruelties,"[2] Sara has been instrumental in perpetuating this legacy.

Underneath these themes of haunting, memory and identity lies the idea of liminality. For Victor Turner, a vital attribute of the liminal experience is its separation from everyday life. This isolation provides liminars with the opportunity to encounter, perhaps through confrontation, wider mysteries that will help them return to society as more enlightened individuals.[3] Liminal space here, most obviously, takes the form of a haunted log cabin. As a vacation retreat, this building functions as a space apart from everyday routine, one in which the boundaries and interactions between life and death, past and present, unearthly and earthly can be explored. Associated from the beginning of the novel with dreams—themselves a special kind of liminal experience—and bound up with ghostly powers and presences, it is a place that comes to signify transition and to offer privileged insight into the history it contains.

Gina Wisker points to the horror genre's potential for disrupting the borderline between reality and fantasy as well as to the pleasure that can be taken from its destabilizing force, which provides readers with a "cultural critique disturbing complacencies and fixities."[4] David A. Oakes highlights the genre's continued potential for such interrogative activity in maintaining that "although its forms appear vastly different than they did in the eighteenth century, the haunted castle continues to serve as a crucial tool in the process of destabilization."[5] I maintain here, as I have throughout this book, that haunted space is intrinsically liminal in nature; in straddling normally-distinct physical, psychological and chronological states, it certainly proves to be a destabilizing influence. *Bag of Bones* works chiefly to challenge its protagonist's preconceptions about his own life.

Once more, the liminality of the haunted house motif generates a narrative arena in which to encounter and reflect upon history. As has ever been the case in this study, haunting here throws up the tensions embedded in twentieth-century American culture. Looking back to Fiedler's view of early American Gothic as a conservative form—particularly in terms of attitudes towards race—from the vantage point of the turn of the twenty-first century, *Bag of Bones* represents a marked shift away from such a reactionary stance, as its haunting functions to condemn racially-motivated violence and to give the wronged Sara a voice. The only King novel examined here with what can be construed as a happy ending—the protagonist not only survives his experience, but learns from it and is able to progress in a positive fashion as a result—

Bag of Bones offers closure. However, as is the case with Matheson's novels, the relatively neat ending threatens to belie the complexity of the history conveyed in the tale. Haunting here thus releases the complex ideologies inherent in shifting social attitudes while also demonstrating the challenges in dealing with such history.

"She had marked his passing"— Memory and Identity

Bag of Bones centers on middle-aged author Mike Noonan, self-acknowledged "V.C. Andrews with a prick."[6] Comparisons between Mike and Jack Torrance from *The Shining*, as fellow writers, reveal much about King's changing attitudes to his craft and its place in his life. Reflective of the twenty-one year gap between the publication of the two novels, and the transformation in King's own authorial status between them, Jack is an up-and-coming young author while Mike is a seasoned publisher of bestsellers. Widowed at the outset, Mike's attempts to cope with his grief and restore his life to some kind of normality form the basis of the narrative.

Having completed a novel in September 1994, one month after his wife, Jo, is buried, he undergoes a physically debilitating and emotionally demoralizing form of writer's block. After the passage of four years, during which he experiences many detailed and terrifying dreams on the subject, Mike feels that the time has come to reacquaint himself with the log cabin retreat called Sara Laughs which he and his wife once shared: "I was decided: I'd go back to the place my subconscious mind had identified as shelter against the deepening dark; I'd go back even though my mind had also suggested that doing so would not be without risks. I would not go back expecting Sara to be Lourdes ... but I would allow myself to hope, and when I saw the evening star peeping out over the lake for the first time, I would allow myself to wish on it [original ellipses]" (*BB*: 63). There is thus a suggestion that Mike returns to this place willingly, yet perhaps not entirely of his own volition. This is confirmed later in the narrative when his brother-in-law Frank tells him that Jo had felt that the house held a supernatural influence over her husband: "She said that when it wanted you, it called you" (343).

This place has never been a permanent home, but rather a vacation residence. This seems significant in terms of the transient nature of the shelter it provides its residents. Not permanently occupied, it has always represented a retreat from the Noonans' daily grind, a place apart in which they were able to escape from the real business of living and working in order to relax. On this basis, it seems a site with inherent liminal potential. Yet this rural resting place proves to be anything but peaceful. Instead, it functions as a site of supernatural horror both physically dangerous—Mike experiences drowning—and psychologically disturbing when the horror of the past is truly brought home to the present.

Mike's reflection on his impetus to return to the house raises several interesting trains of thought, which are variously examined as the tale continues. The repeated phraseology "I'd go back" suggests the idea of literally revisiting a formerly frequently-visited place and, in doing so, re-examining old physical and emotional territory—an idea which lends itself very readily to Gothic notions of confronting the past. The mention of the "subconscious mind" is also highly suggestive of haunting, with its connotations of hidden impulses that shape behavior on the basis of buried, perhaps long-past, events. Further to this, it also has Freudian connotations. Freud's designation of the uncanny "as something which ought to have remained hidden but has come to light,"[7] linked as it is to the return of the repressed, underscores the sense that some past secret is set to be stirred up. It is precisely such an impulse that propels this tale of haunting. Indeed, Mike does appear to be drawn back to Sara Laughs by a potent mix of memory and yearning, and despite his strong suspicion that returning there might mean facing emotional discomfort and real physical peril. In identifying this place as a refuge from the depression and torpor that engulf him after his bereavement, Mike acknowledges the existence of certain dark forces which, although not known to be supernatural at this point, will ultimately demand to be confronted and exorcised as such.

Upon his arrival, Mike inadvertently becomes embroiled in a legal battle involving Max Devore, a powerful local business tycoon, and Devore's daughter-in-law, Mattie. Since the death of Mattie's husband, Lance Devore, Max has sought to obtain custody of granddaughter Kyra. Initially it would seem that this case, distraction as it is from Mike's troubled personal and working life, is to be the main thrust of the narrative. His desire to help a young family stay together, coupled with his growing attraction to Mattie, combine to create an interesting, if rather more conventional, narrative than the supernatural tale discovered to be underpinning it. Eventually Mike learns that he is related to one of those who joined Max Devore's ancestor, Jared, in an attack on a local woman and her son and, through a supernatural legacy, he may well be destined to take Kyra's life. This novel appears to be a romantic drama, while these strands turn out to be only part of a much wider narrative. As Sharon A. Russell remarks, "While *Bag of Bones* is a ghost story, it is also a mystery."[8] The true story—the tragic one of Sara—is revealed only at the end, contingent as it is upon the untangling of confused memories, dreams and ghostly visions, and the liminality of the haunted house motif is crucial to this revelation.

King scholar Tony Magistrale has observed the author's proclivity for depicting "the local raw materials of a cold climate, and the specificity of place that set his readers firmly in a rural Maine world."[9] King works hard here to create an atmosphere evocative of authentic New England. Dark Score Lake, on the shores of which Sara Laughs sits, is relatively isolated, "a place so far up in the western Maine woods that it's not really even in a town at all, but in an unincorporated area designated on state maps as TR-90" (*BB*: 32), or even simply as "the TR" (82). This densely-wooded lakeside community is certainly suggestive of the kind of precarious, remote wilderness settlements so prevalent in early American Gothic. Settings close to nature, and thus on the edges of civilized space, point to lingering fears about the vulnerability of isolated communities from the founding days of the nation.[10] The cobbled-together Sara Laughs itself is an interesting amalgam of different historical periods and the residents that might be said to typify these. At first its history does not appear to be well known, but seems both extensive and troubled, as Mike notes, "The central portion of Sara—the heart of the house—had stood for almost a hundred years and had seen its share of storms" (*BB*: 438). This cabin provides a focal point for much of the supernatural activity that follows.

If "how a nation manipulates and preserves its place and feature names says a lot about its respect for history, minority rights, and indigenous culture,"[11] then the issue of place-names and community in the fictional TR speaks volumes about the impact of its historical treatment of Sara Tidwell and her family. The community's lack of a title, and thus of any of the usual descriptive terminology to help differentiate it from neighboring townships, is highly suggestive. Without an actual name, it somehow seems without character. Anthropologists Pamela J. Stewart and Andrew Strathern highlight the universal centrality of place naming to identity with their assertion that "an important aspect of how landscapes gain their meanings has to do with naming. The names of locations within areas record the forms of human experience that have occurred within them."[12] So the absence of a name for this longstanding community, at least a century old, is improbable and ultimately unconvincing in its implied lack of history: surely there is something to distinguish the area?

Work on landscape and identity suggests that town names may function to transmit memory and tradition.[13] It has been widely acknowledged that the names of places are often used to commemorate the lives and deeds of residents and of their ancestors.[14] The lack of an agreed-upon name for the TR thus suggests a crisis in the shared memory of the township. Unable to acknowledge their past, let alone venerate it, the locals here betray their inability to own their identity by refusing to give their home a name. They may be desirous of hiding their past but, as an understanding of such work on landscape reveals, avoidance of naming is not a strategy that will achieve this. Rather, it flags up the very fissures in their relationship to the land around them.

Despite the area's apparent lack of significance, a certain distinctiveness has clearly been long-imposed upon it by the strong-willed spirit of Sara Tidwell, the turn-of-the-century black blues-style singer who lived there with her family and friends, and whose name associates her so closely with the home of Mike and Jo. So clearly defined is her identity that it isn't even her official name that persists in accounts of her life and music. Her personality transcends this and she achieves the nickname that the Noonans' house eventually acquires: Sara Laughs. Throughout the novel, and over the century since her death, Sara is given the power to name, even from beyond the grave, while the community she haunts remains forever nameless and seemingly powerless to resist her interventions. Though the local community remains nameless, Sara's home bears her name still. Denied the opportunity to commemorate her, and her family's, connection to TR-90 through conventional channels—Mike discovers that they have effectively been omitted from local histories—she is forced to find a way around those. And the Gothic mode permits such an action: the liminal nature of the trope of haunting permits her to engage the reader directly with her untold story.

Naming and identity are both strong themes in this work. Eventually Mike ascertains, as did Jo before him, that Sara's legacy has endured through the act of haunting: her lingering presence causes the long-standing community members to name their offspring in memory of her murdered son, Kito. Observing the prevalence in the phone book of first names beginning with K among the long-time residents of the TR, Mike gradually perceives the full extent of Sara's influence. He specifically labels her actions as commemorative, describing how Kito's name lived on: "She had marked his passing. Memorialized it … almost every longtime family in this part of the world had, in one way or another, named at least one child after Sara Tidwell's dead son" (*BB*: 400). Tellingly, he learns that when she died, Jo was pregnant with a daughter on which she and Mike had always planned to bestow the "African name" (103) of Kia. These discoveries function to bring the full impact of Sara's and Kito's haunting behavior home to the reader; their influence can be seen traced throughout the community both physically, in the actual names of the children, and psychologically, as the memory of the crime still echoes for the descendants of the perpetrators. Clearly, naming and its significance is a key theme in this novel. The TR continues to be identified with and haunted by Sara's presence because of this.

The novel engages directly with one of the key themes of American Gothic fiction—the legacy of slavery and attendant fears and prejudices surrounding the figure of the African American.[15] Maine has long been favored by King as a setting for personal reasons, but the choice of a northern location is an interesting one for this turn-of-the-century tale of racially-motivated violence. The extended African American family who settled in the TR during this post–Reconstruction/Great Migration era, described by historian Rayford Logan as "the nadir of American race relations,"[16] clearly failed to find the kind of welcome that might have been hoped for. The impact of decades of racial segregation has long been a defining feature of American Gothic, so this combination of time and space is one with particular resonance. As Mike (and, through him, the reader) gradually unearths the story of the Tidwells, evidence of prejudice and racism in the TR's past comes to light. Mike reflects on what he has heard of their initial settlement on their lakeside land purchase: "There had been a vast uproar about it in town, and even a meeting to protest 'the advent of these darkies, which come in a Horde'" (*BB:* 170).

After Kyra's mother, Mattie, has been shot and killed by local residents on behalf of the late Max Devore, Mike takes the child back to Sara Laughs—wrongly believing that he is motivated to do so for her protection—and begins to experience the full impact of the ghostly presences that have long surrounded this place. Despite the local inhabitants' early reservations about hosting the Tidwell community in their midst, Mike's supernatural confrontation with a spectral composite of Max Devore and Max's great-grandfather, Jared, reveals that many in the TR actually came to accept them. This was the real source of contention for Jared, who avows to Mike and to his ghostly consorts that "*he never fought that war to free the damned slaves. They can keep slaves down there in the land of cotton until the end of the eternity, as far as Jared Lancelot Devore is concerned*" (473). Confronting the specter of Max, Mike taunts him: "That was what Jared hated most of all, wasn't it? That they didn't turn aside, didn't turn away. She walked on The Street and no one treated her like a nigger. They treated her like a neighbor" (474). As this pivotal scene unfolds, Mike's altercation with "Max-Jared" (470) takes him back to the lakeside in the summer of 1901. Having instilled a paranoid, racist antipathy towards the Tidwell family within the young men of the TR, Devore seeks to put "*uppity bitch*" (473) Sara in her place. Kito, witness to the rape of his mother, is murdered along with her, and their bodies are buried nearby.

Although not foregrounded in the narrative, racism, as with other of the novel's themes, emerges as a key aspect of the story. The hate crime against Sara Tidwell can ultimately be seen as instigating all the other central events of the narrative: Jo's death, Mike's return to the TR and the tragedy of Kyra being orphaned. Only when the nature and details of the crime come to light—along with the exhumation of Sara's and Kito's corpses—does the full story come to be understood. Mike's recurrent description of "the TR crisscrossed with invisible cables, connections that were unseen but as strong as steel" (259) can be seen as an apt metaphor for the nature of the story King is writing about Mike. With this revelation the guilt of the community becomes clear. As Sara is attacked she reflects *"that when men are together like this and full of redeye (she can smell it), they give up thinking for themselves and turn into a pack of dogs"* [original emphasis] (475). At this moment the inherited nature of what the TR has come to stand for crystallizes in Mike's mind: it is a place consumed by the horror of its own communal and historical transgressions.

Contextualized within this history of racism, Sara's supernatural ability to influence the names given by her assailants to their descendants comes to seem particularly salient, especially given the way in which early African American slaves were forced to relinquish their own names in deference to their masters. John C. Inscoe has described the practice of re-naming slaves in the Carolinas:

> Practically all Africans arriving in the New World as slaves found themselves assigned new names in a language they did not understand and derived from a culture equally as foreign to them. A few of these captives stubbornly resisted these new labels and clung to their original names, but the vast majority came not only to accept these strange names but to perpetuate them by passing them on to their children as well. For this reason Anglo-American names dominated slave nomenclature throughout the almost two hundred years in which slavery existed in the Carolinas.[17]

Inherent in this observation is the idea that inflicting a name upon an individual—or a group of individuals—is tantamount to deconstructing and re-designating their identity. In the case of these newly-enslaved people, it was arguably part of an entire process of integration. It certainly can be seen that names have long been used as a device to label; they designate property and assign ownership.

This is particularly interesting here, as Sara's legacy of naming can be seen as a kind of reversal of this process. Whereas slaves began to pass on Anglo-American names to their offspring, it is Kito's decidedly non-American name—angrily denounced by Jared Devore as a *"black-nigger African name"* (*BB*: 473)—which is passed on to the children of the TR. Sara's ghostly enforced naming demonstrates the way in which the community's treatment of her links their mutual destinies. In the same way that Anglo-American identity became inscribed on the children of African slaves, the African identity of Sara and her family becomes indelibly conferred upon the TR. Her ghostly presence reverses her earlier dominance by the white townsfolk and, in so doing, reverses the process of cultural dominance normally associated with the white community rather than with the black one—her haunting is the Gothic return of that which was believed to be repressed.

That naming relates intimately to identity and power relations is also widely discussed.[18] Kimberly W. Benston discusses the key role of naming in slave narratives: "In the narratives of Frederick Douglass and William Wells Brown, for example, the moment when freedom is finally felt to be irrevocable coincides precisely with a ceremonious exchange of slave surname for an agnomen designating a literally liberated 'self,'"[19] making the argument for "the inevitable legacy of naming as an inaugural mark of enslavement."[20] While most emphatically not a slave narrative, and very far from being one as the characters are all fictional and their stories are told in a novel written by a white male author, Sara's story represents a popular cultural engagement with these themes. It raises issues of naming and of passing on names to future generations, as well as exploring how this process has been bound up with culture, identity and power relations over the centuries.

As a popular Gothic novel, *Bag of Bones* is not only distinct from other literary treatments of these themes in terms of its origins, it also treats its subject matter in a far from conventional way. Sara's story is communicated as a disrupted narrative, as it results from the intervention of several sources gathered together over an extended period of time—it comes to light through a combination of memory, dreams, and the research of local history such as newspaper clippings, as well as personal encounters with ghostly presences. How King uses the latter source, drawing on the Gothic mode in general and the trope of haunted space in particular, will be the next focus.

"In the zone"—The power of haunting

The haunted space of the Noonans' vacation home is a liminal arena in which Mike is obliged to confront his ancestral link to a collective past with far-reaching social and historical implications. As a space which links past and present, Sara Laughs is a relatively modern version of the haunted castle of Gothic fiction that originated with Horace Walpole[21] and the sole example in this study of King using a haunted home—as opposed to other kinds of space—as a novel's setting. Much is made of the fact that Mike goes to Sara Laughs as a refuge, but in doing so is forced to confront a troubled past. Mark Jancovich observes that the image of "the house as a monstrous place within which the self is either imprisoned or lost" has endured from the early days of the Gothic into twentieth-century popular fiction by the likes of King.[22] For Mike, this house—long-valued as a "hideout" (*BB*: 32) and, in recent years, cherished for its memories of time spent with Jo—becomes precisely one such site of mystery and menace through the liminality of haunting. It is only when he returns to the TR that he is finally able to confront the past: a past that is actually shaping and motivating his future, as Jo had suspected and feared.

The first example of the Gothic trope of haunting is Mike's dreams—or rather nightmares—of visits to the TR. Though these initially seem to spring simply from the awfulness of his bereavement, it can eventually be seen that these act as extensions of the liminal powers of the haunted space itself: "In the Sara dreams, the major elements were the woods behind me, the house below me, and Michael Noonan himself, frozen in the middle. It's getting dark and there's danger in the woods. It will be frightening to go to the house below, perhaps because it's been empty so long, but I never doubt I must go there; scary or not, it's the only shelter I have" (61). Of course, the content and symbolism here eventually become clear—in providing the impetus for his return to the log cabin, the dreams ensure he is physically in the place through which Sara can use him to exact her revenge. There are many and varied examples of haunting behaviors throughout the novel, including poltergeist activity, automatic writing and inexplicable drowning sensations, among others. The clearest examples in terms of narrative occur when Mike is transported back to the first twentieth-century Fryeburg Fair—where he sees Sara onstage with her band, the Red-Tops—and later when he has the supernatural confrontation with "Max-Jared," along with the ancestors of other TR residents. Here, Mike finally sees for himself how they raped and killed Sara, drowned her child and then concealed the bodies, giving her ample reason to seek retribution.

A further key supernatural element pertains to Mike's authorial activity. For both of King's writer protagonists studied here, the liminal powers of haunting extend to those times when they are engaged in their craft. As examined in *The Shining* chapter, ghostly presences communicate with Jack through his writing and, on overcoming his writer's block, Mike experiences the same phenomenon. A distinctive version of liminality appears here in the form of the alternative mental state that he calls "the zone" (427). He first uses this term to describe his work routine as being "in the writing zone" (149), then later applies the shortened form "the zone" to his encounters with the supernatural. When he starts to interact with the magnetic letters on his fridge, through which he has received messages from the ghosts within the cabin, he observes: "From there I went somewhere else. I don't know where, exactly, because I was tranced out, that intuitive part of my mind up so high a search-party couldn't have found it. I stood in front of my fridge and played with the letters, spelling out little pieces of thought without even thinking about them. You mightn't believe such a thing is possible, but every writer knows it is" (302). The first-person narration style, which is not typical of King, destabilizes the reader once the liminality of haunting takes hold of Mike. Initially, he is largely aware of his tendency to enter this state, but gradually his dipping in and out of the zone compromises the reliability of his narration, as when he believes that taking Kyra to Sara Laughs will help protect her. Examples of those "sleep-like and deathlike states" that Eve Kosofsky Sedgwick sees as typically–Gothic devices,[23] these episodes show the extent to which, once subjected to the liminal experience, Mike's thoughts and behaviors are vulnerable to Sara's ghostly interventions.

In her account of Gothic conventions, Sedgwick includes among their number "such framing devices as found manuscripts."[24] Jo's benevolent spirit—in trying to break Sara's curse by preparing Mike to combat the latter's vengeful ghost—is able to embed messages to him within his work as he writes. As the tale moves to its climax, Jo directs her husband's attention to just one such collection of historical documents, which she collected some months before and placed inside an owl statue to protect them from Sara's spirit. On their retrieval, Mike attains a fuller picture of the TR's history and his own implication in it: "Inside the hole was a small tin box that I recognized.... I shone the lantern on its front, knowing what I'd see: JO'S NOTIONS, written in old-fashioned gilt script.... I spread my hand over the cover and pulled it off. There was a strew of folded papers ... mostly photocopied press clippings from the *Castle Rock Call* and from the *Weekly News*, the paper which had apparently preceded the *Call*" (*BB*: 457–458). These documents comprise reviews of the Red-Tops—characterized by a tone of "unfailing genial contempt" (458)—an article about the 1930s wildfire that allegedly killed the young daughter of Fred Dean, one of Sara's attackers, and research revealing Mike's blood relationship to another of those men. A further ghostly vision reveals that this was no accident: Sara moved Fred to kill Cara, named in memory of her son, as penance for his part in Kito's murder. Finally cutting through the haze in which Mike has brought Kyra to Sara Laughs in order to kill her, and then end his own life, this is a Gothic revelation which drives home the impact of the past on the present.

If, as Teresa A. Goddu suggests, "the gothic serves as a mode of resistance ... by writing their own gothic tales, these authors [Toni Morrison, Harriet Jacobs] combat the master's version of their history; by breaking the silence, they reclaim their history instead of being controlled by it,"[25] then the haunted house motif here permits one such act of defiance. Omitted from the local library's "formal history of Castle County" (*BB*: 265), Sara is denied access to more legitimate, official channels of transmitting her experience and history—all that is said of her is that "when she and her folks—some of them friends, most of them relatives—had left the TR, they had gone on to Castle Rock for a little while ... then had simply disappeared, like a cloud over the horizon or mist on a summer morning [original ellipses]" (128). Yet the haunted house motif of the Gothic genre allows Sara to be the author of her own tragic life story. The restless spirits of these unlawfully and undeservedly executed people thus make their continued presence felt in the community over the course of the century. Here, the Gothic elements of the novel allow the oppressed to speak out, and fight back, against their tormentors.

The liminal haunted house acts as a vehicle whereby several layers of history can coalesce to the extent that the ghosts of Sara and Kito both seemingly merge into one entity, together also with the much more recently-departed spirit of Jo. Their motivations and memories are so very different that Mike struggles to understand and act upon the mixed messages he receives from them. The initial menace appears to be the ghost of Sara herself, and her intent is undoubtedly to cause harm. Thus, according to Stanley Wiater, Christopher Golden and Hank Wagner, Mike defeats the ghostly threat because he comes to identify that "Sara is the root cause of the evil he faces."[26]

Yet Sara has a clear motive for her ghostly actions, and I argue that the real enemy here lies within the community. In other words, while Jared Devore is the instigator of the attacks, it is not the individual members but rather the collective entity of the community itself which must bear the responsibility for what happened.

Other King novels such as *Pet Sematary* (1988) explore rural single-mindedness as a character trait while still allowing the individuals who make up the communities to be sympathetically drawn. Magistrale discerns that King's vision of small-town Maine, with its "acute degree of isolation, pressure to conform, and lack of compassion," gives rise to both heroic and malevolent figures.[27] *Bag of Bones*, with its insistence on the existence of a "town consciousness" (*BB*: 374), takes such traits several steps further in attributing them to whole groups of people and casting them as a united villain. The evil deeds of the original assailants resound through the decades reaching even into Mike's time. So this novel constitutes an examination, not only of the evil inherent within humanity, but more specifically of the potential for evil within collective humanity.

There are other lingering presences in evidence as well. Dying approximately two-thirds of the way through the story, Max Devore continues to act as a potent force for malevolence and disruption, although—aside from the manifestation of the "Max-Jared" hybrid figure—he never actually appears in the more conventional spectral forms exhibited by the other ghosts. Acting chiefly through the community members, he contrives to spread misery by hounding Mike and separating Kyra from her mother, ultimately taking Mattie's life. Heidi Strengell indicates that Max represents an archetypal Gothic villain[28] and, as such, he seems to stand for some kind of timeless evil—one rooted strongly within his community—which may not be entirely expunged even by his death. Sara's construal of Jared Devore as "the worst" (*BB*: 480) of her attackers thus seems equally applicable to his descendant.

In considering the nature of Sara's ghost it is immediately apparent that she is a figure of fear and menace. This is a potentially problematic demonization of Sara the African American woman, as she is forced to occupy both the role of victim and of victimizer in this novel. Speaking of the films *Candyman* (Bernard Rose, 1992), *The Matrix* (The Wachowski Brothers, 1999) and King adaptation *The Green Mile* (Frank Darabont, 1999), Kim D. Hester-Williams concludes that they are part of a problematic body of cinema which suggests "white Americans remain haunted by the history and memory of slavery and are thus the real victims of racial oppression."[29] Yet, through haunting, Sara is not shown solely as a supernatural monster, but also as a person—a strong woman and a loving mother, driven to such desperate acts by human monsters. If we consider Kathleen Brogan's observation that "the ghost gives body to memory, while reminding us that remembering is not a simple or even safe act,"[30] her perceived malevolence seems less threatening. Haunting is a device through which the grisliest details of a troubled history can be laid open for scrutiny. It is inevitable that unpleasant, even dangerous, events will be encountered. In arguing that "frightening ghosts, however, can sometimes be put to rest, not in the sense of being forever banished, but in the sense of being transformed into memories that usefully guide, rather than overwhelm, the present,"[31] Brogan draws attention to the potential of the malevolent specter. Specifically, Sara's ghost functions to inform the present—here, the descendants of her violators—about the true nature of the past.

So it is difficult, even impossible, to see the woman Sara purely as a vengeful monster, punishing innocent future generations simply for the deeds of their ancestors, in light of the revelations that occur towards the story's climax. Although her ghost is indeed bitter, the hauntings do not shy away from revealing the injustice of her earthly plight. Rather, in immersing Mike and the reader in the horror of the situation in which Sara and Kito were placed, the liminality of haunting performs precisely the opposite function. Further, the facts uncovered about her and her family show the extent to which their history of subjugation is buried within a largely prejudiced wider community—a history which cannot be ignored and which Mike is finally led to uncover. Sara can be seen as both subject to, and a subsequent agent of, a violent history.

With Jo's help, as the events of that summer in 1901 unfold in ghostly form, Mike is able to locate the concealed bones and destroy them with lye, thus finally quieting these restless spirits. In the epilogue it is revealed that, having saved Kyra from Sara's curse, he is looking to become her adoptive father. Despite the tragic events of the novel—both historic and contemporary—an optimistic and constructive ending emerges here. Relaying the tale to Frank, emphasizing his repulsion for the Devore patriarchs and his sympathy for Sara, Mike ensures that all the violence and inequity of the Tidwells' story—beyond his own liminal revelations—is made known to others. *Bag of Bones* thus offers a direct engagement with history, acknowledging guilty acts and bringing them openly into the present day. Further, the knowledge yielded here by the liminality of haunting facilitates an end to the devastation and even a chance to forge a new beginning for the protagonist.

However, this broadly positive conclusion can be seen as problematic. Though he is sympathetic, the fact that Mike discovers Sara's haunting behavior only to put an end to it raises other issues. Should the repercussions of her treatment, entrenched as it is in a long and complex history of racism, be stopped? Such an event implies that this history, which can never be expunged, can somehow—through the tropes of supernatural fiction—be managed. It is hardly surprising, at the close of the twentieth century, that a white liberal author like King should produce such an indictment of historic racism. In a post-countercultural era, one where racial discrimination is unacceptable in legal, cultural and moral terms, a novel that deals with race can thus offer a measure of closure denied to a novel like *The Shining* that deals with less overt, still deeply-ingrained, issues like the forces of class and capitalism embedded within the very fabric of American society.

These debates notwithstanding, Sara Laughs' status as a haunted, liminal place is so important because it is precisely the kind of fluidity inherent within liminality that allows the co-existence of disparate historical moments, as well as the conflict and confrontation demanded by the violent and controversial events uncovered in the novel. Without the provision of a motif that gives characters—and readers—the ability to move plausibly back and forth between normally segregated realms such as life and death, past and present, dream and reality, the reader would be less immersed in the narrative and less able to see the full emotional interplay between them. Liminality reveals the full extent to which these forces interact. With its links to potentiality, liminality here can be seen to allow progress in terms of re-visioning history, acknowledging past wrongs and perhaps allowing the opportunity to move on. Inability to progress, stemming from a failure to deal with the past, is dealt with here by the introduction of a Gothic motif that allows direct physical access, via supernatural means, to the horrors of history. Haunting permits an actual encounter with history beyond simply rewriting it for a new generation; it allows a sense of immediacy in enabling direct confrontation with the key figures involved.

Conclusion

The chief function of haunting in *Bag of Bones* is to allow the telling of a story neglected for the duration of the entire twentieth century, a story which intimately concerns an entire community to the extent that it is forced to reproduce its original transgressions in murdering an innocent woman and her child by murdering its own progeny as penance. Without the device of haunting, the horror and injustice experienced by Sara and her relatives and friends would be relegated to the dusty photographs and newspaper clippings left to disintegrate in the bowels of the log cabin that—in bearing her name—stands as testament to her memory. It is only through the evocation of the supernatural that this trauma can be shown for what it was and for what it continues to represent.

Through the haunted house motif, with its potential for exhuming and tackling such events, Mike has a personal encounter with history that helps him to see for himself how the past continues to shape the present. The device of haunting is a means of linking these different, yet crucially inter-linked, spaces—it is bound up with memory, identity, place and heredity. Contingent here upon the presence of an identifiable haunter, this ghostly tale is intimately linked to personal history. It shows how one person's experiences have impacted over time within one place, while also allowing the protagonist who experiences the liminality of haunting to have privileged access to these normally-distinct, yet inter-related, temporal zones.

Bag of Bones, appearing at the close of the twentieth century and thus relatively late in King's writing career, marks a new direction in his treatment of the liminality of haunting. Jack's time at the Overlook, despite the insights it offers into the history of American capitalism, exploits his zeal for success and commandeers his creativity for its own gain, culminating in an explosion that sees him perish and his family left alone. In *Christine*, protagonist Arnie is subjected to a ghoulishly nostalgic evocation of the 1950s—an era riven by conflicts over which subsequent decades still contend—and placed in a liminal state that he is unable to transcend and that ceases only with his violent death. Here, although he encounters a grim history that has led to terrible tragedy in his own life, rather than being overwhelmed by the haunting, Mike is able to use it to finally bring Sara's tale to light, to ensure Kyra's survival and even to carve out a fresh start for himself. His encounter with liminality thus permits a measure of enlightenment and progress denied to King's earlier protagonists.

However, given the thorny nature of the history of which Sara's story is a part, this positive ending brings issues of its own. That Mike, implicated in this situation via familial guilt as he is, effectively silences Sara once and for all is certainly problematic, not least because this deprives of Sara of the ability to tell her own tale. The haunted house motif has given her an opportunity to articulate, even to act upon, her righteous fury. Nonetheless, it should be noted that King's happy ending differs markedly from those tidy conclusions supplied by Matheson. Whereas Matheson's protagonists seek to gloss over uncomfortable truths, Mike is still wholly mindful of the horrors of the history he encounters and keen to lay them bare. Once again, the liminality of haunting here throws up the complexities discernible at the heart of twentieth-century American history and culture.

Return of the Repressed

The Future of the Haunted House Motif

This book has aimed to offer a fresh perspective on one of the most enduring types of popular American Gothic fiction through an analytical focus on what I call the *haunted house motif.* This motif—a recurrent feature of the Gothic as a genre—creates a distinctive narrative space which is characterized by the key quality of liminality, and in which the events and processes of the past intrude directly upon those of the present. While the often disturbing encounters between past and present that erupt within the haunted, liminal spaces of Gothic fictions are imaginary, their staging allows authors to explore the very real and material forces of history and ideology, and to reflect upon as well as intervene in the debates and discourses through which understandings of American social and political identity are forged. Recollecting Fiedler's argument for what he saw as the inherently reactionary bent of American Gothic, it can be seen that the authors discussed here draw on this motif to express the gamut of political stances, from conservative to radical and, sometimes, back again.

The Gothic genre is obsessed by the return of the repressed—the sense that past people and events, even those long gone and (ostensibly) safely buried, might yet come back to unsettle the living—and this fixation is never plainer than it is in tales of haunting. Location, so important to the Gothic, is fundamental to such fiction and reminds us of the relationship between histories and the physical spaces in which they take place. Haunting encounters and ghostly presences are extraordinary. The term liminality, which refers to the state of being on the margins of society—as with an apprentice or initiate—encapsulates the idea that those who experience such things are inevitably set apart from daily life. In this way, they gain a new vantage point and see this life anew. As has been shown in case studies throughout this book, popular tales of haunting offer the chance—for authors and for readers—to reflect upon society in a similar fashion. Forging the trajectory of American Gothic, inspiring later authors and being inspired by them, my chosen authors use the haunted house motif to celebrate, critique—and, above all, to interrogate—twentieth-century American history and culture in all its complexity.

From Past to Present

As we have seen, H. P. Lovecraft, Richard Matheson and Stephen King have been leading lights in twentieth-century American horror, and their individual legacies seem set to live on for the foreseeable future. Yet their tales of haunting belong within a long tradition of Gothic horror fictions that stretches far back into the past and—from the *Twilight* phenomenon of recent years to shows like *True Blood* and the ongoing transmedia narrative *The Walking Dead*—continues to flourish. In Chapter One, I established that Gothic has ever been a means of engaging imaginatively with the times in which it is written and of reflecting critically on change. In holding a mirror up to society, whether safeguarding or contesting the status quo, it is a genre with a propensity for politics. Its preoccupation with the return of the repressed reveals its fascination for looking back, for (on occasion literally) unearthing history. Despite hopes of a fresh start in the New World—or, perhaps, because of it—America was mindful of the link between past, present and future from the outset and Gothic was an ideal means of conveying this. Indicating the centrality of haunting to American Gothic fictions, I then showed that the haunted house motif—especially in the way it draws together the established concerns of the genre, with a particular conception of space and liminality—proves to be an important and original tool for understanding haunted fiction.

Moving into the case studies, the examination of each new author revealed the diverse ways in which they adapted the haunted house motif to different kinds of spaces and thus addressed the changing face of twentieth-century American culture. Writing in the early decades of the century, Lovecraft's absorption in science and discovery—in highlighting humanity's insignificance in cosmic terms—helped shape his idiosyncratic generic blend of Gothic and science fiction. This cosmic turn, along with the regionalism it stirred in him, can be seen as a response to the challenges of life in an era characterized by rapid social, technological and intellectual change. In "The Dreams in the Witch House" (1933), Lovecraft transforms a conventionally troubled and spooky haunted house, regionalized by its setting in a fictionalized version of Salem, into a vehicle for exploring anxieties about America's transition to modernity. In depicting both conservative and progressive impulses, here the liminality of the haunted house motif conjures up the mood of ambivalence and conflict which typified responses to this process.

In the middle part of the twentieth century, Matheson sought to renew Gothic tradition by moving away from the traditional locales favored by Lovecraft, choosing rather to set his tales of haunting squarely in the context of the modern mundane. For instance, haunting in *A Stir of Echoes* (1958) is used to appraise 1950s suburban living and working arrangements, critiquing and endorsing them by turns. Similarly, *Earthbound* (1982; 1989) draws on everyday scenarios to explore how American attitudes towards sexuality and marriage shifted between the 1950s and the 1980s. In both of these novels, which work to bring the Gothic in line with familiar suburban and domestic experience, the haunted house motif lays bare numerous and often fiercely-clashing social and historical forces. Notably, though, where Lovecraft can permit no resolution to the conflicts he locates at the heart of his haunted places, Matheson seeks instead, conservatively, to contain these potentially subversive forces as the novels end.

As a late twentieth-century writer, immersed in horror literature and cinema from a young age, King has been influenced by both Lovecraft and Matheson. Like them, he has contributed to haunted fiction by utilizing new kinds of spaces in which to explore the challenges of history and ideology. For example, the depiction of the haunted hotel in *The Shining* (1977) provides an alternative commentary on the state of America at a time when the recent bicentennial had banished self-critical images in favor of celebratory narratives of national unity and progress. King's popular novel seeks, subversively, to challenge those narratives with images of crisis—manifested in terms of masculinity, class and capitalism—which emerged from the conflicts and struggles of the nation's past that the bicentennial celebrations strove to exclude or repress.

A few years later, *Christine* (1983) offers a critique of Reaganite nostalgia for the supposed "golden age" of the 1950s. The novel's eponymous haunted car is used to destabilize conservative celebrations of the decade as a model of American supremacy, stability and security. Christine— the car and the novel—warns against such nostalgic impulses, revealing them as regressive and deadly. Reflecting once more on how the past intrudes to shape the present, *Bag of Bones* (1998) uses a haunted log cabin to explore a theme found in the very origins of American Gothic— that of racism and the legacy of slavery. The liminality of haunting permits a direct engagement with the case of Sara Tidwell, an African American woman raped and murdered in a small Maine town, whose story has lain dormant throughout the twentieth century. It works to challenge entrenched attitudes on race in revealing, even reversing, Sara's violent past and allowing her a fresh agency. With King, the haunted house motif facilitates a re-evaluation of American society, unleashing all the discord wrought by social change and underscoring the impossibility of any easy resolution to the complexities inherent within unjust, often violent, histories.

What the fictions of these authors all have in common is their capacity to engage with politics and ideology—whether they offer views which are conservative, progressive or even torn between the two—and it is through the haunted house motif that this is exposed. Hauntings are extraordinary: they collapse the boundaries between past and present and generate enlightening, though not always welcome, ways of seeing the world. This study has focused on literary treatments of popular haunted fiction and on how the haunted house motif contributes to an understanding of these forms. Yet the Gothic device of haunting, with its power to nudge at boundaries and challenge preconceptions, extends beyond the page and out to other media forms, and the haunted house motif can offer insights into these narratives as well as into their literary antecedents.

The Future of the Haunted House Motif

In October 2011, a new program entitled simply *American Horror Story* hit the small screen. Building on its early success in terms of critical reception and of ratings, creators Ryan Murphy and Brad Falchuk developed the concept into a horror anthology series and re-branded what was to become Season One as *American Horror Story: Murder House.* This new title, in laying bare the underlying premise of the original show, also indexes the hold that narratives of death and violence—especially ones firmly tied to a domestic context—continue to exert over the American popular imagination.

The troubled Harmon family, desperate for a fresh start after a stillbirth and infidelity threaten to destroy their lives, find their trials are only just beginning with their relocation from Boston to Los Angeles. For, unknown to them, their new home is the infamous "Murder House," the backdrop to many a violent and fatal incident throughout the twentieth century. Mother Vivien learns of the former inhabitants, including a surgeon who performed illegal abortions in the basement and his unhappy wife, on a sightseeing tour that incorporates their home as a ghoulish highlight. Steeped in history and since enshrined in folklore, this house is a twenty-first-century incarnation of the haunted house archetype embedded in the American Gothic tradition and discussed throughout this book.

The Harmons' new home, haunted by a panoply of ghosts whose ranks they themselves are destined to swell, is an imposing and gloomy old mansion, acting as a repository for all the dark deeds committed within its walls. It provides a physical setting in which the past constantly comes back to disturb the present. In this liminal place, increasingly isolated from normal existence, the Harmons not only encounter the sweep of history contained within this edifice but are also forced to confront the secrets, past and present, that beset their own family unit.

Striving to include content relevant to a contemporary audience, *Murder House* is haunted by such ghosts as a disaffected teenage boy responsible for a high school gun massacre. The program also aims to be progressive with the inclusion of same-sex couples and a ghostly housekeeper who problematizes entrenched attitudes towards female sexuality in playing with notions of the male gaze. Yet, in moving finally to restore the Harmon (nuclear) family unit within this sphere of haunted domesticity—glossing over their many problems in doing so— the program ultimately endorses an all too conservative stance on American society. Conventionally atmospheric, yet focused on themes like family, sex and changing social mores, and thus part and parcel of everyday American life, this haunted house from the television series finds common ground with the haunted fictions of all the authors discussed here. The haunted house motif is a persistent and inter-medial form that works to illuminate and critique long-standing issues embedded deep within American society.

This book has demonstrated that the haunted house motif helps us access and interrogate aspects of twentieth-century American history and culture. All three authors included here who draw on the power of this motif remain popular and influential. The last few years have seen the release of several new adaptations of original stories by Lovecraft as comics, while Matheson's fiction is still being adapted for cinema, and a new series of King's 2009 novel *Under the Dome* has been shown on television. A spate of scholarly works—including *New Critical Essays on H. P. Lovecraft* (2013) edited by David Simmons, *TV Horror: Investigating the Dark Side of the Small Screen* (2013) by Lorna Jowett and Stacey Abbott, and *Reading Richard Matheson: A Critical Survey* (2014) edited by Cheyenne Mathews and Janet V. Haedicke, as well as forthcoming collections like *The Age of Lovecraft: Cosmic Horror, Posthumanism, and Popular Culture* edited by Jeffrey A. Weinstock and Carl H. Sederholm— indicates a continued academic interest in new ways of appreciating fictions by these authors as well as in innovative forms of horror.

The haunted house motif itself can both be seen in, and is useful for, the analysis of other Gothic tales in other types of media. Therefore, using my work as a foundation, scholars can draw on its findings to deepen the knowledge of this rich and relevant field. The task that lies ahead is to extend the critical power of this motif to new kinds of Gothic narrative, told through innovative kinds of media forms. Since the early days of the Gothic, haunting has proved to be a potent and stimulating means of engaging with culture. Such tales are proving ripe for translation into movies, television, radio, comics and video games, as well as capable of having new life breathed into them by up-and-coming authors and by fans. Though it may find new modes of expression, the haunted house motif—with all the anxieties, challenges and opportunities for penetrating the murky depths of history and society it comprises—still resonates within American popular culture.

Chapter Notes

Introduction

1. Dale Bailey's *American Nightmares: The Haunted House Formula in American Popular Fiction* (Bowling Green, OH: Bowling Green State University Popular Press, 1999) opens with an account of his adolescent visit to a horror-themed local funhouse one Halloween, 1–3.

2. Jan Harold Brunvand, *The Vanishing Hitchhiker: Urban Legends and Their Meanings* (1981; London: Pan, 1983), 21. Citations are to the 1983 Pan edition.

3. Stephen King, *Danse Macabre* (1981; London: Warner, 1993), 296. Citations are to the 1993 Warner edition.

4. Eino Railo, *The Haunted Castle: A Study of the Elements of English Romanticism* (London: Routledge, 1927), 1–3. Although Walpole's renovations were somewhat artificial, the transformation of his Thames-side home of Strawberry Hill into a vision of antiquarianism through the addition of towers, stained glass and assorted weaponry provided a real life version of the literary Gothic castle.

5. That the castle is haunted by its past is initially evinced by the inexplicable giant helmet that fatally crushes the son and heir of its ruler, Manfred (whose ancestor usurped the true owner, Alfonso). See Horace Walpole, *The Castle of Otranto* (1764; Oxford: Oxford University Press, 1998), 18–19. Later visions of a similarly-proportioned foot and hand, along with the discovery of a vast sword, give these supernatural flashes some historical grounding when the appendages are seen to resemble those on the statue of Alfonso in the nearby church. Yet, as Markman Ellis observes of Walpole's use of the supernatural, "It is not easy for the reader to imagine or literalise the events described"; *The History of Gothic Fiction* (Edinburgh: Edinburgh University Press, 2000), 32.

6. Railo, *The Haunted Castle*, 8. Reeve's novel follows the fortunes of Edmund, young son of a laborer living on the estate of Lovel Castle. This is presided over by Baron Fitz-Owen after the death of Lord Arthur Lovel and the departure of the latter's brother, Walter Lovel, who assumes ownership only briefly. It is eventually revealed that Walter was responsible for the death of Edmund's parents—Arthur and his wife—and his subsequent adoption as a foundling. The exposure of these crimes and the reinstatement of Edmund are made possible after he is visited by the ghosts of his parents in the castle's haunted east wing.

7. Their cognizance of those they haunt reveals their sentience. Appearing to Edmund as he sleeps in the haunted wing, his parents speak to each other to make their relationship known to him. In leaving, they bless him, "One stood on each side of the bed; their hands met over his head, and they gave him a solemn benediction"; Clara Reeve, *The Old English Baron* (1778; London: Oxford University Press, 1967), 45.

8. Ellis, *The History of Gothic Fiction*, 121.

9. Fred Botting, *Gothic* (London: Routledge, 1996), 22. See also Montague Summers, *The Gothic Quest: A History of the*

169

Gothic Novel (London: Fortune Press, 1968), 37.

10. Botting, *Gothic*, 23. The author of *The Return of the Repressed: Gothic Horror from "The Castle of Otranto" to "Alien"* (Albany: State University of New York Press, 1999), Valdine Clemens, puts it this way: "From its inception, Gothic fiction has presented a challenge to enlightened skepticism," 4. This observation indicates that there has long been perceived an opposition between the supernatural on display in such fiction and the rational, Enlightenment context in which it emerged.

11. Brian Stableford, "The Cosmic Horror," in *Icons of Horror and the Supernatural: An Encyclopedia of Our Worst Nightmares* Vol. 1, ed. S. T. Joshi (Westport, CT: Greenwood Press, 2007), 69.

12. Maggie Kilgour, *The Rise of the Gothic Novel* (London: Routledge, 1995), 3.

13. Eve Kosofsky Sedgwick, *The Coherence of Gothic Conventions* (North Stratford, NH: Ayer, 1999), 8–9.

14. Mark Edmundson, *Nightmare on Main Street: Angels, Sadomasochism, and the Culture of Gothic* (Cambridge, MA: Harvard University Press, 1997), 8.

15. Ibid., 20.

16. Botting, 64. Of *The Monk*, Botting observes that "it is the tyrannical nature of, and barbaric superstitions inculcated by, all institutions, including aristocracy, Church and family, that forms the general object of criticism," 78.

17. See Clemens, *The Return of the Repressed*, 3–4; Edmundson, *Nightmare on Main Street*, 114; Chris Baldick, *In Frankenstein's Shadow: Myth, Monstrosity, and Nineteenth-Century Writing* (Oxford: Clarendon Press, 1987), 48, and Allan Lloyd-Smith, *American Gothic Fiction: An Introduction* (New York: Continuum, 2004), 32.

18. Anne Williams, *Art of Darkness: A Poetics of Gothic* (Chicago: University of Chicago Press, 1995), 242.

19. Noël Carroll, *The Philosophy of Horror or Paradoxes of the Heart* (New York: Routledge, 1990), 221.

20. Sigmund Freud, "The 'Uncanny,'" in *The Standard Edition of the Complete Psychological Works of Sigmund Freud: An Infantile Neurosis and Other Works* Vol. 17 (1917–1919), trans. James Strachey (London: Vintage, 2001), 220 and 224.

21. Ibid., 241.

22. Ibid.

23. Edmundson, 157. Edmundson implies that, in theorizing that the human psyche is "haunted" by traumatic personal history, Freud effectively shifted the focus of haunting from without to within, 32. For Manuel Aguirre, whereas the first Gothic hauntings were firmly linked to a castle, Victorian ghosts ended up part of the psyche and thus part of the self; *The Closed Space: Horror Literature and Western Symbolism* (Manchester: Manchester University Press, 1990), 131.

24. Clemens, 5.

25. Ibid., 204.

26. Julia Briggs, *Night Visitors: The Rise and Fall of the English Ghost Story* (London: Faber and Faber, 1977), 15. Jeffrey Andrew Weinstock echoes this sentiment, remarking that ghosts function "to offer a warning, redress a crime, seek revenge"; "Queer Haunting Spaces: Madeline Yale Wynne's 'The Little Room' and Elia Wilkinson Peattie's 'The House That Was Not,'" *American Literature* 79, No. 3 (September 2007): 501.

27. *The Castle of Otranto* details with both more individualized crimes, as in the case of Manfred upholding his ancestor's illegitimate claim to the castle, and social ills. With regard to the latter, Clemens suggests that *Otranto*'s portrayal of domestic violence was indicative of repressive conditions for women at the time of its publication: "The supernatural element could be held responsible ... for the atmosphere of terror and psychic turmoil that also arises from familial abuse," 31.

28. Kilgour, *The Rise of the Gothic Novel*, 3; Clemens, 3–4.

29. Catherine Belsey, *Critical Practice* (London: Routledge, 1980), 144.

30. David A. Oakes, *Science and Destabilization in the Modern American Gothic:*

Lovecraft, Matheson, and King (Westport, CT: Greenwood Press, 2000), 5.

31. Sylvia Grider, "The Haunted House in Literature, Popular Culture, and Tradition: A Consistent Image," *Contemporary Legend* 2 (1999): 180.

32. King, *Danse Macabre*, 66.

33. Ibid., 296.

34. Bailey, *American Nightmares*, uses a variant of the phrase "motif of the haunted house" in explaining how such tales have been adapted to meet the needs of American horror fiction, 6. However, his use of this term quickly gives way to his key designation of such fiction in terms of the eponymous "haunted house formula," 7, 15 and 23.

35. For Judith Halberstam, the move from the eighteenth to the nineteenth century signaled Gothic's thematic shift from "the fear of corrupted aristocracy or clergy, represented by the haunted castle or abbey, to the fear embodied by monstrous bodies"; *Skin Shows: Gothic Horror and the Technology of Monsters* (Durham, NC: Duke University Press, 1995), 16. I argue, rather, that haunting lingers as a key generic trope, one especially pronounced in the case of American Gothic.

36. Railo, 141, and 146–147. Botting acknowledges Gothic's origins in the graveyard poetry and romances decried by Enlightenment thinkers, 32, observing that in the eighteenth century "'Gothic romance' is more applicable than 'Gothic novel' as it highlights the link between medieval romances, the romantic narratives of love, chivalry and adventure, that were imported from France from the late seventeenth century onwards, and the tales that in the later eighteenth century were classified as 'Gothic,'" 24. Railo argues that in nineteenth-century literature "it was the haunted castle that brought to the historical novel those features which entitle it to the name 'romance,'" 147.

37. Lloyd-Smith, *American Gothic Fiction*, 32. For Lloyd-Smith, "Poe's work still shows the effects of late eighteenth-century rationalism in its American form ... the drive toward explanation and understanding of Gothic events through mental disorder, and the sense of stopping short of supernaturalism," 32–33. In other words, while his fiction is very much concerned with Gothic-style settings and themes, the horror can be explained through recourse to natural causes, e.g., delusions, rather than to definitively supernatural ones. Although recognizably Gothic in nature and origin, it can still be made to sit comfortably with Enlightenment modes of explanation. Similar practice is in evidence in early European Gothic, as the novels of Mrs. Radcliffe typically end with apparently-supernatural events being explained away; see Ellis, *The History of Gothic Fiction*, 66–67, perhaps as elaborate deceptions or as outcomes of her heroines' over-active imaginations. Gothic, as a site for contesting rationalism, allowed non-rational events to be explored, if not always fully embraced. As Lloyd-Smith indicates, Poe "explains" his Gothic events through internal factors like individual pathology rather than through external ones.

38. By the mid-nineteenth century, society had changed so much that Gothic settings and characters, already seen as historical by their original audiences, were quite antiquated. Botting describes developments in British and North American fiction at this time in terms of "the domestication of Gothic styles and devices within realistic settings and modes of writing. The architectural and feudal background, the wild landscapes, the aristocratic villains and sentimental heroines, were no longer, in a thoroughly bourgeois culture, objects of terror," 123.

39. Julia Briggs, "The Ghost Story," in *A Companion to the Gothic*, ed. David Punter (Oxford: Blackwell, 2000), 127.

40. Such adaptations include more visceral pure "horror"; see Gina Wisker, *Horror Fiction: An Introduction* (New York: Continuum, 2005), who asserts that "a branch of Gothic writing, horror uses many of its formulae but is more likely to use violence, terror, and bodily harm than the Gothic," 8.

41. Kathleen Brogan, *Cultural Haunting: Ghosts and Ethnicity in Recent American Literature* (Charlottesville: University Press of Virginia, 1998), 62. See also Teresa A. Goddu, *Gothic America: Narrative, History, and Nation* (New York: Columbia University Press, 1997), 154–155, and Lloyd-Smith, *American Gothic Fiction*, 61–62.

42. Toni Morrison, *Beloved* (1987; London: Vintage, 1997), 3.

43. Steven J. Mariconda, "The Haunted House," in *Icons of Horror and the Supernatural*, 269.

44. Michel Foucault, "Of Other Spaces," trans. Jay Miskowiec, *Diacritics* 16, No. 1 (1986): 25.

45. David Punter, *The Literature of Terror: A History of Gothic Fictions from 1765 to the Present Day, Volume 1: The Gothic Tradition*, 2nd ed. (Harlow: Longman, 1996), 165. Citations are to this edition.

46. Allan Lloyd-Smith, "Nineteenth-Century American Gothic," in *A Companion to the Gothic*, 113. Certainly the symbolic resonance of European Gothic architecture made itself felt in America, in material as well as in fictional form. One such example is Eastern State Penitentiary, built on the outskirts of Philadelphia in the 1820s, which was designed to resemble a medieval European castle in order to deter potential criminals; "Façade—Eastern State Penitentiary," accessed August 17, 2012, http://www.easternstate.org/explore/online-360-tour/facade.

47. Goddu, *Gothic America*, 4.

48. Ibid., 3.

49. Ibid., 4.

50. Mark Jancovich, *Horror* (London: B. T. Batsford, 1992), 35.

51. Allan Gardner Lloyd-Smith, *Uncanny American Fiction: Medusa's Face* (Houndmills, Basingstoke: Macmillan, 1989), 151.

52. Charles Brockden Brown, *Edgar Huntly: Or, Memoirs of a Sleep-Walker* (1799; Indianapolis, IN: Hackett, 1998), 4.

53. Renée L. Bergland notes that the United States was engaged in active conflict with Indians from the outset; *The National Uncanny: Indian Ghosts and American Subjects* (Hanover, NH: Dartmouth College/University Press of New England, 2000), 50. She explains, "The goal, both physical and metaphysical, was to secure America's borders, to define the national territory and hence the nation," 50.

54. Lloyd-Smith, *American Gothic Fiction*, 44.

55. Jared Gardner, "Edgar Huntly's Savage Awakening," *American Literature* 66, No. 3 (1994): 430.

56. Bergland, *The National Uncanny*, 53.

57. Lloyd-Smith, *American Gothic Fiction*, 55.

58. Lloyd-Smith, *Uncanny American Fiction*, 64–65.

59. Punter, *The Literature of Terror*, 165.

60. Lloyd-Smith, *American Gothic Fiction*, 34.

61. Leslie A. Fiedler, *Love and Death in the American Novel* (1960; Champaign, IL: Dalkey Archive Press, 1997), 160. Citations are to the 1997 Dalkey Archive edition.

62. Ibid., 160–161.

63. E.J. Clery makes a case for the genre's continued relevance in remarking that "twentieth-century commentators who have insisted that Gothic novels are escapist fictions set in the distant past ignore their steady progress to a present-day setting"; *The Rise of Supernatural Fiction: 1762–1800* (Cambridge: Cambridge University Press, 1995), 129.

64. Lloyd-Smith, *American Gothic Fiction*, 34.

65. Kilgour notes that "The very name 'gothic novel' ... is an oxymoron that reflects its desire to identify conflicting impulses: both towards newness, novelty, originality, and towards a return to nature and revival of the past," 17–18.

66. Stuart Jeffries, "Profile: Stephen King," *The Guardian*, September 18, 2004. Jeffries' interview with King highlights the author's immense popularity: "With so many different publishers, and editions of his novels in print in many different languages all over the world, it is impossible to calculate how many Stephen King books

have been sold. But in 1998 he was widely reported to have earned $40 million," 22–23.

67. Bergland, 52.

68. Aguirre echoes Montague Summers's comment that "the real protagonist of the Gothic novel is the castle" in *The Closed Space*, 92; Lloyd-Smith, *American Gothic Fiction*, 7; Oakes, *Science and Destabilization in the Modern American Gothic*, 55; Edmundson, 54.

69. Bailey, 4.

70. Williams, *Art of Darkness*, 39.

71. Alison Landsberg, *Prosthetic Memory: The Transformation of American Remembrance in the Age of Mass Culture* (New York: Columbia University Press, 2004), 41.

72. Marita Sturken, *Tangled Memories: The Vietnam War, the AIDS Epidemic, and the Politics of Remembering* (Berkeley: University of California Press, 1997), 10–11.

73. Judith Richardson, *Possessions: The History and Uses of Haunting in the Hudson Valley* (Cambridge, MA: Harvard University Press, 2003), 3.

74. Ibid., 122.

75. Jancovich, *Horror*, 41.

76. Gaston Bachelard, *The Poetics of Space*, trans. Maria Jolas (1964; Boston, MA: Beacon, 1994), xxxv. Citations are to the 1994 Beacon edition.

77. Ibid., 3.

78. See Wisker, *Horror Fiction*, 150.

79. Anthony Vidler, *The Architectural Uncanny: Essays in the Modern Unhomely* (Cambridge: MIT Press, 1992), 11.

80. As Irving Malin maintains in his study of twentieth-century American Gothic, "Because the family is usually considered a stable unit, new American Gothic tries to destroy it"; *New American Gothic* (Carbondale: Southern Illinois University Press, 1962), 50. American Gothic thus taps into fears about the stability of the family unit by making domestic space—its physical manifestation—a site of horror.

81. Bachelard, *The Poetics of Space*, 5.

82. Victor Turner, *Dramas, Fields, and Metaphors: Symbolic Action in Human So-ciety* (Ithaca, NY: Cornell University Press, 1974), 231–232.

83. Victor Turner, *The Forest of Symbols: Aspects of Ndembu Ritual* (Ithaca, NY: Cornell University Press, 1967), 93.

84. Arnold van Gennep, *The Rites of Passage*, trans. Monika B. Vizedom and Gabrielle L. Caffee (London: Routledge and Kegan Paul, 1960), 106.

85. Ibid., 105–106.

86. Turner, *Dramas, Fields, and Metaphors*, 238–239.

87. Ibid., 232.

88. Ibid., 237.

89. Ibid., 232.

90. Ibid., 242.

91. Hein Viljoen and Chris N. Van der Merwe, "Introduction: A Poetics of Liminality and Hybridity," in *Beyond the Threshold: Explorations of Liminality in Literature*, eds. Hein Viljoen and Chris N. Van der Merwe (New York: Peter Lang, 2007), 23–24.

92. Manuel Aguirre, Roberta Quance, and Philip Sutton, "Introduction: The Concept of Liminality," in *Margins and Thresholds: An Enquiry into the Concept of Liminality in Text Studies, Studies in Liminality and Literature* 1, eds. Manuel Aguirre, Roberta Quance, and Philip Sutton (Madrid: Gateway Press, 2000), 9.

93. Lucy Kay, et al., "Introduction," in *Mapping Liminalities: Thresholds in Cultural and Literary Texts, Transatlantic Aesthetics and Culture* Vol. 2, eds. Lucy Kay, et al. (Bern: Peter Lang, 2007), 8.

94. Ibid.

95. Terry Phillips, "'No World Between Two Worlds': Liminality in Anglo-Irish Big House Literature, 1925–1932," in ibid., 70.

96. Turner, *Dramas, Fields, and Metaphors*, 232.

97. Though not concerned with liminality, in her study *Ghostly Matters: Haunting and the Sociological Imagination*, Avery F. Gordon casts the ghost as "the merging of the visible and the invisible, the dead and the living, the past and the present" (Minneapolis: University of Minnesota Press, 1997), 24.

98. Peter Messent, "Good Taste? Liminality and the Gothic in Thomas Harris's Hannibal Lecter Novels," in *Betwixt-and-Between: Essays in Liminal Geography, Studies in Liminality and Literature* 3, ed. Philip C. Sutton (Madrid: Gateway Press, 2002), 63.

99. Botting, 4. Gothic was characterized by its "boundlessness" and "over-ornamentation," a genre that "signified an over-abundance of imaginative frenzy," ibid., 3.

100. Kate Ferguson Ellis, *The Contested Castle: Gothic Novels and the Subversion of Domestic Ideology* (Urbana: University of Illinois Press, 1989), 7. In a patriarchal society this included the disenfranchisement of, and violence against, women—a side of eighteenth-century England that was not commonly acknowledged but existed nonetheless.

101. Aguirre, 66.

102. Eric Savoy, "The Face of the Tenant: A Theory of American Gothic," in *American Gothic: New Interventions in a National Narrative*, eds. Robert K. Martin and Eric Savoy (Iowa City: University of Iowa Press, 1998), 9.

103. Lloyd-Smith, *American Gothic Fiction*, 94.

104. Bailey, 56. Briefly, his chief observations are that the setting consists of a house and the characters comprise a middle-class family, or surrogate family, that moves into the house and is subsequently helped by knowledgeable third parties with some experience of the supernatural phenomena the family encounters therein. The plots encompass an ever-increasing array of bizarre events, perhaps including the discovery of how these events began, and culminate in one of three outcomes: the family escaping and the house being destroyed, the family escaping and the house enduring, or "a twist ending which establishes the recurring nature of evil," ibid.

105. Ibid.

106. Ibid., 6.

107. Ken Gelder, *Popular Fiction: The Logics and Practices of a Literary Field* (London: Routledge, 2004), 19. Similarly, Scott McCracken discusses the numerous criticisms of mass culture identified by Stuart Hall and Paddy Whannel, *Pulp: Reading Popular Fiction* (Manchester: Manchester University Press, 1998), 25.

108. Gelder, *Popular Fiction*, 37.

109. Ibid., 22.

110. Clive Bloom, *Bestsellers: Popular Fiction Since 1900*, 2nd ed. (Houndmills, Basingstoke: Palgrave Macmillan, 2008), 25. Citations are to this edition. However, as Gelder explains, the terms "popular fiction" and "bestsellers" are not synonymous, not least because popular fiction does not always sell especially well and literary fiction may do just that, 22.

111. Gelder, 17.

112. Marjorie Ferguson and Peter Golding, "Cultural Studies and Changing Times: An Introduction," in *Cultural Studies in Question*, eds. Marjorie Ferguson and Peter Golding (London: Sage, 1997), xxiii.

113. McCracken, *Pulp*, 2.

114. Ibid.

115. Ibid., 31–34.

116. Ibid., 183.

117. Gelder, 43.

118. Clive Bloom, "Introduction: Death's Own Backyard," in *Gothic Horror: A Reader's Guide from Poe to King and Beyond*, ed. Clive Bloom (Houndmills, Basingstoke: Macmillan, 1998), 2.

119. Ibid., 5. Poe became a staple in periodicals like *Weird Tales*, devoted to tales of horror, fantasy and the supernatural, that were labelled "pulp fiction" because of their inherent disposability. The first critiques of mass culture materialized with the rise of such magazines in the 1920s and 1930s; McCracken, 21.

120. Gelder, 159.

Chapter One

1. S. T. Joshi, *A Dreamer and a Visionary: H. P. Lovecraft in his Time* (Liverpool: Liverpool University Press, 2001), 10. An otherwise happy childhood was marred

by profound family illness. In 1893 his father, Winfield Scott Lovecraft—suffering from what is now believed to have been the tertiary stages of syphilis—was admitted to Providence's Butler Hospital, where he remained until his death in 1898. Lovecraft's mother, Sarah Susan Phillips, felt the effects of this ordeal for many years and was eventually hospitalized herself in 1919. Ibid., 12–14.

2. In 1914 he joined the United Amateur Press Association, an organization whose members made contributions as varied as poetry, fiction, opinion pieces and reviews to amateur journals including the *United Amateur* and the rival publication *National Amateur*. Ibid., 78–79.

3. Donald R. Burleson, *H. P. Lovecraft: A Critical Study* (Westport, CT: Greenwood Press, 1983), 7.

4. Peter Conn, *The Divided Mind: Ideology and Imagination in America, 1898–1917* (Cambridge: Cambridge University Press, 1983), 1.

5. Lawrence W. Levine, *The Unpredictable Past: Explorations in American Cultural History* (New York: Oxford University Press, 1993), 191.

6. Ibid.

7. In the year his father died, Lovecraft experienced his first nervous breakdown in a childhood marked by absences from school and spent largely under "considerable nervous strain," Joshi, *A Dreamer and a Visionary*, 35.

8. Ibid., 17. See also H. P. Lovecraft, "Bernard Austin Dwyer/March 3, 1927," in *H. P. Lovecraft Selected Letters II: 1925–1929*, eds. August Derleth and Donald Wandrei (Sauk City, WI: Arkham House, 1968), 109. Although not individually listed on the bibliography, full bibliographic information for these letters is provided in the endnotes.

9. H. P. Lovecraft, "Reinhardt Kleiner [*sic*]/November 16, 1916," in *H. P. Lovecraft Selected Letters I: 1911–1924*, eds. August Derleth and Donald Wandrei (Sauk City, WI: Arkham House, 1965), 37.

10. Joshi, *A Dreamer and a Visionary*,

28 and 40. Throughout his youth, Lovecraft wrote, then used a hectograph to reproduce, several treatises and periodicals with titles such as *Astronomy, The Scientific Gazette* and *The Rhode Island Journal of Astronomy*. Ibid., 41–42. His first publications took the form of letters, on the subject of astronomy, to the *Providence Sunday Journal* and *Scientific American* in 1906. Ibid., 58. Between 1906 and 1908 he wrote regular astronomy columns for two local papers, the *Pawtuxet Valley Gleaner* and the *Providence Tribune*. Lovecraft, "Reinhardt Kleiner [*sic*]/November 16, 1916," in *H. P. Lovecraft Selected Letters I*, 40.

11. H. P. Lovecraft, "The Dreams in the Witch House," in *"The Dreams in the Witch House" and Other Weird Stories*, ed. S. T. Joshi (London: Penguin, 2005), 300–301. All further references will be included as *TDWH* within the body of the text.

12. Lovecraft, "Edwin Baird/February 3, 1924," in *H. P. Lovecraft Selected Letters I*, 302.

13. Ibid.

14. See Don G. Smith, *H. P. Lovecraft in Popular Culture: The Works and Their Adaptations in Film, Television, Comics, Music and Games* (Jefferson, NC: McFarland, 2006), 2.

15. Quoted in "Expanding Horizons (1921–1924): Literary Development [14]," in *Lord of a Visible World: An Autobiography in Letters—H. P. Lovecraft*, eds. S. T. Joshi and David E. Schultz (Athens: Ohio University Press, 2000), 121–122.

16. H. P. Lovecraft, *Supernatural Horror in Literature* (1927; New York: Dover, 1973), 15. E. F. Bleiler notes that Lovecraft wrote this essay in the mid–1920s and that it was published in amateur magazine *The Recluse* in 1927. It did not appear in print again until its inclusion in *The Outsider and Others* (1939) and was published as a book in its own right in 1945, "Introduction to the Dover Edition," in ibid., iii–iv.

17. Ibid., 15.

18. S. T. Joshi, *The Weird Tale* (Holicong, PA: Wildside Press, 1990), 2–3.

19. Following his 1924 marriage to

Sonia Haft Greene, whom he met in 1921 at an amateur convention, Lovecraft came to reside in New York City. See Maurice Lévy, *Lovecraft: A Study in the Fantastic*, trans. S. T. Joshi (Detroit: Wayne State University Press, 1988), 22. The couple settled in Brooklyn, and Lovecraft remained in New York, even after Sonia's business collapsed and she left to pursue employment in the Midwest, until he returned to Providence to live with the elder of his two maternal aunts. See also S. T. Joshi, *Reader's Guide to H. P. Lovecraft* (Mercer Island, WA: Starmont House, 1982), 12.

20. As S. T. Joshi and David E. Schultz observe, by 1926 Lovecraft was only too eager to return home to Providence; "Introduction," in *From the Pest Zone: The New York Stories*, edited by S. T. Joshi and David E. Schultz (New York: Hippocampus Press, 2003), 7–8.

21. Lovecraft, "James F. Morton/May 16, 1926," in *H. P. Lovecraft Selected Letters II*, 51. Lovecraft lived there until he died in 1937 and the words "I AM PROVIDENCE" appear on his headstone in that city's Swan Point Cemetery.

22. Charles L. Crow, *American Gothic* (Cardiff: University of Wales Press, 2009), 138. I have previously published an article focusing on Lovecraft as a regionalist writer. See Rebecca Janicker, "New England Narratives: Space and Place in the Fiction of H. P. Lovecraft," *Extrapolation* 48, No. 1 (2007): 56–72.

23. Conn, *The Divided Mind*, 12.

24. Lovecraft, *Supernatural Horror in Literature*, 16.

25. Stephen King, *Danse Macabre* (1981; London: Warner, 1993), 80. Citations are to the 1993 Warner edition.

26. S. T. Joshi, "Explanatory Notes," in *"The Dreams in the Witch House" and Other Weird Stories*, 443. Appearing in 1923, *Weird Tales* was the first magazine specializing exclusively in horror and occult fiction; Mike Ashley, *The Time Machines: The Story of the Science-Fiction Pulp Magazines from the Beginning to 1950* (Liverpool: Liverpool University Press, 2000), 41.

27. Focusing on issues of gender, Sara Williams interprets this tale as an expression of Lovecraft's issues with his mother in "'The Infinitude of the Shrieking Abysses': Rooms, Wombs, Tombs, and the Hysterical Female Gothic in 'The Dreams in the Witch-House,'" in *New Critical Essays on H. P. Lovecraft*, ed. David Simmons (New York: Palgrave Macmillan, 2013), 55–72.

28. H. P. Lovecraft, "The Thing on the Doorstep," in *"The Thing on the Doorstep" and Other Weird Stories*, ed. S. T. Joshi (1937; London: Penguin, 2002), 342.

29. Lovecraft, "The Shadow Out of Time," in *"The Dreams in the Witch House" and Other Weird Stories*, 336.

30. Nancy Lusignan Schultz and Dane Anthony Morrison, "Introduction: Salem Enshrined: Myth, Memory, and the Power of Place," in *Salem: Place, Myth, and Memory*, eds. Dane Anthony Morrison and Nancy Lusignan Schultz (Boston, MA: Northeastern University Press/University Press of New England, 2004), 17.

31. Nancy Lusignan Schultz, "Salem as Hawthorne's Creation," in ibid., 164.

32. Carol F. Karlsen, *The Devil in the Shape of a Woman: Witchcraft in Colonial New England* (New York: W. W. Norton, 1998), xi.

33. Ibid., 40–41.

34. Schultz and Morrison, "Introduction," 4.

35. Schultz, "Salem as Hawthorne's Creation," 165. A native and resident of Salem, Hawthorne expressed through literature, e.g., *The House of the Seven Gables* (1851), his disquietude and guilt over his own ancestor—seventeenth-century magistrate Judge John Hathorne—who sentenced witches to death and was said to be cursed by one such accused as a result. See Christopher White, "Salem as Religious Proving Ground," in *Salem*, 49.

36. Gillian Brown, "Hawthorne's American History," in *The Cambridge Companion to Nathaniel Hawthorne*, ed. Richard H. Millington (Cambridge: Cambridge University Press, 2004), 134–135.

37. Robert K. Martin, "Haunted by Jim Crow: Gothic Fictions by Hawthorne and Faulkner," in *American Gothic: New Interventions in a National Narrative*, eds. Robert K. Martin and Eric Savoy (Iowa City: University of Iowa Press, 1998), 130.

38. Schultz, 167.

39. Donald R. Burleson, "H. P. Lovecraft: The Hawthorne Influence," *Extrapolation* 22, No. 3 (1981): 263. See also J. Vernon Shea, "On the Literary Influences Which Shaped Lovecraft's Works," in *H. P. Lovecraft: Four Decades of Criticism*, ed. S. T. Joshi (Athens: Ohio University Press, 1980), 116.

40. White, "Salem as Religious Proving Ground," 53.

41. Ibid., 54.

42. Paul Halpern and Michael C. LaBossiere, "Mind Out of Time: Identity, Perception, and the Fourth Dimension in H. P. Lovecraft's 'The Shadow Out of Time' and 'The Dreams in the Witch House,'" *Extrapolation* 50, No. 3 (Fall 2009): 513.

43. Susan Currell, *American Culture in the 1920s* (Edinburgh: Edinburgh University Press, 2009), 11–14.

44. Ibid., 11.

45. Ashley, *The Time Machines*, 27.

46. Lincoln Geraghty, *American Science Fiction Film and Television* (Oxford: Berg, 2009), 9.

47. Ashley, 49–50.

48. Joshi, *A Dreamer and a Visionary*, 256.

49. H. P. Lovecraft, "Clark Ashton Smith/November 18, 1930," in *H. P. Lovecraft Selected Letters III: 1929–1931*, eds. August Derleth and Donald Wandrei (Sauk City, WI: Arkham House, 1971), 218. Lovecraft averred that "About 1900 I became ... an intense fanatic on the subject of Antarctic exploration"; "Reinhardt Kleiner [*sic*]/November 16, 1916," in *H. P. Lovecraft Selected Letters I*, 37.

50. Lovecraft, "Miss Elizabeth Toldridge/April 1, 1930," in *H. P. Lovecraft Selected Letters III*, 136.

51. David A. Oakes, *Science and Destabilization in the Modern American Gothic: Lovecraft, Matheson, and King* (Westport, CT: Greenwood Press, 2000), 30.

52. Halpern and LaBossiere, "Mind Out of Time," 513.

53. H. P. Lovecraft, "Beyond the Wall of Sleep," in *"The Thing on the Doorstep" and Other Weird Stories*, 17.

54. In "Lovecraft and the Tradition of the Gentleman Narrator," in *An Epicure in the Terrible: A Centennial Anthology of Essays in Honor of H. P. Lovecraft*, eds. David E. Schultz and S. T. Joshi (London: Fairleigh Dickinson University Press/Associated University Presses, 1991), R. Boerem observes that several of Lovecraft's protagonists are artists of various types, writers or medical doctors, while the majority are scholars of some description, whether students or teachers, 266–267.

55. Manuel Aguirre, *The Closed Space: Horror Literature and Western Symbolism* (Manchester: Manchester University Press, 1990), 92. Barton Levi St. Armand notes that many of Lovecraft's "skewed structures" are used to suggest physical and moral corrosion; *The Roots of Horror in the Fiction of H. P. Lovecraft* (Elizabethtown, NY: Dragon Press, 1977), 19.

56. Halpern and LaBossiere, 512.

57. Michael E. Parrish, *Anxious Decades: America in Prosperity and Depression, 1920–1941* (New York: W. W. Norton, 1992), 194. On changing attitudes regarding progressivism, see also Douglas Tallack, *Twentieth-Century America: The Intellectual and Cultural Context* (London: Longman, 1991), 154.

58. Parrish, *Anxious Decades*, 194.

59. Joshi, *H. P. Lovecraft*, 28.

60. Parrish, 195.

61. Paul Goodman and Frank O. Gatell, *America in the Twenties: The Beginnings of Contemporary America* (New York: Holt, Rinehart and Winston, 1972), 70.

62. Parrish, 195.

63. Lovecraft, "Reinhardt Kleiner [*sic*]/June 25, 1920," in *H. P. Lovecraft Selected Letters I*, 120.

64. Lovecraft, "Amateur Journalism (1914–1921): Early Philosophical Views [13]," in *Lord of a Visible World*, 53.

65. Science also nurtured in Lovecraft a profound commitment to materialism. As

Joshi explains, he rejected the possibility that any matter could exist that was not material in nature and thus spurned religion, with its notions of the soul or spirit, on the grounds of its incompatibility with science; *Reader's Guide to H. P. Lovecraft*, 14.

66. Mark Twain, "Letters from the Earth," in *Letters from the Earth*, ed. Bernard DeVoto (1909; New York: Harper and Row, 1962), 7.

67. Ibid., 15.

68. Mark Twain, "The Damned Human Race," in ibid., 215–216.

69. Lin Carter, *Lovecraft: A Look Behind the Cthulhu Mythos* (Mercer Island, WA: Starmont House, 1992), xvii.

70. For example, the narrator of "The Call of Cthulhu" (1928) learns that Cthulhu lies dormant beneath the Pacific, in the submerged city of R'lyeh, to be roused "when the stars were right"to rule Earth as in ages past. See H. P. Lovecraft, "The Call of Cthulhu," in *"The Call of Cthulhu" and Other Weird Stories*, ed. S. T. Joshi (1928; London: Penguin, 2002), 155.

71. Lovecraft, "Homecoming (1926–1930): Theories of Literature and the Weird [17]," in *Lord of a Visible World*, 209.

72. Oakes, *Science and Destabilization in the Modern American Gothic*, 56.

73. Halpern and LaBossiere, 526. Graham Harman echoes this view in remarking of this tale that "science is not a destroyer of irrational illusions, but a dangerous probe into truths too terrifying for rationality to withstand"; *Weird Realism: Lovecraft and Philosophy* (Winchester: Zero Books, 2012), 195.

74. Oakes, 55. Halpern and LaBossiere argue that ghosts are usually scary because they confound science, but with Lovecraft the ghost can actually be explained as part of science, 513.

75. Michael Saler, "Modernity, Disenchantment, and the Ironic Imagination," *Philosophy and Literature* 28, No. 1 (April 2004): 138.

76. Chadwick Hansen, *Witchcraft at Salem* (New York: George Braziller, 1969), 39.

77. Alex Owen, *The Place of Enchantment: British Occultism and the Culture of the Modern* (Chicago: University of Chicago Press, 2004), 11. As Darryl Jones puts it, such scholarship suggests that "occultism should be understood as a major, and seriously neglected, component of modernity"; "Borderlands: spiritualism and the occult in *fin de siècle* and Edwardian Welsh and Irish horror," *Irish Studies Review* 17, No. 1 (February 2009): 32.

78. Michael Saler, "Modern Enchantments: The Canny Wonders and Uncanny Others of H. P. Lovecraft," *The Space Between: Literature and Culture, 1914–1945* 2, No. 1 (2006): 12.

79. Ibid., 15.

80. Ibid., 20.

81. Lovecraft, "James F. Morton/May 16, 1926," in *H. P. Lovecraft Selected Letters II*, 50.

82. Lovecraft, "James Ferdinand Morton/October 19, 1929," in *H. P. Lovecraft Selected Letters III*, 31.

83. Ibid.

84. Lovecraft, "August Derleth/November 21, 1930," in *H. P. Lovecraft Selected Letters III*, 221.

85. Joshi, *H. P. Lovecraft*, 100.

86. David Simmons, "H. P. Lovecraft and the Shadow of England," *Symbiosis: A Journal of Anglo-American Literary Relations* 11, No. 1 (April 2007): 101.

87. Lovecraft, "Frank Belknap Long/May 1, 1926," in *H. P. Lovecraft Selected Letters II*, 46.

88. Conn, 6.

89. Nathan Miller, *New World Coming: The 1920s and the Making of Modern America* (New York: Da Capo Press, 2003), 48–50.

90. Donna R. Gabaccia, *Immigration and American Diversity: A Social and Cultural History* (Malden, MA: Blackwell, 2002), 160.

91. The plight of the urban poor was highlighted by publications such as Jacob Riis's photographic study of New York neighborhoods, *How the Other Half Lives* (1890), while social reformers like Jane Ad-

dams at Chicago's Hull House focused on the concern that urban living could pose as great a threat to spiritual well-being as to physical health. Louis Menand observes that the work done at Hull House, which was in a neighborhood of considerable immigrant diversity, gave reformers ample chance to educate this population about American cultural norms and values; *The Metaphysical Club* (2001; London: Flamingo, 2002), 308. Citations are to the 2002 Flamingo edition.

92. Douglas Tallack, *New York Sights: Visualizing Old and New New York* (Oxford: Berg, 2005), 15.

93. Joshi and Schultz, "Introduction," in *From the Pest Zone*, 9.

94. H. P. Lovecraft, "He," in *"The Call of Cthulhu" and Other Weird Stories*, 129.

95. H. P. Lovecraft, "Cool Air," in ibid., 132.

96. H. P. Lovecraft, "The Horror at Red Hook," *"The Dreams in the Witch House" and Other Weird Stories*, 119.

97. Of Lovecraft's time in New York, Bennett Lovett-Graff remarks that "his memory of its immigrant masses was sufficient to deter him from ever considering living there again"; "Shadows Over Lovecraft: Reactionary Fantasy and Immigrant Eugenics," *Extrapolation* 38, No. 3 (Fall 1997): 182.

98. Levine, *The Unpredictable Past*, 191.

99. Joseph A. Conforti, *Imagining New England: Explorations of Regional Identity from the Pilgrims to the Mid-Twentieth Century* (Chapel Hill: University of North Carolina Press, 2001), 265.

100. James M. Lindgren, *Preserving Historic New England: Preservation, Progressivism, and the Remaking of Memory* (New York: Oxford University Press, 1995), 50.

101. Conforti, *Imagining New England*, 261.

102. Lindgren, *Preserving Historic New England*, 62–63.

103. David Eldridge, *American Culture in the 1930s* (Edinburgh: Edinburgh University Press, 2008), 25.

104. S. T. Joshi and David E. Schultz, "Introduction," in *Lord of a Visible World*, xv.

105. Timothy H. Evans, "A Last Defense against the Dark: Folklore, Horror, and the Uses of Tradition in the Works of H. P. Lovecraft," *Journal of Folklore Research* 42, No. 1 (2005): 126–127.

106. Lovecraft, "Reinhardt Kleiner [*sic*]/ January 11, 1923," in *H. P. Lovecraft Selected Letters I*, 203.

107. Lovecraft, "Frank Belknap Long and Alfred Galpin/May 1, 1923," in ibid, 220.

108. Ibid., 218.

109. Ibid., 221.

110. Paul Boyer and Stephen Nissenbaum, *Salem Possessed: The Social Origins of Witchcraft* (Cambridge, MA: Harvard University Press, 1974), 7.

111. Ibid., 3, 5 and 9–10.

112. Conn, 1.

113. Ibid., 6.

114. Gabaccia, *Immigration and American Diversity*, 138.

115. Conforti, 300.

116. Parrish, 110.

117. Ibid., 110–111. Parrish describes the dubious "scientific research" which suggested that "the human race could be divided up neatly into fixed hereditary types, with Teutons leading the march of civilization while Mediterranean, Oriental, and African peoples brought up the rear." Ibid., 110.

118. John Higham, *Strangers in the Land: Patterns of American Nativism, 1860–1925* (1955; New Brunswick, NJ: Rutgers University Press, 1992), 156. Citations are to the 1992 Rutgers University Press edition.

119. Parrish, 111.

120. Miller observes the dire nativist prediction that American-bound Jewish refugees from Russian pogroms in Eastern Europe would "steal the jobs of native-born Americans"; *New World Coming*, 93.

121. Gabaccia, 139. See also Levine, 195.

122. Gary Gerstle, *American Crucible: Race and Nation in the Twentieth Century* (Princeton, NJ: Princeton University Press, 2001), 104.

123. Lovecraft, "Reinhardt Kleiner [*sic*]/ December 6, 1915," in *H. P. Lovecraft Selected Letters I*, 18. Lovett-Graff sees Lovecraft's attitudes in this regard as a response to his self-image. Perpetually troubled by the infirmity within his family, he was driven to compensate for this shortcoming by fabricating for himself a robust "Nordic pedigree"; "Shadows Over Lovecraft," 178.

124. H. P. Lovecraft, "Lillian D. Clark/ January 11, 1926," in *H. P. Lovecraft: Letters from New York*, eds. S. T. Joshi and David E. Schultz (San Francisco, CA: Night Shade Books, 2005), 270.

125. For a discussion of Lovecraft's "modernist ambivalence towards the racial other," see Tracy Bealer, "'The Innsmouth Look': H. P. Lovecraft's Ambivalent Modernism," *Journal of Philosophy: A Cross-Disciplinary Inquiry* 6, No. 14 (Winter 2011): 46.

126. Quoted in "The Old Gentleman (1931–1937): Supporting Hitler [38]," in *Lord of a Visible World*, 326.

127. Quoted in ibid., 328.

128. Henry James, *The American Scene* (Bloomington: Indiana University Press, 1968), 265.

129. Lovecraft, "Mr Harris/February 25, 1929–March 1, 1929," in *H. P. Lovecraft Selected Letters II*, 306.

130. Niall Palmer, *The Twenties in America: Politics and History* (Edinburgh: Edinburgh University Press, 2006), 4.

Chapter Two

1. Matheson's first horror tale, "Born of Man and Woman," appeared in *The Magazine of Fantasy and Science Fiction* in 1950. The latest film adaptation of Matheson's novel *I Am Legend*, which shared its title with that of its source material, was released by Warner Brothers as recently as 2007. See Paul Stuve and Matthew R. Bradley, "Bibliographies, Filmographies, etc.," in *The Richard Matheson Companion*, eds. Stanley Wiater, Matthew R. Bradley, and Paul Stuve (Colorado Springs: Gauntlet, 2008), 415 and 499.

2. Quoted in Douglas E. Winter, *Faces of Fear: Encounters with the Creators of Modern Horror* (New York: Berkley, 1985), 244.

3. As though to underscore his commitment to literary verisimilitude, Matheson, who worked as a machine parts operator at Douglas Aircraft in Santa Monica, California, in the 1950s to support his own young family, places his protagonist in a living and working situation remarkably like his own. See William F. Nolan, "The Matheson Years: A Profile in Friendship," in *The Twilight and Other Zones: The Dark Worlds of Richard Matheson*, eds. Stanley Wiater, Matthew R. Bradley and Paul Stuve (New York: Citadel Press, 2009), 10.

4. Dean Conrad, in a posthumous piece on Matheson's contribution to science fiction, notes the challenges of trying to categorize his fiction in terms of a single genre, "In Search of Richard Matheson: Science Fiction Screenwriter," *Foundation: The International Review of Science Fiction* 43, No. 117 (Spring 2014): 31.

5. Peter Nicholls, "Richard Matheson," in *Science Fiction Writers: Critical Studies of the Major Authors from the Early Nineteenth Century to the Present Day*, ed. E. F. Bleiler (New York: Charles Scribner's Sons, 1982), 425.

6. Quoted in Nolan, "The Matheson Years," 24.

7. Dara Downey, "'A Labyrinth Without a Clew': Husbands, Houses and Harpies in Richard Matheson's *The Shrinking Man* and Mark Z. Danielewski's *House of Leaves*," in *Heroes of Film, Comics and American Culture: Essays on Real and Fictional Defenders of Home*, ed. Lisa M. DeTora (Jefferson, NC: McFarland, 2009), 24.

8. Nicholls, "Richard Matheson," 430.

9. Ibid., 428.

10. Keith Neilson, "Richard Matheson," in *Supernatural Fiction Writers: Fantasy and Horror* Vol. 2, ed. E. F. Bleiler (New York: Charles Scribner's Sons, 1985), 1074.

11. Quoted in Winter, *Faces of Fear*, 27.

12. Stefan Dziemianowicz, "Horror Begins at Home: Richard Matheson's Fear of

the Familiar," *Studies in Weird Fiction* 14 (1994): 29.

13. Ibid., 30.

14. Bernice M. Murphy, *The Suburban Gothic in American Popular Culture* (Houndmills, Basingstoke: Palgrave Macmillan, 2009), 2.

15. Dziemianowicz, "Horror Begins at Home," 29.

16. Stephen King, *Danse Macabre* (1981; London: Warner, 1993), 431. Citations are to the 1993 Warner edition. Steve Biodrowski's review of David Koepp's 1999 adaptation of *A Stir of Echoes* states that the film does well to follow the source material in utilizing a "believably realistic world where the sudden intrusion of the supernatural is that much more uncanny"; "Classic Horror: Koepp Shocks with Matheson's Psychic Murder Mystery Thriller," *Cinefantastique* 31, No. 8 (October 1999): 61.

17. David A. Oakes, *Science and Destabilization in the Modern American Gothic: Lovecraft, Matheson, and King* (Westport, CT: Greenwood Press, 2000), 88.

18. In addition to the two novels examined here, Matheson published a third novel about haunting, *Hell House* (1971). The tale of a group of experts in the paranormal seeking to grasp the mysterious power of the eponymous Maine mansion, this novel is concerned primarily with the details of their investigation rather than engaging with socio-historical matters, and thus falls beyond the scope of this study.

19. Lucy Kay, et al., "Introduction," in *Mapping Liminalities: Thresholds in Cultural and Literary Texts, Transatlantic Aesthetics and Culture* Vol. 2, eds. Lucy Kay, et al. (Bern: Peter Lang, 2007), 8.

20. Vivian Sobchack, *Screening Space: The American Science Fiction Film*, 2nd ed. (New Brunswick, NJ: Rutgers University Press, 1998), 121. Citations are to this edition.

21. Leslie A. Fiedler, *Love and Death in the American Novel* (1960; Champaign, IL: Dalkey Archive Press, 1997), 160–161. Citations are to the 1997 Dalkey Archive edition.

22. Kenneth T. Jackson, *Crabgrass Fron-* tier: *The Suburbanization of the United States* (New York: Oxford University Press, 1985), 265.

23. Although America became increasingly urbanized during the first half of the twentieth century, it was the latter half that saw "the massive development of the suburban landscape." See Robert Beuka, *SuburbiaNation: Reading Suburban Landscape in Twentieth-Century American Fiction and Film* (New York: Palgrave Macmillan, 2004), 1.

24. Ted Krulik, "Reaching for Immortality: Two Novels of Richard Matheson," in *Critical Encounters II: Writers and Themes in Science Fiction*, ed. Tom Staicar (New York: Frederick Ungar, 1982), 4.

25. Jackson, *Crabgrass Frontier*, 11.

26. Richard Matheson, *A Stir of Echoes* (1958; New York: Tor, 1999), 2. Citations are to the 1999 Tor edition. All further references will be included as *ASOE* within the body of the text.

27. Beuka, *SuburbiaNation*, 152–153.

28. Martin Halliwell, *American Culture in the 1950s* (Edinburgh: Edinburgh University Press, 2007), 34.

29. Howard Davis, *The Culture of Building* (Oxford: Oxford University Press, 2006), 80.

30. Karal Ann Marling, *As Seen on TV: The Visual Culture of Everyday Life in the 1950s* (Cambridge, MA: Harvard University Press, 1994), 253.

31. Jackson, 240.

32. In 1957, Vance Packard's *The Hidden Persuaders* brought the notion that advertisers were manipulating consumers via subliminal techniques. Widespread "fear of brainwashing" in the 1950s fixated on the possibility that people could be "*compelled* to act on a subliminal suggestion"; Robin Waterfield, *Hidden Depths: The Story of Hypnosis* (2002; London: Pan, 2004), 366–367. Citations are to the 2004 Pan edition. Hypnotism might be one means of achieving this, as with the unwitting American soldier turned Communist assassin in Richard Condon's 1959 novel *The Manchurian Candidate*, 377.

33. Murphy, *The Suburban Gothic in American Popular Culture*, 40.

34. Kim Ian Michasiw, "Some Stations of Suburban Gothic," in *American Gothic: New Interventions in a National Narrative*, eds. Robert K. Martin and Eric Savoy (Iowa City: University of Iowa Press, 1998), 242–243.

35. Nicholls, 427.

36. Robin Wood, *Hollywood from Vietnam to Reagan... And Beyond*, rev. and exp. ed. (New York: Columbia University Press, 2003), 78. Citations are to this edition.

37. Marling, *As Seen on TV*, 114.

38. Elaine Tyler May, *Homeward Bound: American Families in the Cold War Era*, rev. and upd. ed. (New York: Basic Books, 1999), 90. Citations are to this edition.

39. Ibid., 151.

40. Though the post-war era undoubtedly saw unusually heightened levels of generalized anxiety in American citizens, the promise of a safe haven from "a host of deep-seated fears" concerning race, poverty and social change was central to perceptions of suburban living from its earliest years. See Robert M. Fogelson, *Bourgeois Nightmares: Suburbia, 1870–1930* (New Haven, CT: Yale University Press, 2005), 24.

41. Marling, 253.

42. I have published elsewhere on Matheson's demonization of Elsie (and of other female characters) for exhibiting sexual desires and engaging in flirtatious behavior. See Rebecca Janicker, "'The Most Monstrous of Monsters': Gender, Sexuality, and Marriage in *A Stir of Echoes* and *Earthbound*," in *Reading Richard Matheson: A Critical Survey*, eds. Cheyenne Mathews and Janet V. Haedicke (Lanham, MD: Rowman and Littlefield, 2014), 119–120.

43. Andrew J. Dunar, *America in the Fifties* (Syracuse, NY: Syracuse University Press, 2006), 189.

44. David Riesman, *The Lonely Crowd: A Study of the Changing American Character*, abr. and rev. ed. (New Haven, CT: Yale Nota Bene/Yale University Press, 2001), 3. Citations are to this edition.

45. Robert N. Bellah, et al., *Habits of the Heart: Individualism and Commitment in American Life*, upd. ed. (Berkeley: University of California Press, 1996), 49. Citations are to this edition.

46. C. Wright Mills, *The Power Elite* (New York: Oxford University Press, 1956), 298–299.

47. Ibid., 304.

48. Ibid., 319.

49. Ibid., 320.

50. Norman Mailer, *The White Negro: Superficial Reflections on the Hipster* (1957; San Francisco, CA: City Lights Books, 1970), 3. Citations are to the 1970 City Lights edition.

51. Halliwell, *American Culture in the 1950s*, 34.

52. Humphrey Carver, *Cities in the Suburbs* (Toronto: University of Toronto Press, 1962), 15.

53. May, *Homeward Bound*, 156. See also Lynn Spigel, *Welcome to the Dreamhouse: Popular Media and Postwar Suburbs* (Durham, NC: Duke University Press, 2001), 110.

54. Marling, 253. Other negative outcomes of this shift in living patterns, in evidence by the late 1950s, were the "suburban jitters" linked to the anxiety associated with upward mobility and constant material acquisition, as well as a paucity of activity for housewives created by the very labor-saving devices they eagerly acquired in the belief that they would improve their lot; ibid., 254–255.

55. Elsa Maxwell, renowned as a gossip columnist and society hostess from the early to mid twentieth century, was widely known by the nickname "the Hostess with the Mostest."

56. Lynn Spigel, "From Theatre to Space Ship: Metaphors of Suburban Domesticity in Postwar America," in *Visions of Suburbia*, ed. Roger Silverstone (London: Routledge, 1997), 221.

57. Catherine Jurca, *White Diaspora: The Suburb and the Twentieth-Century American Novel* (Princeton, NJ: Princeton University Press, 2001), 77.

58. Marling describes a *Saturday Evening Post* cover from 1959 which encapsulates the American Dream with an image of a young couple whose hopes for their future together consist of a boy and a girl, as well as all the trappings of an aspirational suburban environment in which to raise them, 255.

59. Mark Jancovich, *Rational Fears: American Horror in the 1950s* (Manchester: Manchester University Press, 1996), 19.

60. Ibid., 64. Jack Finney's novel *The Body Snatchers* appeared in 1955, then the first film version, *Invasion of the Body Snatchers*, directed by Don Siegel, appeared the following year.

61. Ibid., 26.

62. Adam Roberts, *Science Fiction*, 2nd ed. (London: Routledge, 2006), 60. Citations are to this edition.

63. Jancovich, *Rational Fears*, 95.

64. Dunar, *America in the Fifties*, 191–192.

65. William H. Whyte, *The Organization Man* (1956; Harmondsworth: Penguin, 1960), 246. Citations are to the 1960 Penguin edition.

66. Programs such as "The Monsters are Due On Maple Street," *The Twilight Zone*, DVD, written by Rod Serling (1960; Hollywood, CA: CBS, 2005) point to this potential for horror to lurk and flourish in the very "sameness" and conformity epitomized by suburbia (interestingly enough, this episode precedes one written by Matheson). Despite the final twist, which reveals that aliens do actually exist and pose a threat to America, the narrative shows that they are planning to tap widespread existing social tendencies to ensure that humanity undermines itself.

67. Notably, Helen Driscoll shares a surname with the female protagonist of both Finney's *The Body Snatchers* and Siegel's film adaptation: Becky Driscoll.

68. Allan Lloyd-Smith, *American Gothic Fiction: An Introduction* (New York: Continuum, 2004), 1. See Valdine Clemens, *The Return of the Repressed: Gothic Horror From "The Castle of Otranto" to "Alien"* (Albany: State University of New York Press, 1999), for a discussion of Gothic's preoccupation with the resurgence of that which was believed to be buried.

69. Murphy, 38.

70. H. P. Lovecraft, "The Call of Cthulhu," in *"The Call of Cthulhu" and Other Weird Stories*, H. P. Lovecraft, ed. S. T. Joshi (1928; London: Penguin, 2002), 139.

71. Murphy, 36.

72. Jonathan Engel, *American Therapy: The Rise of Psychotherapy in the United States* (New York: Gotham Books, 2008), 132.

73. May, 21. Interestingly, Jancovich observes that in Ray Bradbury's fiction "it is psychology and psychoanalysis which are seen as the main mechanisms for enforcing conformity and an 'adjustment to reality,'" 110.

74. Neilson, "Richard Matheson," 1077.

75. Sobchack, *Screening Space*, 123. See also Lincoln Geraghty, *American Science Fiction Film and Television* (Oxford: Berg, 2009), 22–23.

76. Neilson, 1077.

Chapter Three

1. Stefan Dziemianowicz, "Horror Begins at Home: Richard Matheson's Fear of the Familiar," *Studies in Weird Fiction* 14 (1994): 36.

2. As the first edition, published in 1982 by Playboy Paperbacks, was not approved by Matheson, it was published under the pseudonym of Logan Swanson. See Paul Stuve and Matthew R. Bradley, "Bibliographies, Filmographies, etc.," in *The Richard Matheson Companion*, eds. Stanley Wiater, Matthew R. Bradley, and Paul Stuve (Colorado Springs: Gauntlet, 2008), 381.

3. In 1989, when Robinson Publishing put out its version of the novel, Matheson's name officially became attached to it. Ibid., 382.

4. Dziemianowicz, "Horror Begins at Home," 30.

5. Kristin Celello, *Making Marriage Work: A History of Marriage and Divorce*

in the Twentieth-Century United States (Chapel Hill: University of North Carolina Press, 2009), 3.

6. Richard Matheson, *Earthbound* (London: Robinson, 1989), 5. All further references will be included as *E* within the body of the text.

7. Gaston Bachelard, *The Poetics of Space*, trans. Maria Jolas (1964; Boston: Beacon, 1994), 3. Citations are to the 1994 Beacon edition.

8. Gina Wisker, *Horror Fiction: An Introduction* (New York: Continuum, 2005), 150.

9. Stephanie Coontz, *Marriage, A History: How Love Conquered Marriage* (New York: Penguin, 2005), 229.

10. Elaine Tyler May, *Homeward Bound: American Families in the Cold War Era*, rev. and upd. ed. (New York: Basic Books, 1999), xviii. Citations are to this edition.

11. Stephanie Coontz, *The Way We Never Were: American Families and the Nostalgia Trap* (1992; New York: Basic Books, 2000), 39. Citations are to the 2000 Basic Books edition.

12. Coontz cites a 1961 survey of young women which discovered that "almost all expected to be married by age twenty-two [and] most hoped to have four children"; *Marriage, A History*, 230. May also notes that "not only did the average age at marriage drop, almost everyone was married by his or her mid-twenties ... most couples had two to four children, born sooner after marriage and spaced closer together than in previous years"; *Homeward Bound*, 14.

13. Coontz, *Marriage, A History*, 231.

14. Ibid.

15. Ibid., 229.

16. Ibid., 233.

17. Ibid., 235.

18. Celello, *Making Marriage Work*, 92 and 97.

19. Ibid., 92.

20. Ibid., 102.

21. Coontz, *Marriage, A History*, 237.

22. Elizabeth Abbott, *A History of Marriage* (London: Duckworth Overlook, 2010), 98. At this time, after the ceremony most newlyweds either went straight to visit those friends and family members who had been unable to attend or simply moved directly into their new marital home, ibid.

23. Coontz, *Marriage, A History*, 167.

24. Ibid.

25. Barry Curtis, *Dark Places: The Haunted House in Film* (London: Reaktion Books, 2008), 171.

26. The physical site to which they retreat for this period, Logan Beach, is a noteworthy one. The inherent liminality of the beach, as a borderland between land and sea, has seen it often cast as an ideal place for contemplation; Zoë Kinsley, "'In moody sadness, on the giddy brink': Liminality and Home Tour Travel," in *Mapping Liminalities: Thresholds in Cultural and Literary Texts, Transatlantic Aesthetics and Culture* Vol. 2, eds. Lucy Kay, et al. (Bern: Peter Lang, 2007), 42. In her analysis of Maui tales, Rose Lovell-Smith also links these liminal properties to the Gothic; "On the Gothic Beach: A New Zealand Reading of House and Landscape in Margaret Mahy's *The Tricksters*," in *The Gothic in Children's Literature: Haunting the Borders*, eds. Anna Jackson, Karen Coats, and Roderick McGillis (New York: Routledge, 2008), 93 and 98.

27. Paul Grainge, *Monochrome Memories: Nostalgia and Style in Retro America* (Westport, CT: Praeger, 2002), 44.

28. Ibid., 45.

29. Celello, 184.

30. May, 98.

31. Anthony Giddens, *The Transformation of Intimacy: Sexuality, Love and Eroticism in Modern Societies* (Cambridge: Polity, 1992), 129.

32. Mary Caputi, *A Kinder, Gentler America: Melancholia and the Mythical 1950s* (Minneapolis: University of Minnesota Press, 2005), 18.

33. Graham Thompson, *American Culture in the 1980s* (Edinburgh: Edinburgh University Press, 2007), 8. See also Carol R. Smith, "Gender and Family Values in the Clinton Presidency and 1990s Hollywood

Film," in *American Film and Politics from Reagan to Bush Jr.*, eds. Philip John Davies and Paul Wells (Manchester: Manchester University Press, 2002), 77.

34. Gil Troy, *Morning in America: How Ronald Reagan Invented the 1980s* (Princeton, NJ: Princeton University Press, 2005), 28.

35. Caputi, *A Kinder, Gentler America*, 2.

36. Troy, *Morning in America*, 12. Troy cites the 1984 campaign advertisement entitled "Morning again in America" which neatly encapsulated Reagan's ethos, 15.

37. Coontz, *Marriage, A History*, 261.

38. Celello, 137.

39. Paul R. Amato, Alan Booth, and David R. Johnson, *Alone Together: How Marriage in America is Changing* (Cambridge, MA: Harvard University Press, 2007), 23.

40. Coontz, *The Way We Never Were*, 167.

41. Celello, 121–123. Barbara Ehrenreich also detects the rise of this trend, citing Mel Krantzler's 1973 popular psychology book *Creative Divorce: A New Opportunity for Personal Growth* as one example; *The Hearts of Men: American Dreams and the Flight from Commitment* (New York: Anchor Books, 1983), 97.

42. Ronald Inglehart and Pippa Norris, *Rising Tide: Gender Equality and Cultural Change Around the World* (Cambridge: Cambridge University Press, 2003), 17.

43. Coontz, *Marriage, A History*, 258. See also Coontz, *The Way We Never Were*, 174.

44. Ehrenreich, *The Hearts of Men*, 90–91.

45. Giddens, *The Transformation of Intimacy*, 30.

46. Inglehart and Norris, *Rising Tide*, 17.

47. Robert N. Bellah, et al., *Habits of the Heart: Individualism and Commitment in American Life*, upd. ed. (Berkeley: University of California Press, 1996), 98. Citations are to this edition.

48. Amato, Booth, and Johnson, *Alone Together*, 4–5.

49. Coontz, *Marriage, A History*, 250.

50. Bellah, et al., *Habits of the Heart*, 90.

51. Ibid., 85.

52. Giddens, 57–58.

53. Mark Jancovich, "The Politics of *Playboy*: Lifestyle, Sexuality and Nonconformity in American Cold War Culture," in *Historicizing Lifestyle: Mediating Taste, Consumption and Identity from the 1900s to 1970s*, eds. David Bell and Joanne Hollows (Aldershot: Ashgate, 2006), 75.

54. Dziemianowicz, 35.

55. Susan Faludi, *Backlash: The Undeclared War Against Women* (1991; London: Vintage, 1993), 441. Citations are to the 1993 Vintage edition.

56. Barbara Creed, *The Monstrous-Feminine: Film, Feminism, Psychoanalysis* (London: Routledge, 1993), 5.

57. Sinikka Elliott and Debra Umberson, "The Performance of Desire: Gender and Sexual Negotiation in Long-Term Marriages," *Journal of Marriage and Family* 70 (May 2008): 392.

58. Bernice M. Murphy, *The Suburban Gothic in American Popular Culture* (Houndmills, Basingstoke: Palgrave Macmillan, 2009), 37.

59. Faludi, *Backlash*, 4.

60. Thompson, *American Culture in the 1980s*, 15.

61. Ibid., 32.

62. Bellah, et al., 110.

63. Troy, 319.

Chapter Four

1. Following in Lovecraft's footsteps, King also found a publishing outlet for his writing efforts in his teenage years courtesy of a family newsletter produced first by a hectograph and then by a home printing press. See Stephen King, *On Writing: A Memoir of the Craft* (London: Hodder and Stoughton, 2000), 35–38. His first professionally published story, "The Glass Floor," appeared in *Startling Mystery Stories* in 1967. See Karin Coddon, "Stephen King: A Biography," in *Readings on Stephen King*, ed. Karin Coddon (Farmington Hills, MI: Greenhaven Press, 2004), 19.

2. In 2006, Stanley Wiater, Christopher Golden, and Hank Wagner noted that *Entertainment Weekly* designated King as "the most significant novelist of the second half of the twentieth century"; *The Complete Stephen King Universe: A Guide to the Worlds of Stephen King*, rev. and upd. ed. (New York: St. Martin's Griffin, 2006), xx. Citations are to this edition.

3. Stephen King, *Danse Macabre* (1981; London: Warner, 1993), 118. Citations are to the 1993 Warner edition.

4. Greg Smith, "The Literary Equivalent of a Big Mac and Fries? Academics, Moralists, and the Stephen King Phenomenon," *Midwest Quarterly: A Journal of Contemporary Thought* 43, No. 4 (2002): 344.

5. Discussions of King's novel in psychoanalytical terms include Clare Hanson's "Stephen King: Powers of Horror," in *American Horror Fiction: From Brockden Brown to Stephen King*, ed. Brian Docherty (Houndmills, Basingstoke: Macmillan, 1990), Ronald T. Curran's "Complex, Archetype, and Primal Fear: King's Use of Fairy Tales in *The Shining*," in *The Dark Descent: Essays Defining Stephen King's Horrorscape*, ed. Tony Magistrale (Westport, CT: Greenwood Press, 1992) and Valdine Clemens's *The Return of the Repressed: Gothic Horror from "The Castle of Otranto" to "Alien"* (Albany: State University of New York Press, 1999). Similar treatments of Kubrick's film include Christopher Hoile's "The Uncanny and the Fairy Tale in Kubrick's *The Shining*," *Literature/Film Quarterly* 12, No. 1 (1984) and Robert Kilker's "All Roads Lead to the Abject: The Monstrous Feminine and Gender Boundaries in Stanley Kubrick's *The Shining*," *Literature/Film Quarterly* 34, No. 1 (2006).

6. For various accounts of the influence of Poe's tales, including "The Masque of the Red Death" and "The Fall of the House of Usher," see Burton R. Pollin, "Stephen King's Fiction and the Heritage of Poe," *Journal of the Fantastic in the Arts* 5, No. 4 (1993), Leonard Mustazza, "Poe's 'The Masque of the Red Death' and King's *The Shining*: Echo, Influence, and Deviation," in *Discovering Stephen King's "The Shining"*:

Essays on the Bestselling Novel by America's Premier Horror Writer, ed. Tony Magistrale (Gillette, NJ: Wildside Press, 1998), and Tony Magistrale and Sidney Poger, *Poe's Children: Connections Between Tales of Terror and Detection* (New York: Peter Lang, 1999). On Norris, see Brian Kent, "Canaries in a Gilded Cage: Mental and Marital Decline in *McTeague* and *The Shining*," in *"The Shining" Reader*, ed. Anthony Magistrale (Mercer Island, WA: Starmont House, 1991), Jeanne Campbell Reesman, "Stephen King and the Tradition of American Naturalism in *The Shining*," in ibid., and Dale Bailey, *American Nightmares: The Haunted House Formula in American Popular Fiction* (Bowling Green, OH: Bowling Green State University Popular Press, 1999). In "Stephen King, Naturalism, and *The Shining*," *Excavatio: Emile Zola and Naturalism* 9 (1997), Tony Williams relates the novel to Zola's *Rougon-Macquart* series.

7. See Patricia Ferreira, "Jack's Nightmare at the Overlook: The American Dream Inverted," in *"The Shining" Reader*.

8. The only reading that takes Jack's role within the Torrance family as a key thematic focus is Frank Manchel's "What About Jack? Another Perspective on Family Relationships in Stanley Kubrick's *The Shining*," *Literature/Film Quarterly* 23, No. 1 (1995). Manchel argues that the much-excoriated cinematic version of Jack is entitled to some measure of empathy because of the "feelings of inadequacy" he experiences with regard to his familial responsibilities, 75.

9. Quoted in "Terror Ink," in *Bare Bones: Conversations on Terror with Stephen King*, eds. Tim Underwood and Chuck Miller (New York: McGraw-Hill, 1988), 105.

10. Quoted in ibid., 99.

11. Sharon Monteith, *American Culture in the 1960s* (Edinburgh: Edinburgh University Press, 2008), 6.

12. Michael S. Kimmel, *Manhood in America: A Cultural History*, 2nd ed. (New York: Oxford University Press, 2006), 174. Citations are to this edition.

13. King, *On Writing*, 62.

14. Pierre Macherey, *A Theory of Liter-*

ary Production, trans. Geoffrey Wall (1966; London: Routledge and Kegan Paul, 1978), 8. Citations are to the 1978 Routledge and Kegan Paul edition.

15. Ibid., 23.

16. Fredric Jameson, *The Ideologies of Theory* (London: Verso, 2008), 130.

17. Joseph Grixti, *Terrors of Uncertainty: The Cultural Contexts of Horror Fiction* (London: Routledge, 1989), 61.

18. Barbara Ehrenreich, *The Hearts of Men: American Dreams and the Flight from Commitment* (New York: Anchor Books: 1983), 7.

19. Stephen King, *The Shining* (Garden City, NY: Doubleday, 1977), 15. All further references will be included as *TS* within the body of the text.

20. Lawrence B. Glickman, *A Living Wage: American Workers and the Making of Consumer Society* (Ithaca, NY: Cornell University Press, 1997), 43.

21. Sara Martín Alegre, "Nightmares of Childhood: The Child and the Monster in Four Novels by Stephen King," *Atlantis: A Journal of the Spanish Association for Anglo-American Studies* 23, No. 1 (June 2001): 105.

22. Kimmel, *Manhood in America*, 13.

23. Sharon A. Russell, *Stephen King: A Critical Companion* (Westport, CT: Greenwood Press, 1996), 55.

24. To take one real-life example, the Hotel del Coronado Heritage Department still boasts that "in the 1920s, England's Prince of Wales was feted at the hotel, as was aviator hero Charles Lindbergh"; *Building the Dream: The Design and Construction of the Hotel del Coronado* (Coronado, CA: Hotel del Coronado Heritage Department, 2008), 79.

25. In a similar vein, the Hotel del Coronado is also deemed noteworthy for its association with polo, which is extolled as "the sport of kings," ibid.

26. Richard T. Hughes, *Myths America Lives By* (Urbana: University of Illinois Press, 2003), 127.

27. Ibid., 128. Hughes joins with Robert N. Bellah in arguing that the equation made between material wealth and moral

virtue at this time led to a pervasive cultural myth, as "Americans since the late nineteenth century have defined the very meaning of life in terms of monetary success and the accumulation of goods," 149.

28. Jeffrey Louis Decker, *Made in America: Self-Styled Success from Horatio Alger to Oprah Winfrey* (Minneapolis: University of Minnesota Press, 1997), 3.

29. Ibid., xxvii. The rise of the business corporation meant that wealth became concentrated in the hands of the few, who then used their positions to remove competition.

30. Ibid., 103.

31. Ibid.

32. Howard Zinn, *The Twentieth Century: A People's History*, rev. and upd. ed. (New York: HarperPerennial, 1998), 335. Citations are to this edition.

33. Karen A. Hohne, "The Power of the Spoken Word in the Works of Stephen King," *Journal of Popular Culture* 28, No. 2 (Fall 1994): 97.

34. Daniel S. Duvall, "Inner Demons: Flawed Protagonists and Haunted Houses in *The Haunting* and *The Shining*," *Creative Screenwriting* 6, No. 4 (1999): 37.

35. The haunting in this encounter is striking in its mimicry of Jack's alcoholism. Despite his continued sobriety, he exhibits symptoms associated with his past, yearning for a drink and "constantly wiping his lips with his hand" (*TS*: 163). The confusion in his thought processes, which deepens as the haunting takes hold, is reminiscent of how he was when he was drinking. As with his writing, his ghostly alcoholism is an experience of haunting through which the Overlook manipulates him and separates him from his family.

36. Kimmel, 156–157.

37. Ehrenreich, *The Hearts of Men*, 12; see also Kimmel, 185.

38. Stephen Meyer, "Work, Play, and Power: Masculine Culture on the Automotive Shop Floor, 1930–1960," in *Boys and Their Toys? Masculinity, Technology, and Class in America*, ed. Roger Horowitz (New York: Routledge, 2001), 22.

39. In this moment, Jack's beleaguered

state of mind resonates with Karl Marx's observation that "Men make their own history, but they do not make it just as they please.... The tradition of all the dead generations weighs like a nightmare on the brain of the living"; *The Eighteenth Brumaire of Louis Bonaparte* (1852; New York: International Publishers, 1963), 15.

40. Mary Jane Dickerson, "The 'Masked Author Strikes Again': Writing and Dying in Stephen King's *The Shining*," in *"The Shining" Reader*, 37.

41. Christopher Lasch, *The Culture of Narcissism: American Life in an Age of Diminishing Expectations* (New York: W. W. Norton, 1979), 61.

42. Ibid.

43. Dennis R. Perry and Carl H. Sederholm, *Poe, "The House of Usher," and the American Gothic* (New York: Palgrave Macmillan, 2009), 155.

44. Ehrenreich, 38.

45. Fredric Jameson, *Signatures of the Visible* (New York: Routledge, 1990), 90.

46. Tyson Lewis and Daniel Cho, "Home is Where the Neurosis Is: A Topography of the Spatial Unconscious," *Cultural Critique* 64, No. 1 (Fall 2006): 79.

47. Christopher Capozzola, "'It Makes You Want to Believe in the Country': Celebrating the Bicentennial in an Age of Limits," in *America in the Seventies*, eds. Beth Bailey and David Farber (Lawrence: University Press of Kansas, 2004), 44.

Chapter Five

1. Stephen King, *Christine* (New York: Viking Press, 1983), 290. All further references will be included as *C* within the body of the text.

2. Jonathan P. Davis, *Stephen King's America* (Bowling Green, OH: Bowling Green State University Popular Press, 1994), 74.

3. James Egan, "Technohorror: The Dystopian Vision of Stephen King," *Extrapolation* 29, No. 2 (1988): 145, Tony Magistrale, *Landscape of Fear: Stephen King's American Gothic* (Bowling Green, OH: Bowling Green

State University Popular Press, 1988), 48; Donald R. Knight, "'Here Comes My Baby, Singin' Like a Nightingale': Stephen King's *Christine*," *Studies in Weird Fiction* 18 (1996): 16; and Mary Findley, "Stephen King's Vintage Ghost-Cars: A Modern-Day Haunting," in *Spectral America: Phantoms and the National Imagination*, ed. Jeffrey Andrew Weinstock (Madison: University of Wisconsin Press/Popular Press, 2004), 212–213.

4. Anthony Magistrale, *The Moral Voyages of Stephen King* (Mercer Island, WA: Starmont House, 1989), 53.

5. Norman Mailer, *Advertisements for Myself* (1961; London: Panther, 1968), 351. Citations are to the 1968 Panther edition.

6. Edward Madden, "Cars Are Girls: Sexual Power and Sexual Panic in Stephen King's *Christine*," in *Imagining the Worst: Stephen King and the Representation of Women*, eds. Kathleen Margaret Lant and Theresa Thompson (Westport, CT: Greenwood Press, 1998), 144.

7. Andrew Schopp, "From Misogyny to Homophobia and Back Again: The Play of Erotic Triangles in Stephen King's *Christine*," *Extrapolation* 38, No. 1 (1997): 67–68.

8. Sylvia Kelso, "Take Me For a Ride in your Man-Eater: Gynophobia in Stephen King's *Christine*," *Paradoxa: Studies in World Literary Genres* 2, No. 2 (1996): 266–267.

9. Victor Turner, *Dramas, Fields, and Metaphors: Symbolic Action in Human Society* (Ithaca, NY: Cornell University Press, 1974), 237.

10. Lucy Kay, et al., "Introduction," in *Mapping Liminalities: Thresholds in Cultural and Literary Texts, Transatlantic Aesthetics and Culture* Vol. 2, eds. Lucy Kay, et al. (Bern: Peter Lang, 2007), 8.

11. Lesley Speed, "Tuesday's Gone: The Nostalgic Teen Film," *Journal of Popular Film and Television* 26, No. 1 (1998): 25.

12. Ibid., 24–26.

13. Fredric Jameson, *Postmodernism, or, The Cultural Logic of Late Capitalism* (London: Verso, 1991), 21.

14. Paul Grainge, *Monochrome Memories: Nostalgia and Style in Retro America* (Westport, CT: Praeger, 2002), 26.

15. Philip Drake, "'Mortgaged to music': new retro movies in 1990s Hollywood cinema," in *Memory and Popular Film*, ed. Paul Grainge (Manchester: Manchester University Press, 2003), 190.

16. Randy Lofficier and Phil Edwards, "Stephen King on *Christine*," *Starburst*, May 1984, 14.

17. Svetlana Boym, *The Future of Nostalgia* (New York: Basic Books, 2001), 54.

18. Linda Badley, *Writing Horror and the Body: The Fiction of Stephen King, Clive Barker, and Anne Rice* (Westport, CT: Greenwood Press, 1996), 29.

19. Douglas E. Winter, *Stephen King: The Art of Darkness*, exp. and upd. ed. (New York: Signet, 1986), 139. Citations are to this edition.

20. Mary Caputi, *A Kinder, Gentler America: Melancholia and the Mythical 1950s* (Minneapolis: University of Minnesota Press, 2005), 1.

21. Ibid., 6.

22. Jameson, *Postmodernism*, 19.

23. Ibid., 279.

24. Joseph Reino, *Stephen King: The First Decade, "Carrie" to "Pet Sematary"* (Boston, MA: Twayne, 1988), 90.

25. James J. Flink, *The Automobile Age* (Cambridge: MIT Press, 1988), 161 and 187.

26. James J. Flink, *The Car Culture* (Cambridge: MIT Press, 1975), 194.

27. Kenneth Hey, "Cars and Films in American Culture, 1929–1959," in *The Automobile and American Culture*, eds. David L. Lewis and Laurence Goldstein (Ann Arbor: University of Michigan Press, 1980), 198.

28. Yasutoshi Ikuta, *Cruise O Matic: Automobile Advertising of the 1950s* (San Francisco, CA: Chronicle Books, 2000), 18.

29. Karal Ann Marling, *As Seen on TV: The Visual Culture of Everyday Life in the 1950s* (Cambridge, MA: Harvard University Press, 1994), 146.

30. Ibid.

31. "Cadillac—Jan. '58," Adflip, accessed June 9, 2011, http://adflip.com/addetails. php?adID=1351&showLargeJpg=yes.

32. "Studebaker Golden Hawks—Jan.

'58," Adflip, accessed June 9, 2011, http://adflip.com/addetails.php?adID=1342&showLargeJpg=yes.

33. "Plymouth: 1956 Plymouth—1956 Plymouth Ad-01," Old Car Advertising, accessed June 22, 2011, http://oldcaradvertising.com/Plymouth/1956%20Plymouth/1956%20Plymouth%20Ad-01.html.

34. "Plymouth: 1957 Plymouth—1957 Plymouth Ad-03," Old Car Advertising, accessed June 22, 2011, http://www.oldcaradvertising.com/Plymouth/1957%20Plymouth/1957%20Plymouth%20Ad-03.html.

35. Ikuta, *Cruise O Matic*, 101.

36. "Plymouth: 1956 Plymouth—1956 Plymouth Ad-01."

37. Marling, *As Seen on TV*, 132.

38. Peter J. Ling, *America and the Automobile: Technology, Reform and Social Change, 1893–1923* (Manchester: Manchester University Press, 1990), 5.

39. Flink, *The Car Culture*, 210.

40. Charles L. Sanford, "'Woman's Place' in American Car Culture," in *The Automobile and American Culture*, 138.

41. Philip Simpson, "The Lonesome Autoerotic Death of Arnie Cunningham in John Carpenter's *Christine*," in *The Films of Stephen King: From "Carrie" to "Secret Window*," ed. Tony Magistrale (New York: Palgrave Macmillan, 2008), 55.

42. Timothy Shary, *Teen Movies: American Youth on Screen* (London: Wallflower, 2005), 17.

43. Speed, "Tuesday's Gone," 28.

44. Ibid.

45. Eric Mottram, *Blood on the Nash Ambassador: Investigations in American Culture* (London: Hutchinson Radius, 1983), 50.

46. Caputi, *A Kinder, Gentler America*, 22–23.

47. Ibid., 106.

48. See Deborah L. Madsen, *American Exceptionalism* (Edinburgh: Edinburgh University Press, 1998) for a discussion of the changing conceptions of exceptionalism in American culture.

49. Caputi, 105–106.

50. Flink, *The Automobile Age*, 373.

51. The Organisation of Arab Petroleum

Exporting Countries (OAPEC) was the predecessor of OPEC, in ibid., 389–390.

52. Flink, *The Car Culture*, 228.

53. Marling, 158–159.

54. Flink, *The Automobile Age*, 327.

55. Caputi, 111.

56. Ibid., 110.

57. Tom Engelhardt, *The End of Victory Culture: Cold War America and the Disillusioning of a Generation* (Amherst: University of Massachusetts Press, 1995), 4–5.

58. Ibid., 15.

59. Thomas Doherty, *Teenagers and Teenpics: The Juvenilization of American Movies in the 1950s*, rev. and exp. ed. (Philadelphia, PA: Temple University Press, 2002), 34–35. Citations are to this edition.

60. Drake, "'Mortgaged to music,'" 190.

61. John Sears, *Stephen King's Gothic* (Cardiff: University of Wales Press, 2011), 94.

62. Caputi, 18.

63. Linda C. Badley, "Love and Death in the American Car: Stephen King's Auto-Erotic Horror," in *The Gothic World of Stephen King: Landscape of Nightmares*, eds. Gary Hoppenstand and Ray B. Browne (Bowling Green, OH: Bowling Green State University Popular Press, 1987), 87.

64. Tom Newhouse, "A Blind Date with Disaster: Adolescent Revolt in the Fiction of Stephen King," in ibid., 54.

65. "Plymouth: 1957 Plymouth—1957 Plymouth Ad-03."

66. "Plymouth: 1957 Plymouth—1957 Plymouth Ad-02," Old Car Advertising, accessed June 22, 2011, http://www.oldcar advertising.com/Plymouth/1957%20Ply mouth/1957%20Plymouth%20Ad-02.html.

67. "Plymouth: 1956 Plymouth—1956 Plymouth Ad-01."

68. Badley, "Love and Death in the American Car," 87.

69. Shary, *Teen Movies*, 21.

70. Doherty, *Teenagers and Teenpics*, 93.

71. Christopher Gair, *The American Counterculture* (Edinburgh: Edinburgh University Press, 2007), 4.

72. Schopp, "From Misogyny to Homophobia and Back Again," 75.

73. Ibid., 76–77.

74. Lawrence Grossberg, *We Gotta Get Out of This Place: Popular Conservatism and Postmodern Culture* (New York: Routledge, 1992), 173.

75. Michael R. Collings, *The Many Facets of Stephen King* (Gillette, NJ: Wildside Press, 1985), 98.

76. David Laird, "Versions of Eden: The Automobile and the American Novel," in *The Automobile and American Culture*, 245.

77. Karin Coddon, "Stephen King: A Biography," in *Readings on Stephen King*, ed. Karin Coddon (Farmington Hills, MI: Greenhaven Press, 2004), 19.

Chapter Six

1. Fred Botting, *Gothic* (London: Routledge, 1996), 129.

2. Lois Parkinson Zamora, "Magical Romance/Magical Realism: Ghosts in U.S. and Latin American Fiction," in *Magical Realism: Theory, History, Community*, eds. Lois Parkinson Zamora and Wendy B. Faris (Durham, NC: Duke University Press, 1995), 497.

3. Victor Turner, *Dramas, Fields, and Metaphors: Symbolic Action in Human Society* (Ithaca, NY: Cornell University Press, 1974), 242.

4. Gina Wisker, *Horror Fiction: An Introduction* (New York: Continuum, 2005), 38.

5. David A. Oakes, *Science and Destabilization in the Modern American Gothic: Lovecraft, Matheson, and King* (Westport, CT: Greenwood Press, 2000), 6.

6. Stephen King, *Bag of Bones* (London: Hodder and Stoughton, 1998), 19. All further references will be included as *BB* within the body of the text. Virginia C. Andrews (1923–1986) was a best-selling American author of Gothic horror and family sagas. Her best-known work is arguably *Flowers in the Attic* (1979), a novel which spawned several successors and a motion picture.

7. Sigmund Freud, "The 'Uncanny,'" in *The Standard Edition of the Complete Psychological Works of Sigmund Freud: An Infantile Neurosis and Other Works* Vol. 17

(1917–1919), trans. James Strachey (London: Vintage, 2001), 241.

8. Sharon A. Russell, *Revisiting Stephen King: A Critical Companion* (Westport, CT: Greenwood Press, 2002), 93.

9. Tony Magistrale, *Landscape of Fear: Stephen King's American Gothic* (Bowling Green, OH: Bowling Green State University Popular Press, 1988), 19.

10. Renée L. Bergland, *The National Uncanny: Indian Ghosts and American Subjects* (Hanover, NH: Dartmouth College/University Press of New England, 2000), 52. Bergland discusses this idea in relation to Leslie A. Fiedler's influential argument, examined earlier in this volume, concerning the shift from Old World to New World Gothic. Ibid., 52–53.

11. Mark Monmonier, *From Squaw Tit to Whorehouse Meadow: How Maps Name, Claim, and Inflame* (Chicago: University of Chicago Press, 2006), 145.

12. Pamela J. Stewart and Andrew Strathern, "Introduction," in *Landscape, Memory and History: Anthropological Perspectives*, eds. Pamela J. Stewart and Andrew Strathern (London: Pluto Press, 2003), 6.

13. Angèle Smith, "Landscape Representation: Place and Identity in Nineteenth-century Ordnance Survey Maps of Ireland," in ibid., 79.

14. Pei-yi Guo, "'Island Builders': Landscape and Historicity Among the Langalanga, Solomon Islands," in ibid., 203. See also Monmonier, *From Squaw Tit to Whorehouse Meadow*, 6.

15. Teresa A. Goddu, *Gothic America: Narrative, History, and Nation* (New York: Columbia University Press, 1997), 7.

16. Quoted in James W. Loewen, *Lies My Teacher Told Me: Everything Your American History Textbook Got Wrong* (New York: Simon and Schuster, 1995), 161; Howard Zinn, *A People's History of the United States: 1492–Present*, rev. and upd. ed. (New York: HarperPerennial, 1995), 339. Citations are to this edition.

17. John C. Inscoe, "Carolina Slave Names: An Index to Acculturation," *The Journal of Southern History* 49, No. 4 (1983): 538–539.

18. Ibid., 533 and 553; Kimberly W. Benston, "I Yam What I Am: The Topos of (Un)Naming in Afro-American Literature," in *Black Literature and Literary Theory*, ed. Henry Louis Gates, Jr. (New York: Methuen, 1984), 152.

19. Benston, ibid.

20. Ibid., 158.

21. Eino Railo, *The Haunted Castle: A Study of the Elements of English Romanticism* (London: Routledge, 1927), 2–3.

22. Mark Jancovich, *Horror* (London: B. T. Batsford, 1992), 41.

23. Eve Kosofsky Sedgwick, *The Coherence of Gothic Conventions* (North Stratford, NH: Ayer, 1999), 8.

24. Ibid.

25. Goddu, *Gothic America*, 155.

26. Stanley Wiater, Christopher Golden and Hank Wagner, *The Complete Stephen King Universe: A Guide to the Worlds of Stephen King*, rev. and upd. ed. (New York: St. Martin's Griffin, 2006), 126. Citations are to this edition.

27. Tony Magistrale, "Native Sons: Regionalism in the Work of Nathaniel Hawthorne and Stephen King," *Journal of the Fantastic in the Arts* 2, no. 1 (Spring 1989): 82.

28. Heidi Strengell, "The Ghost: The Gothic Melodrama in Stephen King's Fiction," *European Journal of American Culture* 24, No. 3 (2005): 228. See also Heidi Strengell, *Dissecting Stephen King: From the Gothic to Literary Naturalism* (Madison: Popular Press/University of Wisconsin Press, 2005), 92–93.

29. Kim D. Hester-Williams, "NeoSlaves: Slavery, Freedom, and African American Apotheosis in *Candyman, The Matrix*, and *The Green Mile*," *Genders* 40 (2004): 43, accessed May 19, 2009, http://www.genders.org/g40/g40_williams.html.

30. Kathleen Brogan, *Cultural Haunting: Ghosts and Ethnicity in Recent American Literature* (Charlottesville: University Press of Virginia, 1998), 29.

31. Ibid., 19.

Bibliography

Abbott, Elizabeth. *A History of Marriage.* London: Duckworth Overlook, 2010.

Adflip. "Cadillac—Jan. '58." Accessed June 9, 2011. http://adflip.com/addetails. php?adID=1351&showLargeJpg=yes.

_____. "Studebaker Golden Hawks—Jan. '58." Accessed June 9, 2011. http://adflip. com/addetails.php?adID=1342&show LargeJpg=yes.

Aguirre, Manuel. *The Closed Space: Horror Literature and Western Symbolism.* Manchester: Manchester University Press, 1990.

Aguirre, Manuel, Roberta Quance, and Philip Sutton. "Introduction: The Concept of Liminality." In *Margins and Thresholds: An Enquiry into the Concept of Liminality in Text Studies; Studies in Liminality and Literature 1,* edited by Manuel Aguirre, Roberta Quance, and Philip Sutton, 1–10. Madrid: Gateway Press, 2000.

_____, _____ and _____, eds. *Margins and Thresholds: An Enquiry into the Concept of Liminality in Text Studies; Studies in Liminality and Literature 1.* Madrid: Gateway Press, 2000.

Amato, Paul R., Alan Booth, and David R. Johnson. *Alone Together: How Marriage in America is Changing.* Cambridge, MA: Harvard University Press, 2007.

Andrews, V. C. *Flowers in the Attic.* 1979. New York: Pocket Books, 2005.

Ashley, Mike. *The Time Machines: The Story of the Science-Fiction Pulp Magazines from the Beginning to 1950.* Liverpool: Liverpool University Press, 2000.

Bachelard, Gaston. *The Poetics of Space.* Translated by Maria Jolas. Boston: Beacon Press, 1994. First published 1964 by Orion Press.

Badley, Linda. *Writing Horror and the Body: The Fiction of Stephen King, Clive Barker, and Anne Rice.* Westport, CT: Greenwood Press, 1996.

Badley, Linda C. "Love and Death in the American Car: Stephen King's Auto-Erotic Horror." In *The Gothic World of Stephen King: Landscape of Nightmares,* edited by Gary Hoppenstand and Ray B. Browne, 84–94. Bowling Green, OH: Bowling Green State University Popular Press, 1987.

Bailey, Beth, and David Farber, eds. *America in the Seventies.* Lawrence: University Press of Kansas, 2004.

Bailey, Dale. *American Nightmares: The Haunted House Formula in American Popular Fiction.* Bowling Green, OH: Bowling Green State University Popular Press, 1999.

Baldick, Chris. *In Frankenstein's Shadow: Myth, Monstrosity, and Nineteenth-Century Writing.* Oxford: Clarendon Press, 1987.

Bealer, Tracy. "'The Innsmouth Look': H. P. Lovecraft's Ambivalent Modernism." *Journal of Philosophy: A Cross-Disciplinary Inquiry* 6, No. 14 (Winter 2011): 44–50.

Bell, David, and Joanne Hollows, eds. *Historicizing Lifestyle: Mediating Taste, Consumption and Identity from the 1900s to 1970s.* Aldershot: Ashgate, 2006.

Bellah, Robert N., Richard Madsen, William M. Sullivan, Ann Swidler, and Steven M. Tipton. *Habits of the Heart:*

Individualism and Commitment in American Life. Upd. ed. Berkeley: University of California Press, 1996.

Belsey, Catherine. *Critical Practice.* London: Routledge, 1980.

Benston, Kimberly W. "I Yam What I Am: The Topos of (Un)Naming in Afro-American Literature." In *Black Literature and Literary Theory,* edited by Henry Louis Gates, Jr., 151–172. New York: Methuen, 1984.

Bergland, Renée L. *The National Uncanny: Indian Ghosts and American Subjects.* Hanover, NH: Dartmouth College/University Press of New England, 2000.

Beuka, Robert. *SuburbiaNation: Reading Suburban Landscape in Twentieth-Century American Fiction and Film.* New York: Palgrave Macmillan, 2004.

Biodrowski, Steve. "Classic Horror: Koepp Shocks with Matheson's Psychic Murder Mystery Thriller." *Cinefantastique* 31, No. 8 (October 1999): 61.

Bleiler, E. F. Introduction to *Supernatural Horror in Literature,* by H. P. Lovecraft, iii–viii. New York: Dover, 1973.

_____, ed. *Science Fiction Writers: Critical Studies of the Major Authors from the Early Nineteenth Century to the Present Day.* New York: Charles Scribner's Sons, 1982.

_____, ed. *Supernatural Fiction Writers: Fantasy and Horror* Vol. 2. New York: Charles Scribner's Sons, 1985.

Bloom, Clive. *Bestsellers: Popular Fiction Since 1900.* 2nd ed. Houndmills, Basingstoke: Palgrave Macmillan, 2008.

_____. "Introduction: Death's Own Backyard." In *Gothic Horror: A Reader's Guide from Poe to King and Beyond,* edited by Clive Bloom, 1–22. Houndmills, Basingstoke: Macmillan, 1998.

_____, ed. *Gothic Horror: A Reader's Guide from Poe to King and Beyond.* Houndmills, Basingstoke: Macmillan, 1998.

Boerem, R. "Lovecraft and the Tradition of the Gentleman Narrator." In *An Epicure in the Terrible: A Centennial Anthology of Essays in Honor of H. P. Lovecraft,* edited by David E. Schultz and S. T. Joshi, 257–272. London: Fairleigh Dickinson University Press/Associated University Presses, 1991.

Botting, Fred. *Gothic.* London: Routledge, 1996.

Boyer, Paul, and Stephen Nissenbaum. *Salem Possessed: The Social Origins of Witchcraft.* Cambridge, MA: Harvard University Press, 1974.

Boym, Svetlana. *The Future of Nostalgia.* New York: Basic Books, 2001.

Briggs, Julia. "The Ghost Story." In *A Companion to the Gothic,* edited by David Punter, 122–131. Oxford: Blackwell, 2000.

_____. *Night Visitors: The Rise and Fall of the English Ghost Story.* London: Faber and Faber, 1977.

Brogan, Kathleen. *Cultural Haunting: Ghosts and Ethnicity in Recent American Literature.* Charlottesville: University Press of Virginia, 1998.

Brown, Charles Brockden. *Edgar Huntly: Or, Memoirs of a Sleep-Walker.* 1799. Indianapolis, IN: Hackett, 1998.

Brown, Gillian. "Hawthorne's American History." In *The Cambridge Companion to Nathaniel Hawthorne,* edited by Richard H. Millington, 121–142. Cambridge: Cambridge University Press, 2004.

Brunvand, Jan Harold. *The Vanishing Hitchhiker: Urban Legends and Their Meanings.* 1981. London: Pan, 1983.

Burleson, Donald R. *H. P. Lovecraft: A Critical Study.* Westport, CT: Greenwood Press, 1983.

_____. "H. P. Lovecraft: The Hawthorne Influence." *Extrapolation* 22, No. 3 (1981): 262–269.

Capozzola, Christopher. "'It Makes You Want to Believe in the Country': Celebrating the Bicentennial in an Age of Limits." In *America in the Seventies,* edited by Beth Bailey and David Farber, 29–49. Lawrence: University Press of Kansas, 2004.

Caputi, Mary. *A Kinder, Gentler America: Melancholia and the Mythical 1950s.* Minneapolis: University of Minnesota Press, 2005.

Carroll, Noël. *The Philosophy of Horror or Paradoxes of the Heart*. New York: Routledge, 1990.

Carter, Lin. *Lovecraft: A Look Behind the Cthulhu Mythos*. Mercer Island, WA: Starmont House, 1992.

Carver, Humphrey. *Cities in the Suburbs*. Toronto: University of Toronto Press, 1962.

Celello, Kristin. *Making Marriage Work: A History of Marriage and Divorce in the Twentieth-Century United States*. Chapel Hill: University of North Carolina Press, 2009.

Clemens, Valdine. *The Return of the Repressed: Gothic Horror from "The Castle of Otranto" to "Alien."* Albany: State University of New York Press, 1999.

Clery, E. J. *The Rise of Supernatural Fiction: 1762–1800*. Cambridge: Cambridge University Press, 1995.

Coddon, Karin. "Stephen King: A Biography." In *Readings on Stephen King*, edited by Karin Coddon, 16–27. Farmington Hills, MI: Greenhaven Press, 2004.

_____, ed. *Readings on Stephen King*. Farmington Hills, MI: Greenhaven Press, 2004.

Collings, Michael R. *The Many Facets of Stephen King*. Gillette, NJ: Wildside Press, 1985.

Conforti, Joseph A. *Imagining New England: Explorations of Regional Identity from the Pilgrims to the Mid-Twentieth Century*. Chapel Hill: University of North Carolina Press, 2001.

Conn, Peter. *The Divided Mind: Ideology and Imagination in America, 1898–1917*. Cambridge: Cambridge University Press, 1983.

Conrad, Dean. "In Search of Richard Matheson: Science Fiction Screenwriter." *Foundation: The International Review of Science Fiction* 43, No.117 (Spring 2014): 31–45.

Coontz, Stephanie. *Marriage, A History: How Love Conquered Marriage*. New York: Penguin, 2005.

_____. *The Way We Never Were: American Families and the Nostalgia Trap*. 1992. New York: Basic Books, 2000.

Creed, Barbara. *The Monstrous-Feminine: Film, Feminism, Psychoanalysis*. London: Routledge, 1993.

Crow, Charles L. *American Gothic*. Cardiff: University of Wales Press, 2009.

Curran, Ronald T. "Complex, Archetype, and Primal Fear: King's Use of Fairy Tales in The Shining." In *The Dark Descent: Essays Defining Stephen King's Horrorscape*, edited by Tony Magistrale, 33–46. Westport, CT: Greenwood Press, 1992.

Currell, Susan. *American Culture in the 1920s*. Edinburgh: Edinburgh University Press, 2009.

Curtis, Barry. *Dark Places: The Haunted House in Film*. London: Reaktion Books, 2008.

Davies, Philip John, and Paul Wells, eds. *American Film and Politics from Reagan to Bush Jr.* Manchester: Manchester University Press, 2002.

Davis, Howard. *The Culture of Building*. Oxford: Oxford University Press, 2006.

Davis, Jonathan P. *Stephen King's America*. Bowling Green, OH: Bowling Green State University Popular Press, 1994.

Decker, Jeffrey Louis. *Made in America: Self-Styled Success from Horatio Alger to Oprah Winfrey*. Minneapolis: University of Minnesota Press, 1997.

Derleth, August, and Donald Wandrei, eds. *H. P. Lovecraft Selected Letters I: 1911–1924*. Sauk City, WI: Arkham House, 1965.

_____, and _____, eds. *H. P. Lovecraft Selected Letters II: 1925–1929*. Sauk City, WI: Arkham House, 1968.

_____, and _____, eds. *H. P. Lovecraft Selected Letters III: 1929–1931*. Sauk City, WI: Arkham House, 1971.

DeTora, Lisa M., ed. *Heroes of Film, Comics and American Culture: Essays on Real and Fictional Defenders of Home*. Jefferson, NC: McFarland, 2009.

DeVoto, Bernard, ed. *Letters from the*

Earth. New York: Harper and Row, 1962.

Dickerson, Mary Jane. "The 'Masked Author Strikes Again': Writing and Dying in Stephen King's *The Shining*." In *"The Shining" Reader*, edited by Anthony Magistrale, 33–46. Mercer Island, WA: Starmont House, 1991.

Docherty, Brian, ed. *American Horror Fiction: From Brockden Brown to Stephen King*. Houndmills, Basingstoke: Macmillan, 1990.

Doherty, Thomas. *Teenagers and Teenpics: The Juvenilization of American Movies in the 1950s*. Rev. and exp. ed. Philadelphia, PA: Temple University Press, 2002.

Downey, Dara. "'A Labyrinth Without a Clew': Husbands, Houses and Harpies in Richard Matheson's *The Shrinking Man* and Mark Z. Danielewski's *House of Leaves*." In *Heroes of Film, Comics and American Culture: Essays on Real and Fictional Defenders of Home*, edited by Lisa M. DeTora, 17–39. Jefferson, NC: McFarland, 2009.

Drake, Philip. "'Mortgaged to Music': New Retro Movies in 1990s Hollywood Cinema." In *Memory and Popular Film*, edited by Paul Grainge, 183–201. Manchester: Manchester University Press, 2003.

Dunar, Andrew J. *America in the Fifties*. Syracuse, NY: Syracuse University Press, 2006.

Duvall, Daniel S. "Inner Demons: Flawed Protagonists and Haunted Houses in *The Haunting* and *The Shining*." *Creative Screenwriting* 6, No. 4 (1999): 32–37.

Dziemianowicz, Stefan. "Horror Begins at Home: Richard Matheson's Fear of the Familiar." *Studies in Weird Fiction* 14 (1994): 29–36.

Eastern State Penitentiary. "Façade—Eastern State Penitentiary." Accessed August 17, 2012. http://www.easternstate.org/explore/online-360-tour/facade.

Edmundson, Mark. *Nightmare on Main Street: Angels, Sadomasochism, and the Culture of Gothic*. Cambridge, MA: Harvard University Press, 1997.

Egan, James. "Technohorror: The Dystopian Vision of Stephen King." *Extrapolation* 29, No. 2 (1988): 140–152.

Ehrenreich, Barbara. *The Hearts of Men: American Dreams and the Flight from Commitment*. New York: Anchor Books, 1983.

Eldridge, David. *American Culture in the 1930s*. Edinburgh: Edinburgh University Press, 2008.

Elliott, Sinikka, and Debra Umberson. "The Performance of Desire: Gender and Sexual Negotiation in Long-Term Marriages." *Journal of Marriage and Family* 70 (May 2008): 391–406.

Ellis, Kate Ferguson. *The Contested Castle: Gothic Novels and the Subversion of Domestic Ideology*. Urbana: University of Illinois Press, 1989.

Ellis, Markman. *The History of Gothic Fiction*. Edinburgh: Edinburgh University Press, 2000.

Engel, Jonathan. *American Therapy: The Rise of Psychotherapy in the United States*. New York: Gotham Books, 2008.

Engelhardt, Tom. *The End of Victory Culture: Cold War America and the Disillusioning of a Generation*. Amherst: University of Massachusetts Press, 1995.

Evans, Timothy H. "A Last Defense Against the Dark: Folklore, Horror, and the Uses of Tradition in the Works of H. P. Lovecraft." *Journal of Folklore Research* 42, No. 1 (2005): 99–135.

Faludi, Susan. *Backlash: The Undeclared War Against Women*. 1991. London: Vintage, 1993.

Ferguson, Marjorie, and Peter Golding. "Cultural Studies and Changing Times: An Introduction." In *Cultural Studies in Question*, edited by Marjorie Ferguson and Peter Golding, xiii–xxvii. London: Sage, 1997.

_____ and _____, eds. *Cultural Studies in Question*. London: Sage, 1997.

Ferreira, Patricia. "Jack's Nightmare at the Overlook: The American Dream Inverted." In *"The Shining" Reader*, edited by Anthony Magistrale, 23–32. Mercer Island, WA: Starmont House, 1991.

Fiedler, Leslie A. *Love and Death in the American Novel*. Champaign, IL: Dalkey Archive Press, 1997. First published 1960 by Stein and Day.

Findley, Mary. "Stephen King's Vintage Ghost-Cars: A Modern-Day Haunting." In *Spectral America: Phantoms and the National Imagination*, edited by Jeffrey Andrew Weinstock, 207–220. Madison: University of Wisconsin Press/Popular Press, 2004.

Finney, Jack. *Invasion of the Body Snatchers*. 1955. New York: Scribner, 1998.

Flink, James J. *The Automobile Age*. Cambridge: MIT Press, 1988.

_____. *The Car Culture*. Cambridge: MIT Press, 1975.

Fogelson, Robert M. *Bourgeois Nightmares: Suburbia, 1870–1930*. New Haven, CT: Yale University Press, 2005.

Foucault, Michel. "Of Other Spaces." Translated by Jay Miskowiec. *Diacritics* 16, No. 1 (1986): 22–27.

Freud, Sigmund. "The 'Uncanny.'" 1919. Translated by James Strachey. In *The Standard Edition of the Complete Psychological Works of Sigmund Freud: An Infantile Neurosis and Other Works* Vol. 17 (1917–1919), 217–256. London: Vintage, 2001.

Gabaccia, Donna R. *Immigration and American Diversity: A Social and Cultural History*. Malden, MA: Blackwell, 2002.

Gair, Christopher. *The American Counterculture*. Edinburgh: Edinburgh University Press, 2007.

Gardner, Jared. "Alien Nation: Edgar Huntly's Savage Awakening." *American Literature* 66, No. 3 (1994): 429–461.

Gates, Henry Louis, Jr., ed. *Black Literature and Literary Theory*. New York: Methuen, 1984.

Gelder, Ken. *Popular Fiction: The Logics and Practices of a Literary Field*. London: Routledge, 2004.

Geraghty, Lincoln. *American Science Fiction Film and Television*. Oxford: Berg, 2009.

Gerstle, Gary. *American Crucible: Race and Nation in the Twentieth Century*. Princeton, NJ: Princeton University Press, 2001.

Giddens, Anthony. *The Transformation of Intimacy: Sexuality, Love and Eroticism in Modern Societies*. Cambridge: Polity, 1992.

Glickman, Lawrence B. *A Living Wage: American Workers and the Making of Consumer Society*. Ithaca, NY: Cornell University Press, 1997.

Goddu, Teresa A. *Gothic America: Narrative, History, and Nation*. New York: Columbia University Press, 1997.

Goodman, Paul, and Frank O. Gatell. *America in the Twenties: The Beginnings of Contemporary America*. New York: Holt, Rinehart and Winston, 1972.

Gordon, Avery F. *Ghostly Matters: Haunting and the Sociological Imagination*. Minneapolis: University of Minnesota Press, 1997.

Grainge, Paul. *Monochrome Memories: Nostalgia and Style in Retro America*. Westport, CT: Praeger, 2002.

_____, ed. *Memory and Popular Film*. Manchester: Manchester University Press, 2003.

Grider, Sylvia. "The Haunted House in Literature, Popular Culture, and Tradition: A Consistent Image." *Contemporary Legend* 2 (1999): 174–204.

Grixti, Joseph. *Terrors of Uncertainty: The Cultural Contexts of Horror Fiction*. London: Routledge, 1989.

Grossberg, Lawrence. *We Gotta Get Out of This Place: Popular Conservatism and Postmodern Culture*. New York: Routledge, 1992.

Guo, Pei-yi. "'Island Builders': Landscape and Historicity Among the Langalanga, Solomon Islands." In *Landscape, Memory and History: Anthropological Perspectives*, edited by Pamela J. Stewart and Andrew Strathern, 189–209. London: Pluto Press, 2003.

Halberstam, Judith. *Skin Shows: Gothic Horror and the Technology of Monsters*. Durham, NC: Duke University Press, 1995.

Halliwell, Martin. *American Culture in the 1950s*. Edinburgh: Edinburgh University Press, 2007.

Halpern, Paul, and Michael C. LaBossiere. "Mind Out of Time: Identity, Perception, and the Fourth Dimension in H. P. Lovecraft's 'The Shadow Out of Time' and 'The Dreams in the Witch House.'" *Extrapolation* 50, No. 3 (Fall 2009): 512–533.

Hansen, Chadwick. *Witchcraft at Salem*. New York: George Braziller, 1969.

Hanson, Clare. "Stephen King: Powers of Horror." In *American Horror Fiction: From Brockden Brown to Stephen King*, edited by Brian Docherty, 135–154. Houndmills, Basingstoke: Macmillan, 1990.

Harman, Graham. *Weird Realism: Lovecraft and Philosophy*. Winchester: Zero Books, 2011.

Hester-Williams, Kim D. "NeoSlaves: Slavery, Freedom, and African American Apotheosis in *Candyman*, *The Matrix*, and *The Green Mile*." *Genders* 40 (2004): 1–43. Accessed May 19, 2009. http://www.genders.org/g40/g40_williams.html.

Hey, Kenneth. "Cars and Films in American Culture, 1929–1959." In *The Automobile and American Culture*, edited by David L. Lewis and Laurence Goldstein, 193–205. Ann Arbor: University of Michigan Press, 1980.

Higham, John. *Strangers in the Land: Patterns of American Nativism, 1860–1925*. 1955. New Brunswick, NJ: Rutgers University Press, 1992.

Hohne, Karen A. "The Power of the Spoken Word in the Works of Stephen King." *Journal of Popular Culture* 28, No. 2 (Fall 1994): 93–103.

Hoile, Christopher. "The Uncanny and the Fairy Tale in Kubrick's The Shining." *Literature/Film Quarterly* 12, No. 1 (1984): 5–12.

Hoppenstand, Gary, and Ray B. Browne, eds. *The Gothic World of Stephen King: Landscape of Nightmares*. Bowling Green, OH: Bowling Green State University Popular Press, 1987.

Horowitz, Roger, ed. *Boys and Their Toys? Masculinity, Technology, and Class in America*. New York: Routledge, 2001.

Hotel del Coronado Heritage Department. *Building the Dream: The Design and Construction of the Hotel del Coronado*. Coronado, CA: Hotel del Coronado Heritage Department, 2008.

Hughes, Richard T. *Myths America Lives By*. Urbana: University of Illinois Press, 2003.

Ikuta, Yasutoshi. *Cruise O Matic: Automobile Advertising of the 1950s*. San Francisco, CA: Chronicle Books, 2000.

Inglehart, Ronald, and Pippa Norris. *Rising Tide: Gender Equality and Cultural Change Around the World*. Cambridge: Cambridge University Press, 2003.

Inscoe, John C. "Carolina Slave Names: An Index to Acculturation." *The Journal of Southern History* 49, No. 4 (1983): 527–554.

Jackson, Anna, Karen Coats, and Roderick McGillis, eds. *The Gothic in Children's Literature: Haunting the Borders*. New York: Routledge, 2008.

Jackson, Kenneth T. *Crabgrass Frontier: The Suburbanization of the United States*. New York: Oxford University Press, 1985.

James, Henry. *The American Scene*. Bloomington: Indiana University Press, 1968.

Jameson, Fredric. *The Ideologies of Theory*. London: Verso, 2008.

_____. *Postmodernism, or, The Cultural Logic of Late Capitalism*. London: Verso, 1991.

_____. *Signatures of the Visible*. London: Routledge, 1990.

Jancovich, Mark. *Horror*. London: B. T. Batsford, 1992.

_____. "The Politics of *Playboy*: Lifestyle, Sexuality and Non-conformity in American Cold War Culture." In *Historicizing Lifestyle: Mediating Taste, Consumption and Identity from the 1900s to 1970s*, edited by David Bell and Joanne Hollows, 70–87. Aldershot, UK: Ashgate, 2006.

_____. *Rational Fears: American Horror in*

the 1950s. Manchester: Manchester University Press, 1996.

Janicker, Rebecca. "'The Most Monstrous of Monsters': Gender, Sexuality, and Marriage in *A Stir of Echoes* and *Earthbound*." In *Reading Richard Matheson: A Critical Survey*, edited by Cheyenne Mathews and Janet V. Haedicke, 117–127. Lanham, MD: Rowman and Littlefield, 2014.

_____. "New England Narratives: Space and Place in the Fiction of H. P. Lovecraft." *Extrapolation* 48, No. 1 (2007): 56–72.

Jeffries, Stuart. "Profile: Stephen King." *The Guardian*, September 18, 2004.

Jones, Darryl. "Borderlands: Spiritualism and the Occult in *fin de siècle* and Edwardian Welsh and Irish Horror." *Irish Studies Review* 17, No. 1 (February 2009): 31–44.

Joshi, S. T. *A Dreamer and a Visionary: H. P. Lovecraft in his Time*. Liverpool: Liverpool University Press, 2001.

_____. "Explanatory Notes." In *"The Dreams in the Witch House" and Other Weird Stories*, edited by S. T. Joshi, 397–453. London: Penguin, 2005.

_____. *Reader's Guide to H. P. Lovecraft*. Mercer Island, WA: Starmont House, 1982.

_____. *The Weird Tale*. Holicong, PA: Wildside Press, 1990.

_____, ed. *"The Call of Cthulhu" and Other Weird Stories*. London: Penguin, 2002.

_____, ed. *"The Dreams in the Witch House" and Other Weird Stories*. London: Penguin, 2005.

_____, ed. *H. P. Lovecraft: Four Decades of Criticism*. Athens: Ohio University Press, 1980.

_____, ed. *Icons of Horror and the Supernatural: An Encyclopedia of Our Worst Nightmares* Vol. 1. Westport, CT: Greenwood Press, 2007.

_____, ed. *"The Thing on the Doorstep" and Other Weird Stories*. London: Penguin, 2002.

Joshi, S. T., and David E. Schultz. "Introduction." In *From the Pest Zone: The New York Stories*, edited by S. T. Joshi and David E. Schultz, 7–31. New York: Hippocampus Press, 2003.

_____ and _____. "Introduction." In *Lord of a Visible World: An Autobiography in Letters—H. P. Lovecraft*, edited by S. T. Joshi and David E. Schultz, vii–xix. Athens: Ohio University Press, 2000.

_____ and _____, eds. *From the Pest Zone: The New York Stories*. New York: Hippocampus Press, 2003.

_____ and _____, eds. *H. P. Lovecraft: Letters from New York*. San Francisco, CA: Night Shade Books, 2005.

_____ and _____, eds. *Lord of a Visible World: An Autobiography in Letters—H. P. Lovecraft*. Athens: Ohio University Press, 2000.

Jowett, Lorna, and Stacey Abbott. *TV Horror: Investigating the Dark Side of the Small Screen*. London: I. B. Tauris, 2013.

Jurca, Catherine. *White Diaspora: The Suburb and the Twentieth-Century American Novel*. Princeton, NJ: Princeton University Press, 2001.

Karlsen, Carol F. *The Devil in the Shape of a Woman: Witchcraft in Colonial New England*. New York: W. W. Norton, 1998.

Kay, Lucy, Zoë Kinsley, Terry Phillips, and Alan Roughley, eds. *Mapping Liminalities: Thresholds in Cultural and Literary Texts, Transatlantic Aesthetics and Culture Vol. 2*. Bern: Peter Lang, 2007.

Kelso, Sylvia. "Take Me For a Ride in your Man-Eater: Gynophobia in Stephen King's *Christine*." *Paradoxa: Studies in World Literary Genres* 2, No. 2 (1996): 263–275.

Kent, Brian. "Canaries in a Gilded Cage: Mental and Marital Decline in *McTeague* and *The Shining*." In *"The Shining" Reader*, edited by Anthony Magistrale, 139–154. Mercer Island, WA: Starmont House, 1991.

Kilgour, Maggie. *The Rise of the Gothic Novel*. London: Routledge, 1995.

Kilker, Robert. "All Roads Lead to the Abject: The Monstrous Feminine and Gender Boundaries in Stanley Kubrick's

The Shining." *Literature/Film Quarterly* 34, No. 1 (2006): 54–63.

Kimmel, Michael S. *Manhood in America: A Cultural History*. 2nd ed. New York: Oxford University Press, 2006.

King, Stephen. *Bag of Bones*. London: Hodder and Stoughton, 1998.

_____. "The Body." 1982. In *Different Seasons*, by Stephen King, 319–481. London: Hodder and Stoughton, 1992.

_____. *Christine*. New York: Viking Press, 1983.

_____. *Danse Macabre*. 1981. London: Warner, 1993.

_____. *Different Seasons*. 1982. London: Hodder and Stoughton, 1992.

_____. *It*. London: Hodder and Stoughton, 1986.

_____. *On Writing: A Memoir of the Craft*. London: Hodder and Stoughton, 2000.

_____. *Pet Sematary*. London: Hodder and Stoughton, 1988.

_____. *The Shining*. Garden City, NY: Doubleday, 1977.

_____. "Terror Ink." In *Bare Bones: Conversations on Terror with Stephen King*, edited by Tim Underwood and Chuck Miller, 93–124. New York: McGraw-Hill, 1988.

Kinsley, Zoë. "'In moody sadness, on the giddy brink': Liminality and Home Tour Travel." In *Mapping Liminalities: Thresholds in Cultural and Literary Texts, Transatlantic Aesthetics and Culture* Vol. 2, edited by Lucy Kay, Zoë Kinsley, Terry Phillips, and Alan Roughley, 41–67. Bern: Peter Lang, 2007.

Knight, Donald R. "'Here Comes My Baby, Singin' Like a Nightingale': Stephen King's Christine." *Studies in Weird Fiction* 18 (1996): 13–16.

Krulik, Ted. "Reaching for Immortality: Two Novels of Richard Matheson." In *Critical Encounters II: Writers and Themes in Science Fiction*, edited by Tom Staicar, 1–14. New York: Frederick Ungar, 1982.

Laird, David. "Versions of Eden: The Automobile and the American Novel." In *The Automobile and American Culture*, edited by David L. Lewis and Laurence Goldstein, 244–256. Ann Arbor: University of Michigan Press, 1980.

Landsberg, Alison. *Prosthetic Memory: The Transformation of American Remembrance in the Age of Mass Culture*. New York: Columbia University Press, 2004.

Lant, Kathleen Margaret, and Theresa Thompson, eds. *Imagining the Worst: Stephen King and the Representation of Women*. Westport, CT: Greenwood Press, 1998.

Lasch, Christopher. *The Culture of Narcissism: American Life in an Age of Diminishing Expectations*. New York: W. W. Norton, 1979.

Levine, Lawrence W. *The Unpredictable Past: Explorations in American Cultural History*. New York: Oxford University Press, 1993.

Lévy, Maurice. *Lovecraft: A Study in the Fantastic*. Translated by S. T. Joshi. Detroit, MI: Wayne State University Press, 1988.

Lewis, David L., and Laurence Goldstein, eds. *The Automobile and American Culture*. Ann Arbor: University of Michigan Press, 1980.

Lewis, Tyson, and Daniel Cho. "Home Is Where the Neurosis Is: A Topography of the Spatial Unconscious." *Cultural Critique* 64, No. 1 (Fall 2006): 69–91.

Lindgren, James M. *Preserving Historic New England: Preservation, Progressivism, and the Remaking of Memory*. New York: Oxford University Press, 1995.

Ling, Peter J. *America and the Automobile: Technology, Reform and Social Change, 1893–1923*. Manchester: Manchester University Press, 1990.

Lloyd-Smith, Allan. *American Gothic Fiction: An Introduction*. New York: Continuum, 2004.

_____. "Nineteenth-Century American Gothic." In *A Companion to the Gothic*, edited by David Punter, 109–121. Oxford: Blackwell, 2000.

Lloyd-Smith, Allan Gardner. *Uncanny American Fiction: Medusa's Face*.

Houndmills, Basingstoke: Macmillan, 1989.

Loewen, James W. *Lies My Teacher Told Me: Everything Your American History Textbook Got Wrong*. New York: Simon and Schuster, 1995.

Lofficier, Randy, and Phil Edwards, "Stephen King on *Christine*." *Starburst*, May 1984.

Lovecraft, H. P. *At the Mountains of Madness*. 1936. In *"The Thing on the Doorstep" and Other Weird Stories*, edited by S. T. Joshi, 246–340. London: Penguin, 2002.

_____. "Beyond the Wall of Sleep." 1919. In *"The Thing on the Doorstep" and Other Weird Stories*, edited by S. T. Joshi, 11–20. London: Penguin, 2002.

_____. "The Call of Cthulhu." 1928. In *"The Call of Cthulhu" and Other Weird Stories*, edited by S. T. Joshi, 139–69. London: Penguin, 2002.

_____. "The Colour Out of Space." 1927. In *"The Call of Cthulhu" and Other Weird Stories*, edited by S. T. Joshi, 170–199. London: Penguin, 2002.

_____. "Cool Air." 1928. In *"The Call of Cthulhu" and Other Weird Stories*, edited by S. T. Joshi, 130–138. London: Penguin, 2002.

_____. "The Dreams in the Witch House." 1933. In *"The Dreams in the Witch House" and Other Weird Stories*, edited by S. T. Joshi, 300–334. London: Penguin, 2005.

_____. "The Dunwich Horror." 1929. In *"The Thing on the Doorstep" and Other Weird Stories*, edited by S. T. Joshi, 206–245. London: Penguin, 2002.

_____. "From Beyond." 1934. In *"The Dreams in the Witch House" and Other Weird Stories*, edited by S. T. Joshi, 23–29. London: Penguin, 2005.

_____. "He." 1926. In *"The Call of Cthulhu" and Other Weird Stories*, edited by S. T. Joshi, 119–129. London: Penguin, 2002.

_____. "The Horror at Red Hook." 1927. In *"The Dreams in the Witch House" and Other Weird Stories*, edited by S. T. Joshi, 116–37. London: Penguin, 2005.

_____. "The Shadow Out of Time." 1936. In *"The Dreams in the Witch House" and Other Weird Stories*, edited by S. T. Joshi, 335–395. London: Penguin, 2005.

_____. "The Shadow Over Innsmouth." 1936. In *"The Call of Cthulhu" and Other Weird Stories*, edited by S. T. Joshi, 268–335. London: Penguin, 2002.

_____. "The Shunned House." 1937. In *"The Dreams in the Witch House" and Other Weird Stories*, edited by S. T. Joshi, 90–115. London: Penguin, 2005.

_____. *Supernatural Horror in Literature*. 1927. New York: Dover, 1973.

_____. "The Thing on the Doorstep." 1937. In *"The Thing on the Doorstep" and Other Weird Stories*, edited by S. T. Joshi, 341–365. London: Penguin, 2002.

Lovell-Smith, Rose. "On the Gothic Beach: A New Zealand Reading of Margaret Mahy's *The Tricksters*." In *The Gothic in Children's Literature: Haunting the Borders*, edited by Anna Jackson, Karen Coats, and Roderick McGillis, 93–115. New York: Routledge, 2008.

Lovett-Graff, Bennett. "Shadows Over Lovecraft: Reactionary Fantasy and Immigrant Eugenics." *Extrapolation* 38, No. 3 (Fall 1997): 175–192.

Macherey, Pierre. *A Theory of Literary Production*. Translated by Geoffrey Wall. London: Routledge and Kegan Paul, 1978. First published 1966 by Librairie François Maspero.

Madden, Edward. "Cars Are Girls: Sexual Power and Sexual Panic in Stephen King's *Christine*." In *Imagining the Worst: Stephen King and the Representation of Women*, edited by Kathleen Margaret Lant and Theresa Thompson, 143–158. Westport, CT: Greenwood Press, 1998.

Madsen, Deborah L. *American Exceptionalism*. Edinburgh: Edinburgh University Press, 1998.

Magistrale, Tony. *Landscape of Fear: Stephen King's American Gothic*. Bowling Green, OH: Bowling Green State University Popular Press, 1988.

_____. *The Moral Voyages of Stephen King*. Mercer Island, WA: Starmont House, 1989.

_____. "Native Sons: Regionalism in the Work of Nathaniel Hawthorne and Stephen King." *Journal of the Fantastic in the Arts* 2, No. 1 (Spring 1989): 76–86.

_____, ed. *The Dark Descent: Essays Defining Stephen King's Horrorscape.* Westport, CT: Greenwood Press, 1992.

_____, ed. *Discovering Stephen King's "The Shining": Essays on the Bestselling Novel by America's Premier Horror Writer.* Gillette, NJ: Wildside Press, 1998.

_____, ed. *The Films of Stephen King: From "Carrie" to "Secret Window."* New York: Palgrave Macmillan, 2008.

_____, ed. *"The Shining" Reader.* Mercer Island, WA: Starmont House, 1991.

Magistrale, Tony, and Sidney Poger. *Poe's Children: Connections between Tales of Terror and Detection.* New York: Peter Lang, 1999.

Mailer, Norman. *Advertisements for Myself.* London: Panther, 1968. First published 1961 by Andre Deutsch Limited.

_____. *The White Negro: Superficial Reflections on the Hipster.* San Francisco, CA: City Lights Books, 1970. First published 1957 by Dissent Publishing Associates.

Malin, Irving. *New American Gothic.* Carbondale: Southern Illinois University Press, 1962.

Manchel, Frank. "What about Jack? Another Perspective on Family Relationships in Stanley Kubrick's The Shining." Literature/Film Quarterly 23, No. 1 (1995): 68–78.

Mariconda, Steven J. "The Haunted House." In *Icons of Horror and the Supernatural: An Encyclopedia of Our Worst Nightmares* Vol. 1, edited by S. T. Joshi, 267–305. Westport, CT: Greenwood Press, 2007

Marling, Karal Ann. *As Seen on TV: The Visual Culture of Everyday Life in the 1950s.* Cambridge, MA: Harvard University Press, 1994.

Martin, Robert K. "Haunted by Jim Crow: Gothic Fictions by Haw-thorne and Faulkner." In *American Gothic: New Interventions in a National Narrative,* edited by Robert K. Martin and Eric Savoy, 129–142. Iowa City: University of Iowa Press, 1998.

Martin, Robert K., and Eric Savoy, eds. *American Gothic: New Interventions in a National Narrative.* Iowa City: University of Iowa Press, 1998.

Martín Alegre, Sara. "Nightmares of Childhood: The Child and the Monster in Four Novels by Stephen King." *Atlantis: A Journal of the Spanish Association for Anglo-American Studies* 23, No. 1 (June 2001): 105–114.

Marx, Karl. *The Eighteenth Brumaire of Louis Bonaparte.* 1852. New York: International Publishers, 1963.

Matheson, Richard. *Earthbound.* London: Robinson, 1989.

_____. *Hell House.* 1971. New York: Tor, 1999.

_____. *A Stir of Echoes.* 1958. New York: Tor, 1999.

Mathews, Cheyenne, and Janet V. Haedicke, eds. *Reading Richard Matheson: A Critical Survey.* Lanham, MD: Rowman and Littlefield, 2014.

May, Elaine Tyler. *Homeward Bound: American Families in the Cold War Era.* Rev. and upd. ed. New York: Basic Books, 1999.

McCracken, Scott. *Pulp: Reading Popular Fiction.* Manchester: Manchester University Press, 1998.

Menand, Louis. *The Metaphysical Club.* 2001. London: Flamingo, 2002.

Messent, Peter. "Good Taste? Liminality and the Gothic in Thomas Harris's Hannibal Lecter Novels." In *Betwixt-and-Between: Essays in Liminal Geography, Studies in Liminality and Literature* 3, edited by Philip C. Sutton, 63–85. Madrid: Gateway Press, 2002.

Meyer, Stephen. "Work, Play, and Power: Masculine Culture on the Automotive Shop Floor, 1930–1960." In *Boys and Their Toys? Masculinity, Technology, and Class in America,* edited by Roger Horowitz, 13–32. New York: Routledge, 2001.

Michasiw, Kim Ian. "Some Stations of Suburban Gothic." In *American Gothic: New Interventions in a National Narrative*, edited by Robert K. Martin and Eric Savoy, 237–257. Iowa City: University of Iowa Press, 1998.

Miller, Nathan. *New World Coming: The 1920s and the Making of Modern America*. New York: Da Capo Press, 2003.

Millington, Richard H. *The Cambridge Companion to Nathaniel Hawthorne*. Cambridge: Cambridge University Press, 2004.

Mills, C. Wright. *The Power Elite*. New York: Oxford University Press, 1956.

Monmonier, Mark. *From Squaw Tit to Whorehouse Meadow: How Maps Name, Claim, and Inflame*. Chicago: University of Chicago Press, 2006.

Monteith, Sharon. *American Culture in the 1960s*. Edinburgh: Edinburgh University Press, 2008.

Morrison, Dane Anthony, and Nancy Lusignan Schultz, eds. *Salem: Place, Myth, and Memory*. Boston, MA: Northeastern University Press/University Press of New England, 2004.

Morrison, Toni. *Beloved*. 1987. London: Vintage, 1997.

Mottram, Eric. *Blood on the Nash Ambassador: Investigations in American Culture*. London: Hutchinson Radius, 1983.

Murphy, Bernice M. *The Suburban Gothic in American Popular Culture*. Houndmills, Basingstoke: Palgrave Macmillan, 2009.

Mustazza, Leonard. "Poe's 'The Masque of the Red Death' and King's *The Shining*: Echo, Influence, and Deviation." In *Discovering Stephen King's 'The Shining': Essays on the Bestselling Novel by America's Premier Horror Writer*, edited by Tony Magistrale, 62–73. Gillette, NJ: Wildside Press, 1998.

Neilson, Keith. "Richard Matheson." In *Supernatural Fiction Writers: Fantasy and Horror* Vol. 2, edited by E. F. Bleiler, 1073–1080. New York: Charles Scribner's Sons, 1985.

Newhouse, Tom. "A Blind Date with Disaster: Adolescent Revolt in the Fiction of Stephen King." In *The Gothic World of Stephen King: Landscape of Nightmares*, edited by Gary Hoppenstand and Ray B. Browne, 49–55. Bowling Green, OH: Bowling Green State University Popular Press, 1987.

Nicholls, Peter. "Richard Matheson." In *Science Fiction Writers: Critical Studies of the Major Authors from the Early Nineteenth Century to the Present Day*, edited by E. F. Bleiler, 425–431. New York: Charles Scribner's Sons, 1982.

Nolan, William F. "The Matheson Years: A Profile in Friendship." In *The Twilight and Other Zones: The Dark Worlds of Richard Matheson*, edited by Stanley Wiater, Matthew R. Bradley, and Paul Stuve, 9–29. New York: Citadel Press, 2009.

Oakes, David A. *Science and Destabilization in the Modern American Gothic: Lovecraft, Matheson, and King*. Westport, CT: Greenwood Press, 2000.

Old Car Advertising. "Plymouth: 1956 Plymouth—1956 Plymouth Ad-01." Accessed June 22, 2011. http://oldcaradvertising.com/Plymouth/1956%20Plymouth/1956%20Plymouth%20Ad-01.html.

_____. "Plymouth: 1957 Plymouth—1957 Plymouth Ad-02." Accessed June 22, 2011. http://www.oldcaradvertising.com/Plymouth/1957%20Plymouth/1957%20Plymouth%20Ad-02.html.

_____. Plymouth: 1957 Plymouth—1957 Plymouth Ad-03." Accessed June 22, 2011. http://www.oldcaradvertising.com/Plymouth/1957%20Plymouth/1957%20Plymouth%20Ad-03.html.

Orr, John, and Colin Nicholson, eds. *Cinema and Fiction: New Modes of Adapting, 1950–1990*. Edinburgh: Edinburgh University Press, 1992.

Owen, Alex. *The Place of Enchantment: British Occultism and the Culture of the Modern*. Chicago: University of Chicago Press, 2004.

Palmer, Niall. *The Twenties in America: Politics and History*. Edinburgh: Edinburgh University Press, 2006.

Parrish, Michael E. *Anxious Decades: America in Prosperity and Depression, 1920–1941.* New York: W. W. Norton, 1992.

Perry, Dennis R., and Carl H. Sederholm. *Poe, "The House of Usher," and the American Gothic.* New York: Palgrave Macmillan, 2009.

Phillips, Terry. "'No World Between Two Worlds': Liminality in Anglo-Irish Big House Literature, 1925–1932." In *Mapping Liminalities: Thresholds in Cultural and Literary Texts, Transatlantic Aesthetics and Culture* Vol. 2, edited by Lucy Kay, Zoë Kinsley, Terry Phillips, and Alan Roughley, 69–90. Bern: Peter Lang, 2007.

Pollin, Burton R. "Stephen King's Fiction and the Heritage of Poe." *Journal of the Fantastic in the Arts* 5, No. 4 (1993): 2–25.

Punter, David. *The Literature of Terror: A History of Gothic Fictions from 1765 to the Present Day, Volume 1: The Gothic Tradition.* 2nd ed. Harlow: Longman, 1996.

_____, ed. *A Companion to the Gothic.* Oxford: Blackwell, 2000.

Railo, Eino. *The Haunted Castle: A Study of the Elements of English Romanticism.* London: Routledge, 1927.

Reesman, Jeanne Campbell. "Stephen King and the Tradition of American Naturalism in *The Shining.*" In *"The Shining" Reader*, edited by Anthony Magistrale, 121–137. Mercer Island, WA: Starmont House, 1991.

Reeve, Clara. *The Old English Baron.* 1778. London: Oxford University Press, 1967.

Reino, Joseph. *Stephen King: The First Decade, "Carrie" to "Pet Sematary."* Boston, MA: Twayne Publishers, 1988.

Richardson, Judith. *Possessions: The History and Uses of Haunting in the Hudson Valley.* Cambridge, MA: Harvard University Press, 2003.

Riesman, David. *The Lonely Crowd: A Study of the Changing American Character.* Abr. and rev. ed. New Haven, CT: Yale Nota Bene/Yale University Press, 2001.

Roberts, Adam. *Science Fiction.* 2nd ed. London: Routledge, 2006.

Russell, Sharon A. *Revisiting Stephen King: A Critical Companion.* Westport, CT: Greenwood Press, 2002.

_____. *Stephen King: A Critical Companion.* Westport, CT: Greenwood Press, 1996.

St. Armand, Barton Levi. *The Roots of Horror in the Fiction of H. P. Lovecraft.* Elizabethtown, NY: Dragon Press, 1977.

Saler, Michael. "Modern Enchantments: The Canny Wonders and Uncanny Others of H. P. Lovecraft." *The Space Between: Literature and Culture, 1914–1945* 2, No. 1 (2006): 11–32.

_____. "Modernity, Disenchantment, and the Ironic Imagination." *Philosophy and Literature* 28, No. 1 (April 2004): 137–149.

Sanford, Charles L. "'Woman's Place' in American Car Culture." In *The Automobile and American Culture*, edited by David L. Lewis and Laurence Goldstein, 137–152. Ann Arbor: University of Michigan Press, 1980.

Savoy, Eric. "The Face of the Tenant: A Theory of American Gothic." In *American Gothic: New Interventions in a National Narrative*, edited by Robert K. Martin and Eric Savoy, 3–19. Iowa City: University of Iowa Press, 1998.

Schopp, Andrew. "From Misogyny to Homophobia and Back Again: The Play of Erotic Triangles in Stephen King's *Christine.*" *Extrapolation* 38, No. 1 (1997): 66–78.

Schultz, David E., and S. T. Joshi, eds. *An Epicure in the Terrible: A Centennial Anthology of Essays in Honor of H. P. Lovecraft.* London: Fairleigh Dickinson University Press/Associated University Presses, 1991.

Schultz, Nancy Lusignan. "Salem as Hawthorne's Creation." In *Salem: Place, Myth, and Memory*, edited by Dane Anthony Morrison and Nancy Lusignan Schultz, 163–183. Boston: Northeastern University Press/University Press of New England, 2004.

Schultz, Nancy Lusignan, and Dane Anthony Morrison. "Introduction: Salem Enshrined: Myth, Memory, and the Power of Place." In *Salem: Place, Myth, and Memory*, edited by Dane Anthony Morrison and Nancy Lusignan Schultz, 3–19. Boston: Northeastern University Press/University Press of New England, 2004.

Sears, John. *Stephen King's Gothic.* Cardiff: University of Wales Press, 2011.

Sedgwick, Eve Kosofsky. *The Coherence of Gothic Conventions.* North Stratford, NH: Ayer, 1999.

Shary, Timothy. *Teen Movies: American Youth on Screen.* London: Wallflower, 2005.

Shea, J. Vernon. "On the Literary Influences Which Shaped Lovecraft's Works." In *H. P. Lovecraft: Four Decades of Criticism*, edited by S. T. Joshi, 113–139. Athens: Ohio University Press, 1980.

Silverstone, Roger, ed. *Visions of Suburbia.* London: Routledge, 1997.

Simmons, David. "H. P. Lovecraft and the Shadow of England." *Symbiosis: A Journal of Anglo-American Literary Relations* 11, No. 1 (April 2007): 89–104.

_____, ed. *New Critical Essays on H. P. Lovecraft.* New York: Palgrave Macmillan, 2013.

Simpson, Philip. "The Lonesome Autoerotic Death of Arnie Cunningham in John Carpenter's *Christine.*" In *The Films of Stephen King: From "Carrie" to "Secret Window,"* edited by Tony Magistrale, 51–64. New York: Palgrave Macmillan, 2008.

Smith, Angèle. "Landscape Representation: Place and Identity in Nineteenth-century Ordnance Survey Maps of Ireland." In *Landscape, Memory and History: Anthropological Perspectives*, edited by Pamela J. Stewart and Andrew Strathern, 71–88. London: Pluto Press, 2003.

Smith, Carol R. "Gender and Family Values in the Clinton Presidency and 1990s Hollywood Film." In *American Film and Politics from Reagan to Bush Jr.,* edited by Philip John Davies and Paul Wells, 77–88. Manchester: Manchester University Press, 2002.

Smith, Don G. *H. P. Lovecraft in Popular Culture: The Works and Their Adaptations in Film, Television, Comics, Music and Games.* Jefferson, NC: McFarland, 2006.

Smith, Greg. "The Literary Equivalent of a Big Mac and Fries? Academics, Moralists, and the Stephen King Phenomenon." *Midwest Quarterly: A Journal of Contemporary Thought* 43, No. 4 (2002): 329–345.

Sobchack, Vivian. *Screening Space: The American Science Fiction Film.* 2nd ed. New Brunswick, NJ: Rutgers University Press, 1998.

Speed, Lesley. "Tuesday's Gone: The Nostalgic Teen Film." *Journal of Popular Film and Television* 26, No. 1 (1998): 24–32.

Spigel, Lynn. "From Theatre to Space Ship: Metaphors of Suburban Domesticity in Postwar America." In *Visions of Suburbia*, edited by Roger Silverstone, 217–239. London: Routledge, 1997.

_____. *Welcome to the Dreamhouse: Popular Media and Postwar Suburbs.* Durham, NC: Duke University Press, 2001.

Stableford, Brian. "The Cosmic Horror." In *Icons of Horror and the Supernatural: An Encyclopedia of Our Worst Nightmares* Vol. 1, edited by S. T. Joshi, 65–96. Westport, CT: Greenwood Press, 2007.

Staicar, Tom, ed. *Critical Encounters II: Writers and Themes in Science Fiction.* New York: Frederick Ungar, 1982.

Stewart, Pamela J., and Andrew Strathern. "Introduction." In *Landscape, Memory and History: Anthropological Perspectives*, edited by Pamela J. Stewart and Andrew Strathern, 1–15. London: Pluto Press, 2003.

_____ and _____, eds. *Landscape, Memory and History: Anthropological Perspectives.* London: Pluto Press, 2003.

Strengell, Heidi. *Dissecting Stephen King: From the Gothic to Literary Naturalism.* Madison: Popular Press/The University of Wisconsin Press, 2005.

_____. "The Ghost: The Gothic Melodrama in Stephen King's Fiction." *European Journal of American Culture* 24, No. 3 (2005): 221–238.

Sturken, Marita. *Tangled Memories: The Vietnam War, the AIDS Epidemic, and the Politics of Remembering.* Berkeley, CA: University of California Press, 1997.

Stuve, Paul, and Matthew R. Bradley. "Bibliographies, Filmographies, etc." In *The Richard Matheson Companion,* edited by Stanley Wiater, Matthew R. Bradley, and Paul Stuve, 373–559. Colorado Springs: Gauntlet, 2008.

Summers, Montague. *The Gothic Quest: A History of the Gothic Novel.* London: Fortune Press, 1968.

Sutton, Philip C., ed. *Betwixt-and-Between: Essays in Liminal Geography, Studies in Liminality and Literature* 3. Madrid: Gateway Press, 2002.

Tallack, Douglas. *New York Sights: Visualizing Old and New New York.* Oxford: Berg, 2005.

_____. *Twentieth-Century America: The Intellectual and Cultural Context.* London: Longman, 1991.

Thompson, Graham. *American Culture in the 1980s.* Edinburgh: Edinburgh University Press, 2007.

Troy, Gil. *Morning in America: How Ronald Reagan Invented the 1980s.* Princeton, NJ: Princeton University Press, 2005

Turner, Victor. *Dramas, Fields, and Metaphors: Symbolic Action in Human Society.* Ithaca, NY: Cornell University Press, 1974.

_____. *The Forest of Symbols: Aspects of Ndembu Ritual.* Ithaca, NY: Cornell University Press, 1967.

Twain, Mark. "The Damned Human Race." circa 1905–1909. In *Letters from the Earth,* edited by Bernard DeVoto, 211–232. New York: Harper and Row, 1962.

_____. "Letters from the Earth." 1909. In *Letters from the Earth,* edited by Bernard DeVoto, 3–55. New York: Harper and Row, 1962.

Underwood, Tim, and Chuck Miller, eds. *Bare Bones: Conversations on Terror with Stephen King.* New York: McGraw-Hill, 1988.

Van Gennep, Arnold. *The Rites of Passage.* Translated by Monika B.Vizedom and Gabrielle L. Caffee. London: Routledge and Kegan Paul, 1960.

Vidler, Anthony. *The Architectural Uncanny: Essays in the Modern Unhomely.* Cambridge: MIT Press, 1992.

Viljoen, Hein, and Chris N. van der Merwe. "Introduction: A Poetics of Liminality and Hybridity." In *Beyond the Threshold: Explorations of Liminality in Literature,* edited by Hein Viljoen and Chris N. van der Merwe, 1–26. New York: Peter Lang, 2007.

_____ and _____, eds. *Beyond the Threshold: Explorations of Liminality in Literature.* New York: Peter Lang, 2007.

Walpole, Horace. *The Castle of Otranto.* 1764. Oxford: Oxford University Press, 1998.

Waterfield, Robin. *Hidden Depths: The Story of Hypnosis.* London: Pan, 2004. First published 2002 by Macmillan.

Weinstock, Jeffrey Andrew. "Queer Haunting Spaces: Madeline Yale Wynne's 'The Little Room' and Elia Wilkinson Peattie's 'The House That Was Not.'" *American Literature* 79, No. 3 (September 2007): 501–525.

Weinstock, Jeffrey Andrew, ed. *Spectral America: Phantoms and the National Imagination.* Madison: University of Wisconsin Press/Popular Press, 2004.

Weinstock, Jeffrey A., and Carl H. Sederholm, eds. *The Age of Lovecraft: Cosmic Horror, Posthumanism, and Popular Culture.* Forthcoming.

White, Christopher. "Salem as Religious Proving Ground." In *Salem: Place, Myth, and Memory,* edited by Dane Anthony Morrison and Nancy Lusignan Schultz, 43–61. Boston: Northeastern University Press/University Press of New England, 2004.

Whyte, William H. *The Organization Man*. Harmondsworth: Penguin, 1960. First published 1956 by Simon and Schuster.

Wiater, Stanley, Christopher Golden, and Hank Wagner. *The Complete Stephen King Universe: A Guide to the Worlds of Stephen King*. Rev. and upd. ed. New York: St. Martin's Griffin, 2006.

Wiater, Stanley, Matthew R. Bradley, and Paul Stuve, eds. *The Richard Matheson Companion*. Colorado Springs: Gauntlet, 2008.

_____, _____ and _____, eds. *The Twilight and Other Zones: The Dark Worlds of Richard Matheson*. New York: Citadel Press, 2009.

Williams, Anne. *Art of Darkness: A Poetics of Gothic*. Chicago: University of Chicago Press, 1995.

Williams, Sara. "'The Infinitude of the Shrieking Abysses': Rooms, Wombs, Tombs, and the Hysterical Female Gothic in 'The Dreams in the Witch-House.'" In *New Critical Essays on H. P. Lovecraft*, edited by David Simmons, 55–72. New York: Palgrave Macmillan, 2013.

Williams, Tony. "Stephen King, Naturalism, and The Shining." *Excavatio: Emile Zola and Naturalism* 9 (1997): 156–165.

Winter, Douglas E. *Faces of Fear: Encounters with the Creators of Modern Horror*. New York: Berkley, 1985.

_____. *Stephen King: The Art of Darkness*. Exp. and upd. ed. New York: Signet, 1986.

Wisker, Gina. *Horror Fiction: An Introduction*. New York: Continuum, 2005.

Wood, Robin. *Hollywood from Vietnam to Reagan ... and Beyond*. Rev. and exp. ed. New York: Columbia University Press, 2003.

Zamora, Lois Parkinson. "Magical Romance/Magical Realism: Ghosts in U.S. and Latin American Fiction." In *Magical Realism: Theory, History, Community*, edited by Lois Parkinson Zamora and Wendy B. Faris, 497–550. Durham, NC: Duke University Press, 1995.

Zamora, Lois Parkinson, and Wendy B. Faris, eds. *Magical Realism: Theory, History, Community*. Durham, NC: Duke University Press, 1995.

Zinn, Howard. *A People's History of the United States: 1492–Present*. Rev. and upd. ed. New York: HarperPerennial, 1995.

_____. *The Twentieth Century: A People's History*. Rev. and upd. ed. New York: HarperPerennial, 1998.

Index

207